Karen Morrison an̶d̶ ̶.̶.̶.̶n̶e

Cambridge IGCSE®

Mathematics

Extended Practice Book

CAMBRIDGE
UNIVERSITY PRESS

CAMBRIDGE
UNIVERSITY PRESS

University Printing House, Cambridge CB2 8BS, United Kingdom

Cambridge University Press is part of the University of Cambridge.

It furthers the University's mission by disseminating knowledge in the pursuit of education, learning and research at the highest international levels of excellence.

Information on this title: education.cambridge.org

© Cambridge University Press 2013

First published 2013
6th printing 2015

Printed in Poland by Opolgraf

A catalogue record for this publication is available from the British Library

ISBN-13 978-1-107-67272-7 Paperback

Cover image: Seamus Ditmeyer/Alamy

Contents

Unit 4

Unit 5

Unit 6

Example practice papers can be found online, visit education.cambridge.org/extendedpracticebook

Introduction

This highly illustrated practice book has been written by experienced teachers to help students revise the *Cambridge IGCSE Mathematics* (0580) Extended syllabus. Packed full of exercises, the only narrative consists of helpful bulleted lists of key reminders and useful hints in the margins for students needing more support.

There is plenty of practice offered via 'drill' exercises throughout each chapter. These consist of progressive and repetitive questions that allow the student to practise methods applicable to each subtopic. At the end of each chapter there are 'Mixed exercises' that bring together all the subtopics of a chapter in such a way that students have to decide for themselves what methods to use. The answers to *all* of these questions are supplied at the back of the book. This encourages students to assess their progress as they go along, choosing to do more or less practice as required.

The book has been written with a clear progression from start to finish, with some later chapters requiring knowledge learned in earlier chapters. There are useful signposts throughout that link the content of the chapters, allowing the individual to follow their own course through the book: where the content in one chapter might require knowledge from a previous chapter, a comment is included in a 'Rewind' box; and where content will be practised in more detail later on, a comment is included in a 'Fast forward' box. Examples of both are included below:

◀ REWIND

You learned how to plot lines from equations in chapter 10. ◀

FAST FORWARD ▶

You will learn much more about sets in chapter 9. For now, just think of a set as a list of numbers or other items that are often placed inside curly brackets. ▶

Other helpful guides in the margin of the book are as follows:

Hints: these are general comments to remind students of important or key information that is useful when tackling an exercise, or simply useful to know. They often provide extra information or support in potentially tricky topics.

Remember 'coefficient' is the *number* in the term.

Tip

It is essential that you remember to work out *both* unknowns. Every pair of simultaneous linear equations will have a pair of solutions.

Tip: these are tips that relate to good practice in examinations, and also just generally in mathematics! They cover common pitfalls based on the **authors'** experiences of their students, and give students things to be wary of or to remember in order to score marks in the exam.

The *Extended Practice Book* mirrors the chapters and subtopics of the *Cambridge IGCSE Mathematics Core and Extended Coursebook* written by Karen Morrison and Nick Hamshaw (9781107606272). **However**, this book has been written such that it can be used **without the coursebook**; it can be used as a revision tool by any student regardless of what coursebook they are using. Various aspects of the Core syllabus are also revised for complete coverage.

Also in the *Cambridge IGCSE Mathematics* series:

Cambridge IGCSE Mathematics Core and Extended Coursebook (9781107606272)

Cambridge IGCSE Mathematics Core Practice Book (9781107609884)

Cambridge IGCSE Mathematics Teacher's Resource CD-ROM (9781107627529)

1 Reviewing number concepts

1.1 Different types of numbers

- Real numbers can be divided into rational and irrational numbers. You will deal with rational numbers in this chapter. Irrational numbers are covered in chapter 9.
- Rational numbers can be written as fractions in the form of $\frac{a}{b}$ where a and b are integers and $b \neq 0$.
  (Integers are negative and positive whole numbers, and zero.)
- Integers, fractions and terminating decimals are all rational numbers.

> **Tip**
> Make sure you know what the following sets of numbers are: natural numbers, integers, odd and even numbers and prime numbers.

Exercise 1.1

1 Tick the correct columns in the table to classify each number.

Number	Natural	Integer	Prime	Fraction
−0.2				
−57				
3.142				
0				
$0.\dot{3}$				
1				
51				
10 270				
$-\frac{1}{4}$				
$\frac{2}{7}$				
11				
$\sqrt[3]{512}$				

2 List:

(a) four square numbers greater than 100.

(b) four rational numbers smaller than $\frac{1}{3}$.

(c) two prime numbers that are > 80.

(d) the prime numbers < 10.

1.2 Multiples and factors

- A multiple of a number is the product obtained when multiplying that number and an integer. The lowest common multiple (LCM) of two or more numbers is the lowest number that is a multiple of both (or all) of the numbers.
- A factor of a number is any number that will divide into the number exactly.
- The highest common factor (HCF) of two or more numbers is the highest number that is a factor of all the given numbers.

To find the LCM of a set of numbers, you can list the multiples of each number until you find the first multiple that is in the lists for all of the numbers in the set.

FAST FORWARD

You will use LCM again when you work with fractions to find the lowest common denominator of two or more fractions. See chapter 5. ▶

You need to work out whether to use LCM or HCF to find the answers. Problems involving LCM usually include repeating events. Problems involving HCF usually involve splitting things into smaller pieces or arranging things in equal groups or rows.

Exercise 1.2 A

1 Find the LCM of the given numbers.

    (a) 9 and 18   **(b)** 12 and 18   **(c)** 15 and 18   **(d)** 24 and 12

    (e) 36 and 9   **(f)** 4, 12 and 8   **(g)** 3, 9 and 24   **(h)** 12, 16 and 32

2 Find the HCF of the given numbers.

    (a) 12 and 18   **(b)** 18 and 36   **(c)** 27 and 90   **(d)** 12 and 15

    (e) 20 and 30   **(f)** 19 and 45   **(g)** 60 and 72   **(h)** 250 and 900

Exercise 1.2 B

1 Amira has two rolls of cotton fabric. One roll has 72 metres on it and the other has 90 metres on it. She wants to cut the fabric to make as many equal length pieces as possible of the longest possible length. How long should each piece be?

2 In a shopping mall promotion every 30th shopper gets a $10 voucher and every 120th shopper gets a free meal. How many shoppers must enter the mall before one receives a voucher and a free meal?

3 Amanda has 40 pieces of fruit and 100 sweets to share amongst the students in her class. She is able to give each student an equal number of pieces of fruit and an equal number of sweets. What is the largest possible number of students in her class?

4 Francesca, Ayuba and Claire are Olympic and Paralympic contenders. They share a training slot on a running track. Francesca cycles and completes a lap in 20 seconds, Ayuba runs the lap in 84 seconds and Claire, in her wheelchair, takes 105 seconds. They start training together. After how long will all three be at the same point again and how many laps will each have completed?

5 Mr Smit wants to tile a rectangular veranda with dimensions 3.2 m × 6.4 m with a whole number of identical square tiles. Mrs Smit wants the tiles to be as large as possible.

    (a) Find the area of the largest possible tiles in cm².

    (b) How many 3.2 m × 3.2 m tiles will Mr Smit need to tile the veranda?

1.3 Prime numbers

- Prime numbers only have two factors: 1 and the number itself.
- Prime factors are factors of a number that are also prime numbers.
- You can write any number as a product of prime factors. But remember the number 1 itself is *not* a prime number so you cannot use it to write a number as the product of its prime factors.
- You can use the product of prime factors to find the HCF or LCM of two or more numbers.

You can use a tree diagram or division to find the prime factors of a composite whole number.

Exercise 1.3

1 Identify the prime numbers in each set.

   (a) 1, 2, 3, 4, 5, 6, 7, 8, 9, 10

   (b) 50, 51, 52, 53, 54, 55, 56, 57, 58, 59, 60

   (c) 95, 96, 97, 98, 99, 100, 101, 102, 103, 104, 105

2 Express the following numbers as a product of their prime factors.

   (a) 36   **(b)** 65   **(c)** 64   **(d)** 84

   (e) 80   **(f)** 1000   **(g)** 1270   **(h)** 1963

3 Find the LCM and the HCF of the following numbers by means of prime factors.

   (a) 27 and 14   **(b)** 85 and 15   **(c)** 96 and 27   **(d)** 53 and 16

   (e) 674 and 72   **(f)** 234 and 66   **(g)** 550 and 128   **(h)** 315 and 275

1.4 Powers and roots

- A number is squared (n^2) when it is multiplied by itself ($n \times n$).
- The square root ($\sqrt{n}$) of a number is the number that is multiplied by itself to get the number.
- A number is cubed (n^3) when it is multiplied by itself and then multiplied by itself again ($n \times n \times n$).
- The cube root ($\sqrt[3]{n}$) of a number is the number that is multiplied by itself twice to get the number.

FAST FORWARD

Powers greater than 3 are dealt with in chapter 2. See topic 2.5 indices. ▶

Exercise 1.4

1 Find all the square and cube numbers between 100 and 300.

2 Simplify.

   (a) $\sqrt{9} + \sqrt{16}$ **(b)** $\sqrt{9+16}$ **(c)** $\sqrt{64} + \sqrt{36}$ **(d)** $\sqrt{64+36}$

   (e) $\sqrt{\dfrac{36}{4}}$ **(f)** $\left(\sqrt{25}\right)^2$ **(g)** $\dfrac{\sqrt{9}}{\sqrt{16}}$ **(h)** $\sqrt{169-144}$

   (i) $\sqrt[3]{27} - \sqrt[3]{1}$ **(j)** $\sqrt{100 \div 4}$ **(k)** $\sqrt[3]{1} + \sqrt{\dfrac{9}{16}}$ **(l)** $\sqrt{16} \times \sqrt[3]{27}$

   (m) $\sqrt{(-5)^2} \times \sqrt[3]{-1}$ **(n)** $\sqrt{\dfrac{1}{4} + \sqrt{\left(\dfrac{1}{3}\right)^2}}$ **(o)** $\sqrt[3]{1} - \sqrt[3]{-125}$

3 A cube has a volume of 12 167 cm³. Calculate:

   (a) the height of the cube.

   (b) the area of one face of the cube.

1.5 Working with directed numbers .

- Integers are directed whole numbers.
- Negative integers are written with a minus (–) sign. Positive integers may be written with a plus (+) sign, but usually they are not.
- In real life, negative numbers are used to represent temperatures below zero; movements downwards or left; depths; distances below sea level; bank withdrawals and overdrawn amounts, and many more things.

Exercise 1.5

1 If the temperature is 4 °C in the evening and it drops 7 °C overnight, what will the temperature be in the morning?

2 Which is colder in each pair of temperatures?

(a) 0 °C or –2 °C   (b) 9 °C or –9 °C   (c) –4 °C or –12 °C

Draw a number line to help you.

3 An office block has three basement levels (level –1, –2 and –3), a ground floor and 15 floors above the ground floor (1 to 15). Where will the lift be in the following situations?

(a) Starts on ground and goes down one floor then up five?
(b) Starts on level –3 and goes up 10 floors?
(c) Starts on floor 12 and goes down 13 floors?
(d) Starts on floor 15 and goes down 17 floors?
(e) Starts on level –2, goes up seven floors and then down eight?

1.6 Order of operations

- When there is more than one operation to be done in a calculation you must work out the parts in brackets first. Then do any division or multiplication (from left to right) before adding and subtracting (from left to right).
- The word 'of' means × and a fraction line means divide.
- Long fraction lines and square or cube root signs act like brackets, indicating parts of the calculation that have to be done first.

Remember the order of operations using BODMAS:

Brackets
Of
Divide
Multiply
Add
Subtract

Exercise 1.6

 Tip

Most modern scientific calculators apply the rules for order of operations automatically. If there are brackets, fractions or roots in your calculation you need to enter these correctly on the calculator. When there is more than one term in the denominator, the calculator will divide by the first term only unless you enter brackets.

FAST FORWARD ▶

The next section will remind you of the rules for rounding numbers. ▶

1 Calculate and give your answer correct to two decimal places.

(a) $8 + 3 \times 6$

(b) $(8 + 3) \times 6$

(c) $8 \times 3 - 4 \div 5$

(d) $12.64 + 2.32 \times 1.3$

(e) $6.5 \times 1.3 - 5.06$

(f) $(6.7 \div 8) + 1.6$

(g) $1.453 + \dfrac{7.6}{3.2}$

(h) $\dfrac{5.34 + 3.315}{4.03}$

(i) $\dfrac{6.54}{2.3} - 1.08$

(j) $\dfrac{5.27}{1.4 \times 1.35}$

(k) $\dfrac{11.5}{2.9 - 1.43}$

(l) $\dfrac{0.23 \times 4.26}{1.32 + 3.43}$

(m) $8.9 - \dfrac{8.9}{10.4}$

(n) $\dfrac{12.6}{8.3} - \dfrac{1.98}{4.62}$

(o) $12.9 - 2.03^2$

(p) $(9.4 - 2.67)^3$

(q) $12.02^2 - 7.05^2$

(r) $\left(\dfrac{16.8}{9.3} - 1.01\right)^2$

(s) $\dfrac{4.07^2}{8.2 - 4.09}$

(t) $6.8 + \dfrac{1.4}{6.9} - \dfrac{1.2}{9.3}$

(u) $4.3 + \left(1.2 + \dfrac{1.6}{5}\right)^2$

(v) $\dfrac{6.1}{2.8} + \left(\dfrac{2.1}{1.6}\right)^2$

(w) $6.4 - (1.2^2 + 1.9^2)^2$

(x) $\left(4.8 - \dfrac{1}{9.6}\right) \times 4.3$

1.7 Rounding numbers

- You may be asked to round numbers to a given number of decimal places or to a given number of significant figures.
- To round to a decimal place:
  - look at the value of the digit to the right of the place you are rounding to
  - if this value is ≥ 5 then you round up (add 1 to the digit you are rounding to)
  - if this value is ≤ 4 then leave the digit you are rounding to as it is.
- To round to a significant figure:
  - the first non-zero digit (before or after the decimal place in a number) is the first significant figure
  - find the correct digit and then round off from that digit using the rules above.

Exercise 1.7

FAST FORWARD

Rounding is very useful when you have to estimate an answer. You will deal with this in more detail in chapter 5. ▶

1 Round these numbers to:

  (i)   two decimal places
  (ii) one decimal place
  (iii) the nearest whole number.

  (a) 5.6543   (b) 9.8774   (c) 12.8706
  (d) 0.0098   (e) 10.099   (f) 45.439
  (g) 13.999   (h) 26.001

2 Round each of these numbers to three significant figures.

  (a) 53 217   (b) 712 984   (c) 17.364   (d) 0.007279

3 Round the following numbers to two significant figures.

  (a) 35.8   (b) 5.234   (c) 12 345   (d) 0.00875
  (e) 432 128   (f) 120.09   (g) 0.00456   (h) 10.002

Mixed exercise

1 State whether each number is natural, rational, an integer and/or a prime number.

$-\dfrac{3}{4}$ 24   0.65 -12 $3\dfrac{1}{2}$ 0   0.66   17

2 List the factors of 36.

(a) How many of these factors are prime numbers?

(b) Express 36 as the product of its prime factors.

(c) List two numbers that are factors of both 36 and 72.

(e) What is the highest number that is a factor of both 36 and 72?

3 Write each number as a product of its prime factors.

(a) 196   (b) 1845   (c) 8820

4 Amira starts an exercise programme on the 3rd of March. She decides she will swim every 3 days and cycle every 4 days. On which dates in March will she swim and cycle on the same day?

5 State whether each equation is true or false.

(a) $18 \div 6 + (5 + 3 \times 4) = 20$

(b) $6 \times (5 - 4) + 3 = 9$

(c) $\dfrac{30+10}{30} - 10 = 1$

(d) $(6 + 3)^2 = 45$

6 Simplify:

(a) $\sqrt{100} \div \sqrt{4}$ (b) $\sqrt{100 \div 4}$ (c) $\left(\sqrt[3]{64}\right)^3$ (d) $4^3 + 9^2$

7 Calculate. Give your answer correct to two decimal places.

(a) $\dfrac{5.4 \times 12.2}{4.1}$ (b) $\dfrac{12.2^2}{3.9^2}$ (c) $\dfrac{12.65}{2.04} + 1.7 \times 4.3$

(d) $\dfrac{3.8 \times 12.6}{4.35}$ (e) $\dfrac{2.8 \times 4.2^2}{3.3^2 \times 6.2^2}$ (f) $2.5 - \left(3.1 + \dfrac{0.5}{5}\right)^2$

8 Round each number to three significant figures.

(a) 1235.6   (b) 0.76513   (c) 0.0237548   (d) 31.4596

9 A building supply store is selling tiles with an area of 790 cm².

(a) Is it possible to have square tiles whose area is not a square number? Explain.

(b) Find the length of each side of the tile correct to 3 significant figures.

(c) What is the minimum number of tiles you would need to tile a rectangular floor 3.6 m long and 2.4 m wide?

Making sense of algebra

2.1 Using letters to represent unknown values

- Letters in algebra are called variables because they can have many different values (the value varies). Any letter can be used as a variable, but *x* and *y* are used most often.
- A number on its own is called a constant.
- A term is a group of numbers and/or variables combined by the operations multiplying and/or dividing only.
- An algebraic expression links terms by using the + and − operation signs. An expression does not have an equals sign (unlike an equation). An expression could have just one term.

Exercise 2.1

> **Tip**
>
> An expression in terms of *x* means that the variable letter used in the expression is *x*.

1 Write expressions, in terms of *x*, to represent:

   (a) 3 times the sum of a number and 2
   (b) 6 times the difference of a number and 1
   (c) twice the sum of 11 and a number
   (d) a number times the difference of 12 and −6
   (e) 4 added to 3 times the square of a number
   (f) a number squared added to 4 times the difference of 7 and 5
   (g) a number subtracted from the result of 4 divided by 20
   (h) a number added to the result of 3 divided 9
   (i) the sum of 8 times $\frac{1}{2}$ and a number times 3
   (j) the difference of a number times −5 and 6 times −2

2 A boy is *p* years old.

   (a) How old will the boy be in five years' time?
   (b) How old was the boy four years ago?
   (c) His father is four times the boy's age. How old is the father?

3 Three people win a prize of $*x*.

   (a) If they share the prize equally, how much will each of them receive?
   (b) If the prize is divided so that the first person gets half as much money as the second person and the third person gets three times as much as the second person, how much will each receive?

2.2 Substitution

- Substitution involves replacing variables with given numbers to work out the value of an expression. For example, you may be told to evaluate $5x$ when $x = -2$. To do this you work out $5 \times (-2) = -10$

Exercise 2.2

1 The formula for finding the area (A) of a triangle is $A = \frac{1}{2}bh$, where b is the length of the base and h is the perpendicular height of the triangle.

Find the area of a triangle if:

(a) the base is 12 cm and the height is 9 cm

(b) the base is 2.5 m and the height is 1.5 m

(c) the base is 21 cm and the height is half as long as the base

(d) the height is 2 cm and the base is the cube of the height.

◀ REWIND

Remember that the BODMAS rules always apply in these calculations. ◀

2 Evaluate $3xy - 4(2x - 3y)$ when $x = 4$ and $y = -3$.

3 Given that $a = 3$, $b = -2$ and $c = -4$, evaluate $(a + 2b)^2 - 4c$.

Take special care when substituting negative numbers. If you replace x with -3 in the expression $4x$, you will obtain $4 \times -3 = -12$, but in the expression $-4x$, you will obtain $-4 \times -3 = 12$.

4 When $m = 2$ and $n = -3$, what is the value of $m^3 - \dfrac{n^3}{m^2} + mn + n^2$?

5 The number of games that can be played among x competitors in a chess tournament is given by the expression $\frac{1}{2}x^2 - \frac{1}{2}x$.

(a) How many games will be played if there are 4 competitors?

(b) How many games will be played if there are 14 competitors?

2.3 Simplifying expressions

- To simplify an expression you add or subtract like terms.
- Like terms are those that have exactly the same variables (including powers of variables).
- You can also multiply and divide to simplify expressions. Both like and unlike terms can be multiplied or divided.

Remember, like terms must have exactly the same variables with exactly the same indices. So $3x$ and $2x$ are like terms but $3x^2$ and $2x$ are not like terms.

Exercise 2.3

1 Simplify the following expressions.

(a) $3x^2 + 6x - 8x + 3$

(b) $x^2y + 3x^2y - 2yx$

(c) $2ab - 4ac + 3ba$

(d) $x^2 + 2x - 4 + 3x^2 - y + 3x - 1$

(e) $-6m \times 5n$

(f) $3xy \times 2x$

Remember, multiplication can be done in any order so, although it is better to put variable letters in a term in alphabetical order, $ab = ba$. So, $3ab + 2ba$ can be simplified to $5ab$.

(g) $-2xy \times -3y^2$

(h) $-2xy \times 2x^2$

(i) $12ab \div 3a$

(j) $12x \div 48xy$

(k) $\dfrac{33abc}{11ca}$

(l) $\dfrac{45mn}{20n}$

(m) $\dfrac{80xy^2}{12x^2y}$

(n) $\dfrac{-36x^3}{-12xy}$

Remember,
$x \times x = x^2$
$y \times y \times y = y^3$
$x \div x = 1$

(o) $\dfrac{y}{x} \times \dfrac{2y}{x}$

(p) $\dfrac{xy}{2} \times \dfrac{y}{x}$

(q) $5a \times \dfrac{3a}{4}$

(r) $7 \times \dfrac{-2y}{5}$

(s) $\dfrac{x}{4} \times \dfrac{2}{3y}$

(t) $\dfrac{3x}{5} \times \dfrac{9x}{2}$

2.4 Working with brackets

- You can remove brackets from an expression by multiplying everything inside the brackets by the value (or values) in front of the bracket.
- Removing brackets is also called expanding the expression.
- When you remove brackets in part of an expression you may end up with like terms. Add or subtract any like terms to simplify the expression fully.
- In general terms $a(b+c) = ab + ac$

Exercise 2.4

Remember the rules for multiplying integers:

$+ \times + = +$

$- \times - = +$

$+ \times - = -$

If the quantity in front of a bracket is negative, the signs of the terms inside the bracket will change when the brackets are expanded.

1 Remove the brackets and simplify where possible.

(a) $2x(x-2)$ (b) $(y-3)x$ (c) $(x-2)-3x$ (d) $-2x-(x-2)$

(e) $(x-3)(-2x)$ (f) $2(x+1)-(1-x)$ (g) $x(x^2-2x-1)$

(h) $-x(1-x)+2(x+3)-4$

2 Remove the brackets and simplify where possible.

(a) $2x(\frac{1}{2}x+\frac{1}{4})$ (b) $-3x(x-y)-2x(y-2x)$ (c) $-2x(4x^2-2x-1)$

(d) $(x+y)-(\frac{1}{2}x-\frac{1}{2}y)$ (e) $5x+x(3-2x)$ (f) $2x(2x-2)-x(x+2)$

(g) $x(1-x)+x(2x-5)-2x(1+3x)$

2.5 Indices

- An index (also called a power or exponent) shows how many times the base is multiplied by itself.
- x^2 means $x \times x$ and $(3y)^4$ means $3y \times 3y \times 3y \times 3y$.
- The laws of indices are used to simplify algebraic terms and expressions. Make sure you know the laws and understand how they work (see below).
- When an expression contains negative indices you apply the same laws as for other indices to simplify it.

Exercise 2.5 A

Tip

Memorise this summary of the **index laws**:

$x^m \times x^n = x^{m+n}$

$x^m \div x^n = x^{m-n}$

$(x^m)^n = x^{mn}$

$x^0 = 1$

$x^{-m} = \dfrac{1}{x^m}$

$x^{\frac{m}{n}} = \left(x^{\frac{1}{n}}\right)^m = \left(\sqrt[n]{x}\right)^m$

1 Simplify.

(a) $\dfrac{x^4 y \times y^2 x^6}{x^4 y^5}$ (b) $\dfrac{2x^2 y^4 \times 3x^3 y}{2xy^4}$ (c) $\dfrac{2x^5 y^4 \times 2xy^3}{2x^2 y^5 \times 3x^2 y^3}$

(d) $\dfrac{x^3 y^7}{xy^4} \times \dfrac{x^2 y^8}{x^3 y}$ (e) $\dfrac{2x^7 y^2}{4x^3 y^7} \times \dfrac{10x^8 y^4}{2x^3 y^2}$ (f) $\dfrac{x^9 y^6}{x^4 y^2} \div \dfrac{x^3 y^2}{x^5 y}$

(g) $\dfrac{10x^5 y^2}{9x^6 y^6} \div \dfrac{3x^3 y}{5x^7 y^4}$ (h) $\dfrac{7y^3 x^2}{5y^5 x^4} \div \dfrac{5x^6 y^2}{7x^5 y^3}$ (i) $\dfrac{\left(x^5 y\right)^2 \times \left(x^3 y^4\right)^2}{\left(x^3 y^3\right)^3}$

(j) $\dfrac{\left(2x^4 y^2\right)^3}{\left(y^3 x^2\right)^3} \times \dfrac{\left(x^4 y^4\right)^2}{3\left(x^2 y\right)^2}$ (k) $\left(\dfrac{x^2}{y^4}\right)^3 \times \left(\dfrac{x^5}{y^2}\right)^2$ (l) $\dfrac{\left(5x^3 y^2\right)^3}{4x^7 y^6} \div \left(\dfrac{2xy^3}{5x^2 y^4}\right)^2$

Tip

Some exam questions will accept simplified expressions with negative indices, such as $5x^{-4}$.
If, however, the question states positive indices only, you can use the law

$x^{-m} = \dfrac{1}{x^m}$ so that $5x^{-4} = \dfrac{5}{x^4}$.

Similarly, $\dfrac{y}{x^{-2}} = x^2 y$.

2 Simplify each expression and give your answer using positive indices only.

(a) $\dfrac{x^5 y^{-4}}{x^{-3} y^{-2}}$

(b) $\dfrac{x^{-4} y^3}{x^2 y^{-1}} \times \dfrac{x^7 y^{-5}}{x^{-4} y^3}$

(c) $\dfrac{\left(2x^{-3} y^{-1}\right)^3}{\left(y^2 x^{-2}\right)^2}$

(d) $\left(\dfrac{x}{y^3}\right)^{-1} \div \dfrac{\left(x^2\right)^4}{y^{-3}}$

(e) $\dfrac{x^{-10}}{\left(y^{-4}\right)^2} \div \left(\dfrac{y^2}{x^3}\right)^{-4}$

(f) $\left(\dfrac{x^4 y^{-1}}{x^5 y^{-3}}\right)^2 \times \dfrac{\left(x^{-2} y^6\right)^2}{2\left(xy^3\right)^{-2}}$

3 Simplify.

(a) $x^{\frac{1}{4}} \times x^{\frac{1}{4}}$

(b) $x^{\frac{1}{3}} \times x^{\frac{1}{5}}$

(c) $\dfrac{x^{\frac{1}{2}}}{x^{\frac{1}{3}}}$

(d) $\left(x^{\frac{1}{3}}\right)^{\frac{1}{3}}$

(e) $\left(64x^6\right)^{\frac{1}{2}}$

(f) $\left(8x^9 y\right)^{\frac{1}{3}}$

(g) $\sqrt{xy^8}$

(h) $\left(\dfrac{x^6}{y^2}\right)^{\frac{1}{2}}$

(i) $\left(x^{\frac{1}{2}}\right)^8 \times \dfrac{x^2}{x^3}$

(j) $\left(x^6 y^3\right)^{\frac{1}{3}} \times \left(x^{-8} y^{-10}\right)^{\frac{1}{2}}$

(k) $\left(xy^3\right)^{\frac{1}{2}} \times \dfrac{x^{\frac{1}{2}} y^{\frac{1}{2}}}{xy^4}$

4 Simplify.

(a) $\left(x^{\frac{2}{3}}\right)^{\frac{1}{2}} \times \dfrac{x}{x^{\frac{2}{3}}}$

(b) $\left(x^{\frac{5}{2}}\right)^{\frac{3}{5}} \times \dfrac{x}{x^{\frac{1}{2}}}$

(c) $\left(x^{\frac{1}{2}} y^2\right)^{\frac{1}{2}} \times \left(x^{-\frac{3}{4}} y^4\right)^{\frac{1}{3}}$

(d) $\left(x^{\frac{2}{3}} y^{\frac{1}{3}}\right)^4 \times \dfrac{x^{\frac{1}{3}} y^{\frac{2}{3}}}{xy^2}$

(e) $\dfrac{y^{\frac{1}{3}}}{x^{\frac{1}{2}}} \div \left(\dfrac{x^{\frac{1}{2}} y^{\frac{2}{3}}}{x^3 y^4}\right)^{\frac{1}{2}}$

(f) $\dfrac{x^{\frac{1}{4}}}{y^{\frac{1}{2}}} \times \left(\dfrac{xy^{\frac{3}{4}}}{x^3 y^2}\right)^{\frac{1}{4}}$

Tip

Apply the index laws and work in this order:

- simplify any terms in brackets
- apply the multiplication law to numerators and then to denominators
- cancel numbers if you can
- apply the division law if the same letter appears in the numerator and denominator
- express your answer using positive indices

Exercise 2.5 B

1 Evaluate:

(a) $(-3^4)(-4)^2$

(b) $\dfrac{-2^4}{(-2)^4}$

(c) $\dfrac{6^3}{(-3)^4}$

(d) $8^{\frac{1}{3}}$

(e) $256^{-\frac{1}{4}}$

(f) $125^{-\frac{4}{3}}$

(g) $\left(\tfrac{1}{4}\right)^{-\frac{5}{2}}$

(h) $\left(\tfrac{1}{8}\right)^{-\frac{2}{3}}$

(i) $\left(\tfrac{8}{27}\right)^{-\frac{1}{3}}$

(j) $\left(\tfrac{8}{18}\right)^{-\frac{1}{2}}$

2 Calculate.

(a) $5 - 7(23 - 5^2) - 16 \div 2^3$

(b) $3(5^2) - 6(-3^2 - 4^2) \div -15$

(c) $-2(-3^2) + 24 \div (-2)^3$

(d) $-2(3)^4 - (6 - 7)^6$

3 Solve for x.

(a) $81^x = 3$

(b) $3^x = 81$

(c) $3^x = \tfrac{1}{81}$

(d) $16^x = 8$

(e) $16^x = 256$

(f) $5^{-x} = \tfrac{1}{25}$

(g) $3^{2x-4} = 1$

(h) $2^{2x+1} = 16$

Mixed exercise

1 Write each of the following as an algebraic expression. Use x to represent 'the number'.

(a) A number increased by 12.

(b) A number decreased by four.

(c) Five times a number.

(d) A number divided by three.

(e) The product of a number and four.

(f) A quarter of a number.

(g) A number subtracted from 12.

(h) The difference between a number and its cube.

2 Determine the value of $x^2 - 5x$ if:

(a) $x = 2$

(b) $x = -3$

(c) $x = \frac{1}{3}$

3 Evaluate each expression if $a = -1$, $b = 2$ and $c = 0$.

(a) $\dfrac{-2a + 3b}{2ab}$

(b) $\dfrac{b(c - a)}{b - a}$

(c) $\dfrac{a - b^2}{c - a^2}$

(d) $\dfrac{3 - 2(a - 1)}{c - a(b - 1)}$

(e) $a^3 b^2 - 2a^2 + a^4 b^2 - ac^3$

4 Simplify each of the following expressions as fully as possible.

(a) $3a + 4b + 6a - 3b$

(b) $x^2 + 4x - x - 2$

(c) $-2a^2 b(2a^2 - 3b^2)$

(d) $2x(x - 3) - (x - 4) - 2x^2$

(e) $16x^2 y \div 4y^2 x$

(f) $\dfrac{10x^2 - 5xy}{2x}$

5 Expand and simplify if possible.

(a) $2(4x - 3) + 3(x + 1)$

(b) $3x(2x + 3) - 2(4 - 3x)$

(c) $x(x + 2) + 3x - 3(x^2 - 4)$

(d) $x^2(x + 3) - 2x^3 - (x - 5)$

6 Simplify. Give all answers with positive indices only.

(a) $\dfrac{15x^7}{18x^2}$

(b) $5x^2 \times \dfrac{3x^5}{x^7}$

(c) $\dfrac{\left(x^3\right)^4}{\left(x^2\right)^8}$

(d) $\left(2xy^2\right)^4$

(e) $\left(\dfrac{4x^3}{y^5}\right)^3$

(f) $\left(x^3 y\right)^2 \times \dfrac{\left(x^2 y^4\right)^3}{\left(xy^2\right)^3}$

(g) $\left(2xy^3\right)^{-2} \times \left(3x^2 y\right)^3$

(h) $\dfrac{\left(x^{-3} y^2\right)^4}{2\left(xy^2\right)^{-3}} \div \left(\dfrac{x^{-3} y^3}{x^2 y^{-1}}\right)^2$

7 Simplify each of the following expressions.

(a) $\left(125x^3 y\right)^{\frac{1}{3}}$

(b) $\left(x^6 y^3\right)^{\frac{1}{2}} \times \dfrac{x^{\frac{1}{2}} y^{\frac{1}{2}}}{x^3 y^2}$

(c) $\left(x^2 y^{-3}\right)^{\frac{1}{2}} \times \left(x^{-4} y\right)^{\frac{5}{2}}$

(d) $\left(\dfrac{x^{\frac{1}{3}} y^{\frac{2}{3}}}{xy^{\frac{1}{3}}}\right)^2 \div \dfrac{\left(x^{\frac{1}{2}} y\right)^4}{2x^3 y^5}$

3 Lines, angles and shapes

3.1 Lines and angles

- Angles can be classified according to their size:
  - acute angles are < 90°
  - right angles are 90°
  - obtuse angles are > 90° but < 180°
  - reflex angles are > 180° but < 360°.
- Two angles that add up to 90° are called complementary angles. Two angles that add up to 180° are called supplementary angles.
- The sum of adjacent angles on a straight line is 180°.
- The sum of the angles around a point is 360°.
- When two lines intersect (cross), two pairs of vertically opposite angles are formed. Vertically opposite angles are equal.
- When two parallel lines are cut by a transversal, alternate angles are equal, corresponding angles are equal and co-interior angles add up to 180°.
- When alternate or corresponding angles are equal, or when co-interior angles add up to 180°, the lines are parallel.

Exercise 3.1 A

1 Look at the clock face on the left. Calculate the following.

(a) The smallest angle between the hands of the clock at:
   (i) 5 o'clock   (ii) 1800 hours   (iii) 1.30 a.m.

(b) Through how many degrees does the hour hand move between 4 p.m. and 5.30 p.m.?

(c) Through how many degrees does the minute hand turn in:

   (i) $2\frac{1}{4}$ hours?   (ii) 12 minutes?

(d) A clock shows 12 noon. What will the time be when the minute hand has moved 270° clockwise?

2 Will doubling an acute angle always produce an obtuse angle? Explain your answer.

3 Will halving an obtuse angle always produce an acute angle? Explain your answer.

4 What is the complement of each the following angles?

(a) 45°   (b) $x°$ (c) $(90 - x)°$

5 What is the supplement of each of the following angles?

(a) 45°   (b) 90°   (c) $x°$
(d) $(180 - x)°$ (e) $(90 - x)°$ (f) $(90 + x)°$

Exercise 3.1 B

In this exercise, calculate (do not measure from the diagrams) the values of the lettered angles. You should also state your reasons.

1 In the following diagram, *MN* and *PQ* are straight lines. Find the size of angle *a*.

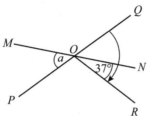

$Q\hat{O}R = 85°$

2 Calculate the value of *x* in each of the following figures.

(a)
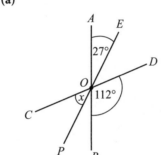

(b)
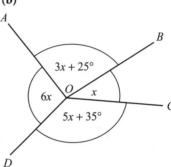

Exercise 3.1 C

1 Find the values of the angles marked *x* and *y* in each diagram.

(a)
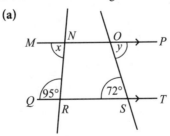

(b)
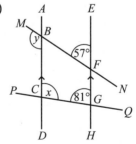

(c)
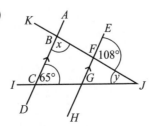

(d)
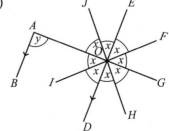

2 Calculate the value of x in each of the following figures. Give reasons for your answers.

(a)

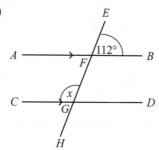

(b)

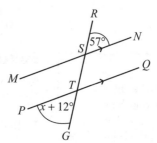

(c)

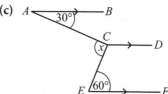

(d)

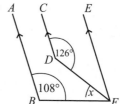

(e)

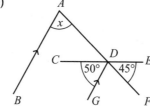

3.2 Triangles

- Scalene triangles have no equal sides and no equal angles.
- Isosceles triangles have two equal sides. The angles at the bases of the equal sides are equal in size. The converse is also true – if a triangle has two equal angles, then it is isosceles.
- Equilateral triangles have three equal sides and three equal angles (each being 60°).
- The sum of the interior angles of any triangle is 180°.
- The exterior angle of a triangle is equal to the sum of the two opposite interior angles.

Exercise 3.2

◀ REWIND

You may also need to apply the angle relationships for points, lines and parallel lines to find the missing angles in triangles. ◀

1 Find the angles marked with letters. Give reasons for any statements.

(a)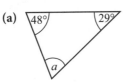

(b)

(c)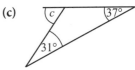

(d)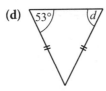

(e)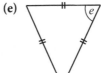

(f)

(g)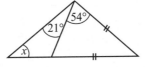

(h)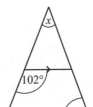

(i)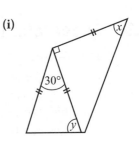

2 Calculate the value of *x* and hence find the size of the marked angles.

(a)

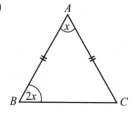

(b)

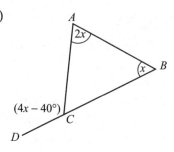

(c)

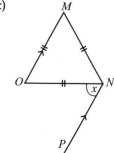

(d)

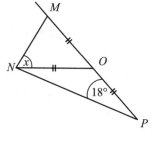

3 In △*ABC*, ∠*A* = 78°, ∠*B* = *x* and ∠*C* = 2*x*.

Calculate the size of angles *B* and *C* in degrees.

> **! Tip**
> For word problems
> where you are not given a
> diagram, a rough sketch
> may help you work out the
> answers.

3.3 Quadrilaterals

- A quadrilateral is a four-sided shape.
  - A trapezium has one pair of parallel sides.
  - A kite has two pairs of adjacent sides equal in length. The diagonals intersect at 90° and the longer diagonal bisects the shorter one. Only one pair of opposite angles is equal. The diagonals bisect the opposite angles.
  - A parallelogram has opposite sides equal and parallel. The opposite angles are equal in size and the diagonals bisect each other.
  - A rectangle has opposite sides equal and parallel and interior angles each equal to 90°. The diagonals are equal in length and they bisect each other.
  - A rhombus is a parallelogram with all four sides equal in length. The diagonals bisect each other at 90° and bisect the opposite angles.
  - A square has four equal sides and four angles each equal to 90°. The opposite sides are parallel. The diagonals are equal in length, they bisect each other at right angles and they bisect the opposite angles.
- The sum of the interior angles of a quadrilateral is 360°.

Exercise 3.3

REWIND

The angle relationships for parallel lines will apply when a quadrilateral has parallel sides. ◄

1   Each of the following statements applies to one or more quadrilaterals. For each one, name the quadrilateral(s) to which it always applies.

(a) All sides are equal in length.

(b) All angles are equal in size.

(c) The diagonals are the same length.

(d) The diagonals bisect each other.

(e) The angles are all 90° and the diagonals bisect each other.

(f) Opposite angles are equal in size.

(g) The diagonals intersect at right angles.

(h) The diagonals bisect the opposite angles.

(i) One diagonal divides the quadrilateral into two isosceles triangles.

2   Copy the diagrams below. Fill in the sizes of all the angles.

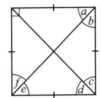 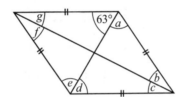

3   Calculate the size of the marked angles in the following figures. Give reasons or state the properties you are using.

(a)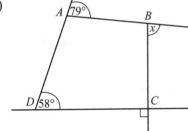

(b)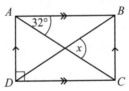

(c)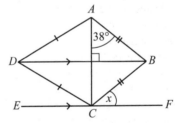

(d)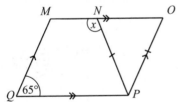

(e)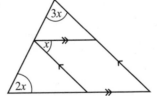

(f)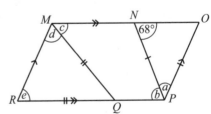

4   Quadrilateral $PQRS$ has $\angle P = \angle S = 75°$ and $\angle R = 2\angle Q$.

Calculate the size of:

(a) $\angle R + \angle Q$ (b) $\angle R$ (c) $\angle Q$.

5   A kite $PMNO$ has diagonals PN and MO that intersect at Q. $\angle QMN = 48°$ and $\angle PNO = 62°$.
Calculate the size of:

(a) $\angle MNP$ (b) $\angle MNO$ (c) $\angle PON$.

3.4 Polygons

- A polygon is a two-dimensional shape with three or more sides. Polygons are named according the number of sides they have:

  - triangle (3)
  - heptagon (7)
  - quadrilateral (4)
  - octagon (8)
  - pentagon (5)
  - nonagon (9)
  - hexagon (6)
  - decagon (10).

- A regular polygon has all its sides equal and all its angles equal.
- The interior angle sum of any polygon can be worked out using the formula $(n-2) \times 180°$ where n is the number of sides. Once you have the angle sum, you can find the size of one angle of a regular polygon by dividing the total by the number of angles.
- The sum of the exterior angles of any convex polygon is 360°.

Exercise 3.4

Tip

If you can't remember the formula, you can find the size of one interior angle of a regular polygon using the fact that the exterior angles add up to 360°. Divide 360 by the number of angles to find the size of one exterior angle. Then use the fact that the exterior and interior angles form a straight line (180°) to work out the size of the interior angle.

1 For each of the following find:

   (i)   the sum of the interior angles   (ii) the size of one interior angle

   (a) a regular octagon
   (b) a regular decagon
   (c) a regular 15-sided polygon.

2 A coin is made in the shape of a regular 7-sided polygon. Calculate the size of each interior angle.

3 The interior angle of a regular polygon is 162°. How many sides does the polygon have?

4 One exterior angle of a regular polygon is 14.4°.

   (a) What is the size of each interior angle?
   (b) How many sides does the polygon have?

5 Calculate the value of the angles marked with letters in each of these irregular polygons.

   (a)

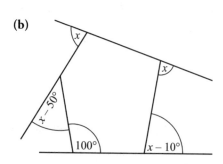

   (b)

   (c)

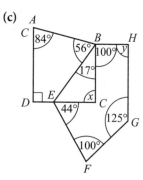

3.5 Circles

- A circle is a set of points equidistant from a fixed centre. Half a circle is a semi-circle.
- The perimeter of a circle is called its circumference.
- The distance across a circle (through the centre) is called its diameter. A radius is half a diameter.
- An arc is part of the circumference of a circle.
- A chord is a line joining two points on the circumference. A chord cuts the circle into two segments.
- A 'slice' of a circle, made by two radii and the arc between them on the circumference, is called a sector.
- A tangent is a line that touches a circle at only one point.

Exercise 3.5

1 Draw a circle with a radius of 4 cm and centre O. By drawing the parts and labelling them, indicate the following on your diagram:

   (a) a sector with an angle of 50°
   (b) chord DE
   (c) MON, the diameter of the circle
   (d) a tangent that touches the circle at M
   (e) the major arc MP.

3.6 Construction

- You need to be able to use a ruler and a pair of compasses to construct triangles (given the lengths of three sides) and bisect lines and angles. You also need to be able to construct other simple geometric figures from given specifications.
- The diagrams below show you how to bisect an angle and how to draw the perpendicular bisector of a line:

How to bisect an angle.

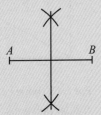

How to draw the perpendicular bisector of a line.

Tip

Always start with a rough sketch. Label your rough sketch so you know what lengths you need to measure.

Exercise 3.6

1 Draw angle $A\hat{B}C = 105°$. Accurately bisect the angle.

2 Construct $\triangle ABC$ with $AC = 7\,\text{cm}$, $CB = 6\,\text{cm}$ and $AB = 8\,\text{cm}$.

3 Construct $\triangle MNO$ with $MN = 4.5\,\text{cm}$, $NO = 5.5\,\text{cm}$ and $MO = 8\,\text{cm}$. Construct the perpendicular bisector of NO to cut NO at X and extend the line to cut MO at Y. Measure the length of XY to the nearest millimetre.

4 Construct △*DEF* with *DE* = 100 mm, *FE* = 70 mm and *DF* = 50 mm.

    (a) What type of triangle is *DEF*?

    (b) Bisect each angle of the triangle. Do the angle bisectors meet at the same point?

5 Accurately construct a square of side 4.7 cm. What is the length of a diagonal of the square?

Mixed exercise

1 Find the value of the marked angles in each of the following.

(a)

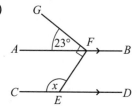

(b)

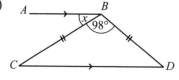

(c)

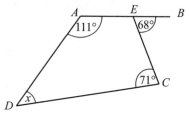

(d)

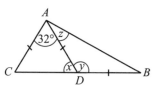

(e)

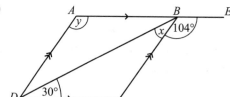

(f)

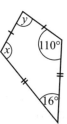

(g)

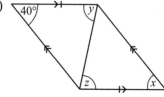

(h)

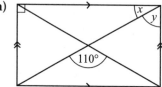

2 For each shape combination find the size of angle *x*. The shapes in parts (a) and (b) are regular polygons.

(a)

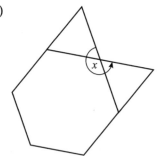

(b)

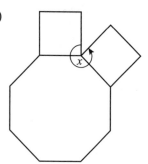

(c)

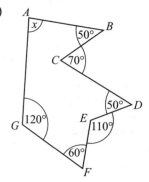

3 Use the diagram of the circle with centre O to answer these questions.

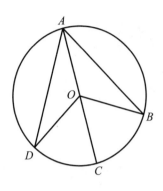

(a) What are the correct mathematical names for:
   (i) DO (ii) AB (iii) AC?

(b) Four radii are shown on the diagram. Name them.

(c) If OB is 12.4 cm long, how long is AC?

(d) Draw a copy of the circle and on to it draw the tangent to the circle that passes through point B.

4 Use a ruler and a protractor to draw line segment AB 11 cm long. Construct XY, the perpendicular bisector of AB with point X on AB. Bisect angle $B\hat{X}Y$.

5 Construct $\triangle ABC$ with $AB = BC = AC = 6.5$ cm. Construct the perpendicular bisector of AB. Where does this intersect with the triangle?

Collecting, organising and displaying data

4.1 Collecting and classifying data

- Data is a set of facts, numbers or other information, collected to try to answer a question.
- Primary data is 'original' data and can be collected by measuring, observation, doing experiments, carrying out surveys or asking people to complete questionnaires.
- Secondary data is data drawn from a non-original source. For example you could find the area of each of the world's oceans by referring to an atlas.
- You can classify data as qualitative or quantitative.
- Qualitative data is non-numeric such as colour, make of vehicle or favourite flavour.
- Quantitative data is numerical data that was counted or measured. For example age, marks in a test, shoe size, height.
- Quantitative data can be discrete or continuous.
- Discrete data can only take certain values and is usually something counted. For example, the number of children in your family. There are no in-between values; you can't have $2\frac{1}{2}$ children in a family.
- Continuous data can take any value and is usually something measured. For example the heights of trees in a rainforest could range from 50 to 60 metres. Any value in-between those two heights is possible.

Exercise 4.1

The following table of data was collected about ten students in a high school. Study the table and then answer the questions about the data.

Student	1	2	3	4	5	6	7	8	9	10
Gender	F	F	M	M	M	F	M	F	F	M
Height (m)	1.55	1.61	1.63	1.60	1.61	1.62	1.64	1.69	1.61	1.65
Shoe size	3	4	7	6	9	7	8	7	5	10
Mass (kg)	40	51	52	54	60	43	55	56	51	55
Eye colour	Br	Gr	Gr	Br	Br	Br	Br	Gr	Bl	Br
Hair colour	Bl	Bl	Blo	Br	Br	Br	Bl	Bl	Bl	Bl
No. of brothers/ sisters	0	3	4	2	1	2	3	1	0	3

(a) Which of these data categories are qualitative?
(b) Which of these data categories are quantitative?
(c) Which sets of numerical data are discrete data?
(d) Which sets of numerical data are continuous data?
(e) How do you think each set of data was collected? Give a reason for your answers.

4.2 Organising data

- Once data has been collected, it needs to be arranged and organised so that it is easier to work with, interpret and make inferences about.
- Tally tables and frequency tables are used to organise data and to show the totals of different values or categories.
- When you have a large set of numerical data, with lots of different scores, you can group the data into intervals called class intervals. Class intervals should not overlap.
- A two way table can be used to show the frequency of results for two or more sets of data.

Exercise 4.2

In data handling, the word **frequency** means the number of times a score or observation occurs.

1 Sesh did a survey to find out how many phone calls a group of 40 students received in one hour. These are his results.

6	5	6	7	4	5	8	6	7	10
7	6	5	6	1	9	4	4	2	6
5	5	7	3	4	5	8	3	5	8
10	9	9	7	5	5	7	6	4	2

Copy and complete this tally table to organise the data.

Phone calls	Tally	Frequency
1		
2		

2 Nika counted the number of mosquitoes in her bedroom for 50 nights in a row and got these results.

6	6	6	5	4	3	2	0	0	6
5	0	4	0	0	0	0	2	1	4
1	1	3	2	5	4	3	3	3	2
1	6	5	5	4	4	3	2	5	4
6	3	2	4	2	1	2	2	1	5

(a) Copy and complete this frequency table to organise the data.

Number of mosquitoes	0	1	2	3	4	5	6
Frequency							

(b) Does Nika have a mosquito problem? Give a reason for your answer.

Score	Frequency
0–29	
30–39	
40–49	
50–59	
60–69	
70–79	
80–100	

3 These are the percentage scores of 50 students in an examination.

54	26	60	40	55	82	67	59	57	70
67	44	63	56	46	48	55	63	42	58
45	54	76	65	63	61	49	54	54	53
67	56	69	57	38	57	51	55	59	78
65	52	55	78	69	71	73	88	80	91

(a) Copy and complete this grouped frequency table to organise the results.
(b) How many students scored at least 70%?
(c) How many students scored lower than 40%?
(d) How many students scored at least 40% but less than 60%?
(e) The first and last class interval in the table are greater than the others. Suggest why this is the case.

4 This is a section of the table you worked with in Exercise 4.1.

Student	1	2	3	4	5	6	7	8	9	10
Gender	F	F	M	M	M	F	M	F	F	M
Eye colour	Br	Gr	Gr	Br	Br	Br	Br	Gr	Bl	Br
Hair colour	Bl	Bl	Blo	Br	Br	Br	Bl	Bl	Bl	Bl
No. of siblings (brothers/sisters)	0	3	4	2	1	2	3	1	0	3

(a) Copy and complete this two way table using data from the table.

Eye colour	Brown	Blue	Green
Male			
Female			

(b) Draw and complete two similar two way tables of your own to show the hair colour and number of brothers or sisters by gender.
(c) Write a sentence to summarise what you found out for each table.

4.3 Using charts to display data

- Charts usually help you to see patterns and trends in data more easily than in tables.
- Pictograms use symbols to show the frequency of data in different categories. They are useful for discrete, categorical and ungrouped data.
- Bar charts are useful for categorical and ungrouped data. A bar chart has bars of equal width which are equally spaced.
- Bar charts can be drawn as horizontal or vertical charts. They can also show two or more sets of data on the same set of axes.
- Pie charts are circular graphs that use sectors of circle to show the proportion of data in each category.
- All charts should have a heading and clearly labelled scales, axes or keys.

Exercise 4.3

1 Study the diagram carefully and answer the questions about it.

Number of students in each year

Year 8	
Year 9	
Year 10	
Year 11	
Year 12	

Key

⚇ = 30 students

(a) What type of chart is this?

(b) What does the chart show?

(c) What does each full symbol represent?

(d) How are 15 students shown on the chart?

(e) How many students are there in Year 8?

(f) Which year group has the most students? How many are there in this year group?

(g) Do you think these are accurate or rounded figures? Why?

> **Tip**
>
> Choose symbols that are easy to draw and to divide into parts. If it is not given, choose a suitable scale for your symbols so you don't have to draw too many.

2 The table shows the population (in millions) of five of the world's largest cities.

City	Tokyo	Seoul	Mexico City	New York	Mumbai
Population (millions)	32.5	20.6	20.5	19.75	19.2

Draw a pictogram to show this data.

> **Tip**
>
> Compound bar charts show two or more sets of data on the same pair of axes. A key is needed to show which set each bar represents.

3 Study the two bar charts below.

(a) What does chart A show?

(b) How many boys are there in Class 10A?

(c) How many students are there in 10A altogether?

(d) What does chart B show?

(e) Which sport is most popular with boys?

(f) Which sport is most popular with girls?

(g) How many students chose basketball as their favourite sport?

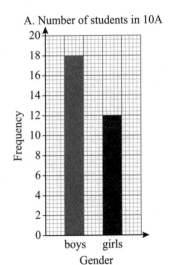

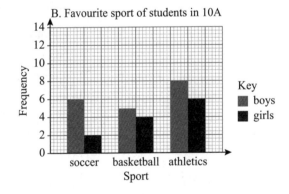

4 The table below shows the type of food that a group of students in a hostel chose for breakfast.

	Cereal	Hot porridge	Bread
Girls	8	16	12
Boys	2	12	10

(a) Draw a single bar chart to show the choice of cereal against bread.

(b) Draw a compound bar chart to show the breakfast food choice for girls and boys.

> ## Tip
>
> To work out the percentage that an angle in a pie chart represents, use the formula:
>
> $\frac{n}{360} \times 100$
>
> where n is the size of the angle.

5 Jyoti recorded the number and type of 180 vehicles passing her home in Bangalore. She drew this pie chart to show her results.

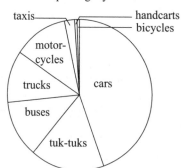

Traffic passing my home

(a) Which type of vehicle was most common?

(b) What percentage of the vehicles were tuk-tuks?

(c) How many trucks passed Jyoti's home?

(d) Which types of vehicles were least common?

6 In an IGCSE exam the results for 120 students were: 5% attained an A grade, 12% attained a B grade, 41% attained a C grade, 25% attained a D grade and the rest attained E grade or lower.

(a) Represent this information on a pie chart.

(b) How many students attained an A?

(c) How many students attained a D or lower?

(d) Which grade was attained by most of the students?

7 The graphs below represent the average monthly temperature and the average monthly rainfall in the desert in Egypt.

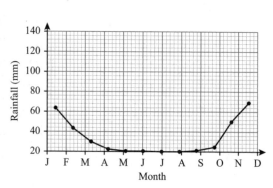

Average monthly temperature

Average monthly rainfall

(a) What is the maximum temperature?

(b) In what months is the average temperature above 20 °C?

(c)   Is Egypt in the northern or southern hemisphere?
(d)   Is the temperature ever below freezing point?
(e)   What is the average rainfall in November?
(f)   In which month is the average rainfall 2 mm?
(g)   Looking at both graphs, what can you say about the rainfall when the temperatures are high?

Mixed exercise

1   Mika collected data about how many children different families in her community had. These are her results.

0	3	4	3	3	2	2	2	2	1	1	1
3	3	4	3	6	2	2	2	0	0	2	1
5	4	3	2	4	3	3	3	2	1	1	0
3	1	1	1	1	0	0	0	2	4	5	3

(a)   How do you think Mika collected the data?
(b)   Is this data discrete or continuous? Why?
(c)   Is this data qualitative or quantitative? Why?
(d)   Draw up a frequency table, with tallies, to organise the data.
(e)   Represent the data on a pie chart.
(f)   Draw a bar chart to compare the number of families that have three or fewer children with those that have four or more children.

2   Mrs Sanchez bakes and sells cookies. One week she sells 420 peanut crunchies, 488 chocolate cups and 320 coconut munchies. Draw a pictogram to represent this data.

3   Study the chart in the margin.

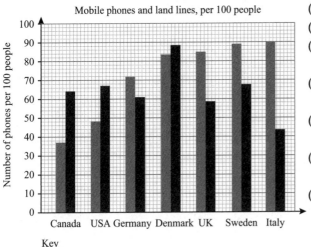

Mobile phones and land lines, per 100 people

Key
■ Mobile phones   ■ Land lines

(a)   What do you call this type of chart?
(b)   What does the chart show?
(c)   Can you tell how many people in each country have a mobile phone from this chart? Explain your answer.
(d)   In which countries do a greater proportion of the people have a land line than a mobile phone?
(e)   In which countries do more people have mobile phones than land lines?
(f)   In which country do more than 80% of the population have a land line and a mobile phone?
(g)   What do you think the bars would look like for your country? Why?

4 Use the table of data from Exercise 4.1 (repeated below) about the ten students for this question.

Student	1	2	3	4	5	6	7	8	9	10
Gender	F	F	M	M	M	F	M	F	F	M
Height (m)	1.55	1.61	1.63	1.60	1.61	1.62	1.64	1.69	1.61	1.65
Shoe size	3	4	7	6	9	7	8	7	5	10
Mass (kg)	40	51	52	54	60	43	55	56	51	55
Eye colour	Br	Gr	Gr	Br	Br	Br	Br	Gr	Bl	Br
Hair colour	Bl	Bl	Blo	Br	Br	Br	Bl	Bl	Bl	Bl
No. of brothers/sisters	0	3	4	2	1	2	3	1	0	3

(a) Draw a pie chart to show the data about the number of siblings.

(b) Represent the height of students using an appropriate chart.

(c) Draw a compound bar chart showing eye and hair colour by gender.

5 Amy bought a new Vauxhall Corsa in 2008. Its value is shown in the table below.

Year	Value of car
2008	$13 900
2009	$7 000
2010	$5 700
2011	$4 700
2012	$4 000

(a) Draw a line graph to represent this information.

(b) What is the percentage depreciation in the first year she owned the car?

(c) Use your graph to estimate the value of the car in 2013.

FAST FORWARD ▶

In part (b), the 'percentage depreciation' requires you to first calculate how much the car's value decreased in the year she had it, and then calculate this as a percentage of the original value. You will see more about percentage decrease in chapter 5. ▶

5 Fractions

5.1 Equivalent fractions

- Equivalent means, 'has the same value'.
- To find equivalent fractions either multiply both the numerator and denominator by the same number or divide both the numerator and denominator by the same number.

You can cross multiply to make an equation and then solve it. For example:

$$\frac{1}{2} \diagdown \frac{x}{28}$$

$2x = 28$

$x = 14$

Exercise 5.1

1 Find the missing value in each pair of equivalent fractions.

(a) $\dfrac{2}{5} = \dfrac{26}{x}$

(b) $\dfrac{5}{7} = \dfrac{120}{x}$

(c) $\dfrac{6}{5} = \dfrac{66}{x}$

(d) $\dfrac{11}{9} = \dfrac{143}{x}$

(e) $\dfrac{5}{3} = \dfrac{80}{x}$

(f) $\dfrac{8}{12} = \dfrac{x}{156}$

5.2 Operations on fractions

- To multiply fractions, multiply numerators by numerators and denominators by denominators. Mixed numbers should be rewritten as improper fractions before multiplying or dividing.
- To add or subtract fractions change them to equivalent fractions with the same denominator, then add (or subtract) the numerators only.
- To divide by a fraction, invert the fraction (turn it upside down) and change the ÷ sign to a × sign.
- Unless you are specifically asked for a mixed number, give answers to calculations with fractions as proper or improper fractions in their simplest form.

Tip

If you can simplify the fraction part first you will have smaller numbers to multiply to get the improper fraction.

Remember: you can cancel to simplify when you are multiplying fractions; and the word 'of' means ×.

Exercise 5.2

1 Rewrite each mixed number as an improper fraction in its simplest form.

(a) $3\dfrac{5}{40}$

(b) $1\dfrac{12}{22}$

(c) $11\dfrac{24}{30}$

(d) $3\dfrac{75}{100}$

(e) $14\dfrac{3}{4}$

(f) $2\dfrac{35}{45}$

2 Calculate.

(a) $1\dfrac{4}{5} \times 12$

(b) $\dfrac{9}{13} \times 7$

(c) $3\dfrac{1}{2} \times 4$

(d) $2\dfrac{1}{3} \times 2\dfrac{2}{5}$

(e) $2 \times 4\dfrac{1}{2} \times \dfrac{1}{3}$

(f) $\dfrac{1}{5} \times \dfrac{12}{19} \times 2\dfrac{1}{2}$

(g) $\dfrac{1}{3}$ of 360

(h) $\dfrac{3}{4}$ of $\dfrac{2}{7}$

(i) $\dfrac{8}{9}$ of 81

(j) $\dfrac{2}{3}$ of $4\dfrac{1}{2}$

(k) $\dfrac{1}{2}$ of $9\dfrac{16}{50}$

(l) $\dfrac{3}{4}$ of $2\dfrac{1}{3}$

Tip

You can use any common denominator but it is easier to simplify if you use the lowest one.

3 Calculate, giving your answer as a fraction in simplest form.

(a) $\frac{1}{6} + \frac{3}{8}$

(b) $\frac{9}{10} - \frac{7}{12}$

(c) $\frac{4}{7} + \frac{1}{3}$

(d) $2\frac{1}{2} + 3\frac{1}{3}$

(e) $2\frac{1}{8} + 1\frac{1}{7}$

(f) $4\frac{3}{10} + 3\frac{3}{4}$

(g) $1\frac{1}{13} - \frac{4}{5}$

(h) $3\frac{9}{10} - 2\frac{7}{8}$

(i) $2\frac{5}{7} - 1\frac{1}{3}$

(j) $1\frac{1}{2} - \frac{7}{3}$

(k) $2\frac{1}{3} - \frac{17}{3}$

(l) $1\frac{4}{9} - \frac{13}{3}$

4 Calculate.

(a) $8 \div \frac{1}{3}$

(b) $12 \div \frac{7}{8}$

(c) $\frac{7}{8} \div 12$

(d) $\frac{2}{9} \div \frac{18}{30}$

(e) $\frac{8}{9} \div \frac{4}{5}$

(f) $1\frac{3}{7} \div 2\frac{2}{9}$

(g) $1\frac{14}{26} \div \frac{10}{13}$

(h) $3\frac{6}{15} \div 5\frac{2}{3}$

(i) $5\frac{1}{5} \div 1\frac{3}{10}$

REWIND

The order of operations rules (BODMAS) that were covered in chapter 1 apply here too. ◄

5 Simplify the following.

(a) $4 + \frac{2}{3} \times \frac{1}{3}$

(b) $2\frac{1}{8} - \left(2\frac{1}{5} - \frac{7}{8}\right)$

(c) $\frac{3}{7} \times \left(\frac{2}{3} + 6 \div \frac{2}{3}\right) + 5 \times \frac{2}{7}$

(d) $2\frac{7}{8} + \left(8\frac{1}{4} - 6\frac{3}{8}\right)$

(e) $\frac{5}{6} \times \frac{1}{4} + \frac{5}{8} \times \frac{1}{3}$

(f) $\left(5 \div \frac{3}{11} - \frac{5}{12}\right) \times \frac{1}{6}$

(g) $\left(\frac{5}{8} \div \frac{15}{4}\right) - \left(\frac{5}{6} \times \frac{1}{5}\right)$

(h) $\left(2\frac{2}{3} \div 4 - \frac{3}{10}\right) \times \frac{3}{17}$

(i) $\left(7 \div \frac{2}{9} - \frac{1}{3}\right) \times \frac{2}{3}$

6 Mrs West has \$900 dollars in her account. She spends $\frac{7}{12}$ of this.

(a) How much does she spend?

(b) How much does she have left?

7 It takes a builder $\frac{3}{4}$ of an hour to lay 50 tiles.

(a) How many tiles will he lay in $4\frac{1}{2}$ hours?

(b) How long will it take him to complete a floor needing 462 tiles?

5.3 Percentages

- Per cent means per hundred. A percentage is a fraction with a denominator of 100.
- To write one quantity as a percentage of another, express it as a fraction and then convert the fraction to a percentage.
- To find a percentage of a quantity, multiply the percentage by the quantity.
- To increase or decrease an amount by a percentage, find the percentage amount and add or subtract it from the original amount.

Exercise 5.3 A

1 Express the following as percentages. Round your answers to one decimal place.

(a) $\frac{1}{6}$

(b) $\frac{5}{8}$

(c) $\frac{93}{312}$

(d) 0.3

(e) 0.04

(f) 0.47

(g) 1.12

(h) 2.07

2 Express the following percentages as common fractions in their simplest form.

(a) 12.5% (b) 50% (c) 98% (d) 60% (e) 22%

3 Express the following decimals as percentages.

(a) 0.83 (b) 0.6 (c) 0.07 (d) 0.375

(e) 1.25 (f) 2.5

4 Calculate.

(a) 30% of 200 kg (b) 40% of $60 (c) 25% of 600 litres (d) 22% of 250 ml

(e) 50% of $128 (f) 65% of £30 (g) 15% of 120 km (h) 0.5% of 40 grams

(i) 2.6% of $80 (j) 9.5% of 5000 cubic metres

> **Tip**
> When finding a percentage of a quantity, your answer will have a unit and not a percentage sign because you are working out an amount.

5 Calculate the percentage increase or decrease and copy and complete the table. Round your answers to one decimal place.

	Original amount	New amount	Percentage increase or decrease
(a)	40	48	
(b)	4000	3600	
(c)	1.5	2.3	
(d)	12 000	12 400	
(e)	12 000	8600	
(f)	9.6	12.8	
(g)	90	2400	

6 Increase each amount by the given percentage.

(a) $48 increased by 14% (b) $700 increased by 35%

(c) $30 increased by 7.6% (d) $40 000 increased by 0.59%

(e) $90 increased by 9.5% (f) $80 increased by 24.6%

7 Decrease each amount by the given percentage.

(a) $68 decreased by 14% (b) $800 decreased by 35%

(c) $90 decreased by 7.6% (d) $20 000 decreased by 0.59%

(e) $85 decreased by 9.5% (f) $60 decreased by 24.6%

Exercise 5.3 B

1 75 250 tickets were available for an international cricket match. 62% of the tickets were sold within a day. How many tickets are left?

2 Mrs Rajah owns 15% of a company. If the company issues 12 000 shares, how many shares should she get?

3 A building, which cost $125 000 to build, increased in value by $3\frac{1}{2}$ %. What is the building worth now?

4 A player scored 18 out of the 82 points in a basketball match. What percentage of the points did he score?

5 A company has a budget of $24 000 for printing brochures. The marketing department has spent 34.6% of the budget already. How much money is left in the budget?

6 Josh currently earns $6000 per month. If he receives an increase of 3.8%, what will his new monthly earnings be?

7 A company advertises that its cottage cheese is 99.5% fat free. If this is correct, how many grams of fat would there be in a 500 gram tub of the cottage cheese?

8 Sally earns $25 per shift. Her boss says she can either have $7 more per shift or a 20% increase. Which is the better offer?

Exercise 5.3 C

Tip

Finding an original amount involves reverse percentages. Note that there are different ways of saying 'original amount', such as old amount, previous amount, amount before the increase or decrease, and so on.

1 Misha paid $40 for a DVD set at a 20% off sale. What was the original price of the DVD set?

2 In a large school 240 students are in Grade 8. This is 20% of the school population.
(a) How many students are there in total in the school?
(b) How many students are in the rest of the school?

3 Suki, the waitress, has her wages increased by 15%. Her new wages are $172.50. What was her wage before the increase?

4 This summer, an amusement park increased its entry prices by 25% to $15.00. This summer, the number of people entering the park dropped by 8% from the previous summer to 25 530.
(a) What was the entry price the previous summer?
(b) How many visitors did the park have the previous summer?
(c) If the running costs of the amusement park remained the same as the previous summer and they made a 30% profit on the entry fees in this summer, how much was their profit amount in dollars?

5.4 Standard form

- A number in standard form is written as a number between 1 and 10 multiplied by 10 raised to a power e.g., $a \times 10^k$
- Standard form is also called scientific notation.
- To write a number in standard form:
  - 1. place a decimal point after the first significant digit
  - 2. count the number of place orders the first significant digit has to move to get from this new number to the original number, this gives the power of 10
  - 3. if the significant digit has moved to the left (note this *looks* like the decimal point has moved to the right), the power of 10 is positive, but if the significant digit has moved to the right (or decimal to the left), the power of 10 is negative.
- To write a number in standard form as an ordinary number, multiply the decimal fraction by 10 to the given power.

Tip

Make sure you know how your calculator deals with standard form.

Exercise 5.4 A

1 Write the following numbers in standard form.
(a) 45 000 (b) 800 000 (c) 80 (d) 2 345 000
(e) 4 190 000 (f) 32 000 000 000 (g) 0.0065 (h) 0.009
(i) 0.00045 (j) 0.0000008 (k) 0.00675 (l) 0.00000000045

If the number part of your standard form answer is a whole number, there is no need to add a decimal point.

2 Write the following as ordinary numbers.

(a) 2.5×10^3 (b) 3.9×10^4 (c) 4.265×10^5 (d) 1.045×10^{-5}

(e) 9.15×10^{-6} (f) 1×10^{-9} (g) 2.8×10^{-5} (h) 9.4×10^7

(i) 2.45×10^{-3}

REWIND

Remember, the first significant figure is the first non-zero digit from the left. ◀

Exercise 5.4 B

1 Calculate, giving your answers in standard form correct to three significant figures.

(a) $(0.00009)^4$ (b) $0.0002 \div 2500^3$ (c) $65\,000\,000 \div 0.0000045$

(d) $(0.0029)^3 \times (0.00365)^5$ (e) $(48 \times 987)^4$ (f) $\dfrac{4525 \times 8760}{0.00002}$

(g) $\dfrac{9500}{0.0005^4}$ (h) $\sqrt{5.25} \times 10^8$ (i) $\sqrt[3]{9.1 \times 10^{-8}}$

2 Simplify each of the following. Give your answer in standard form.

(a) $(3 \times 10^{12}) \times (4 \times 10^{18})$ (b) $(1.5 \times 10^6) \times (3 \times 10^5)$ (c) $(1.5 \times 10^{12})^3$

(d) $(1.2 \times 10^{-5}) \times (1.1 \times 10^{-6})$ (e) $(0.4 \times 10^{15}) \times (0.5 \times 10^{12})$ (f) $(8 \times 10^{17}) \div (3 \times 10^{12})$

(g) $(1.44 \times 10^8) \div (1.2 \times 10^6)$ (h) $(8 \times 10^{-15}) \div (4 \times 10^{-12})$ (i) $\sqrt[3]{9.1} \times 10^{-8}$

3 The Sun has a mass of approximately 1.998×10^{27} tonnes. The planet Mercury has a mass of approximately 3.302×10^{20} tonnes.

(a) Which has the greater mass?

(b) How many times heavier is the greater mass compared with the smaller mass?

4 Light travels at a speed of 3×10^8 metres per second. The Earth is an average distance of 1.5×10^{11} m from the Sun and Pluto is an average 5.9×10^{12} m from the Sun.

(a) Work out how long it takes light from the Sun to reach Earth (in seconds). Give your answer in both ordinary numbers and standard form.

(b) How much longer does it take for the light to reach Pluto? Give your answer in both ordinary numbers and standard form.

5.5 Estimation

- Estimating involves rounding values in a calculation to numbers that are easy to work with (usually without the need for a calculator).
- An estimate allows you to check that your calculations make sense.

Exercise 5.5

Remember, the symbol ≈ means 'is approximately equal to'.

1 Use whole numbers to show why these estimates are correct.

(a) $3.9 \times 5.1 \approx 20$ (b) $68 \times 5.03 \approx 350$

(c) $999 \times 6.9 \approx 7000$ (d) $42.02 \div 5.96 \approx 7$

2 Estimate the answers to each of these calculations to the nearest whole number.

(a) $5.2 + 16.9 - 8.9 + 7.1$ (b) $(23.86 + 9.07) \div (15.99 - 4.59)$

(c) $\dfrac{9.3 \times 7.6}{5.9 \times 0.95}$ (d) $8.9^2 \times \sqrt{8.98}$

Mixed exercise

1 Estimate the answer to each of these calculations to the nearest whole number.

(a) 9.75×4.108 (b) $0.0387 \div 0.00732$ (c) $\dfrac{36.4 \times 6.32}{9.987}$ (d) $\sqrt{64.25} \times 3.098^2$

2 Simplify.

(a) $\dfrac{160}{200}$ (b) $\dfrac{48}{72}$ (c) $\dfrac{36}{54}$

3 Calculate.

(a) $\dfrac{4}{9} \times \dfrac{3}{8}$ (b) $84 \times \dfrac{3}{4}$ (c) $\dfrac{5}{9} \div \dfrac{1}{3}$ (d) $\dfrac{9}{11} - \dfrac{3}{4}$ (e) $\dfrac{5}{24} + \dfrac{7}{16}$

(f) $2\dfrac{1}{3} + 9\dfrac{1}{2}$ (g) $\left(4\dfrac{3}{4}\right)^2$ (h) $9\dfrac{1}{5} - 1\dfrac{7}{9}$ (i) $9\dfrac{1}{5} - 1\dfrac{7}{9} \times 2\dfrac{5}{8}$ (j) $\dfrac{4}{5} \div \dfrac{18}{25} + \left(\dfrac{2}{3}\right)^2$

4 Joshua is paid \$20.45 per hour. He normally works a 38-hour week.

(a) Estimate his weekly earnings to the nearest dollar.

(b) Estimate his annual earnings.

5 The value of a plot of land increased by 5% to \$10 500. What was its previous value?

6 In an election, 2.5% of the 28 765 ballot papers were rejected as spoiled votes.

(a) How many votes were spoiled?

(b) Of the rest of the votes, 42% were for Candidate A. How many votes did Candidate A receive?

7 A baby had a mass of 3.25 kg when she was born. After 12 weeks, her mass had increased to 5.45 kg. Express this as a percentage increase, correct to one decimal place.

8 Pluto is 5.9×10^{12} m from the Sun.

(a) Express this in kilometres, giving your answer in standard form.

(b) In a certain position, the Earth is 1.47×10^8 km from the Sun. If Pluto, the Earth and the Sun are in a straight line in this position (and both planets are the same side of the Sun), calculate the approximate distance, in km, between the Earth and Pluto. Give your answer in standard form.

9 A light year is the distance that light travels in one year, 9 463 700 000 000 km.

(a) Write one light year in standard form.

(b) The Sun is 0.000016 light years from Earth. Express this distance in light years in standard form.

(c) Proxima centauri, a star, is 4.2 light years from Earth. How many kilometres is this? Give your answer in standard form.

Equations and transforming formulae

6.1 Further expansions of brackets

- Expand means to remove the brackets by multiplying out.
- Each term inside the bracket must be multiplied by the term outside the bracket.
- Negative terms in front of the brackets will affect the signs of the expanded terms.

Remember:

$+ \times - = -$

$- \times + = -$

$+ \times + = +$

$- + - = +$

Exercise 6.1

1 Expand and simplify if possible.

(a) $-2(x+y)$ (b) $-5(a-b)$ (c) $-3(-2x+y)$

(d) $2x(4-2y)$ (e) $-2x(x+3y)$ (f) $-9(x-1)$

(g) $3(4-2a)$ (h) $3-(4x+y)$ (i) $2x-(2x-3)$

(j) $-(3x+7)$ (k) $2x(x-y)$ (l) $-3x(x-2y)$

2 Expand and simplify as far as possible.

(a) $2(x-y)+3x(4-3)$ (b) $-4x(y-3)-(2x+xy)$ (c) $-2(x+3y)-2x(y-4)$

(d) $-\frac{1}{2}x(4-2y)-2y(3+x)$ (e) $12xy-(2+y)-3(4-x)$ (f) $2x^2(2-2y)-y(3-2x^2)$

(g) $-\frac{1}{4}x(4x-8)+2-(x^2-3)$ (h) $-2(x^2-2y)+4x(2x-2y)$ (i) $-\frac{1}{2}(8x-2)+3-(x+7)$

6.2 Solving linear equations

- To solve an equation, you find the value of the unknown letter (variable) that makes the equation true.
- If you add or subtract the same number (or term) to both sides of the equation, you produce an equivalent equation and the solution remains unchanged.
- If you multiply or divide each term on both sides of the equation by the same number (or term), you produce an equivalent equation and the solution remains unchanged.

Exercise 6.2

In this exercise leave answers as fractions rather than decimals, where necessary.

1 Solve these equations for x. Show the steps in your working.

(a) $2x+7=3x+4$ (b) $4x+6=x+18$ (c) $5x-2=3x+7$ (d) $9x-5=7x+3$

(e) $11x-4=x+32$ (f) $2x-1=14-x$ (g) $20-4x=5x+2$ (h) $3+4x=2x-7$

(i) $4x+5=7x-7$ (j) $2x-6=4x-3$ (k) $3x+2=5x-9$ (l) $x+9=5x-3$

2 Solve these equations for x.

> When an equation has brackets it is usually best to expand them first.

(a) $3(x-2)=24$ (b) $5(x+4)=10$ (c) $3(3x+10)=6$ (d) $3(2x-1)=5$

(e) $-3(x-6)=-6$ (f) $4(3-5x)=7$ (g) $4(x+3)=x$ (h) $6(x+3)=4x$

(i) $3x+2=2(x-4)$ (j) $x-3=2(x+5)$ (k) $4(x+7)-3(x-5)=9$

(l) $2(x-1)-7(3x-2)=7(x-4)$

3 Solve these equations for x.

> To remove the denominators of fractions in an equation, multiply each term on both sides by the common denominator.

(a) $\frac{x}{2}-3=6$ (b) $\frac{x}{3}+2=11$ (c) $\frac{4x}{6}=16$ (d) $\frac{28-x}{6}=12$

(e) $\frac{x-2}{3}=5$ (f) $\frac{12x-1}{5}=9$ (g) $\frac{5x+2}{3}=-1$ (h) $\frac{5-2x}{4}=-1$

(i) $\frac{2x-1}{5}=x$ (j) $\frac{2x-3}{5}=x-6$ (k) $\frac{10x+2}{3}=6-x$ (l) $\frac{x}{2}-\frac{x}{5}=3$

(m) $\frac{2x}{3}-\frac{x}{2}=7$ (n) $-2\frac{(x+4)}{2}=x+7$

6.3 Factorising algebraic expressions

- The first step in factorising is to identify and 'take out' ALL common factors.
- Common factors can be numbers, variables, brackets or a combination of these.
- Factorising is the opposite of expanding – when you factorise you put brackets back into the expression.

Exercise 6.3

1 Find the highest common factor of each pair.

> Remember, x^2 means $x \times x$, so x is a factor of x^2

(a) $3x$ and 21 (b) 40 and $8x$ (c) $15a$ and $5b$

(d) $2a$ and ab (e) $3xy$ and $12yz$ (f) $5a^2b$ and $20ab^2$

(g) $8xy$ and $28xyz$ (h) $9pq$ and p^2q^2 (i) $14abc$ and $7a^2b$

(j) x^2y^3z and $2xy^2z^2$ (k) $2a^2b^4$ and ab^3 (l) $3x^3y^2$ and $15xy$

2 Factorise as fully as possible.

> Find the HCF of the numbers first. Then find the HCF of the variables, if there is one, in alphabetical order.

(a) $12x+48$ (b) $2+8y$ (c) $4a-16$ (d) $3x-xy$

(e) $ab+5a$ (f) $3x-15y$ (g) $24xyz-8xz$ (h) $9ab-12bc$

(i) $6xy-4yz$ (j) $14x-26xy$

3 Factorise the following.

> Remember, if one of the terms is exactly the same as the common factor, you must put a 1 where the term would appear in the bracket.

(a) x^2+8x (b) $12a-a^2$ (c) $9x^2+4x$ (d) $22x-16x^2$

(e) $6ab^2+8b$ (f) $18xy-36x^2y$ (g) $6x-9x^2$ (h) $14x^2y^2-6xy^2$

(i) $9abc^3-3a^2b^2c^2$ (j) $4x^2-7xy$ (k) $3ab^2-4b^2c$ (l) $14a^2b-21ab^2$

4 Remove a common factor to factorise each of the following expressions.

(a) $x(3+y)+4(3+y)$ (b) $x(y-3)+5(y-3)$

(c) $3(a+2b)-2a(a+2b)$ (d) $4a(2a-b)-3(2a-b)$

(e) $x(2-y)+(2-y)$ (f) $x(x-3)+4(x-3)$

(g) $9(2+y)-x(y+2)$ (h) $4a(2b-c)-(c-2b)$

(i) $3x(x-6)-5(x-6)$ (j) $x(x-y)-(2x-2y)$

(k) $3x(2x+3)+y(3+2x)$ (l) $4(x-y)-x(3x-3y)$

6.4 Transformation of a formula

- A formula is a general rule, usually involving several variables, for example, the area of a rectangle, $A=bh$.
- A variable is called the subject of the formula when it is on its own on one side of the equals sign.
- You can transform a formula to make any variable the subject. You use the same rules that you used to solve equations.

Exercise 6.4 A

1 Make m the subject if $D=km$

2 Make c the subject if $y=mx+c$

3 Given that $P=ab-c$, make b the subject of the formula.

4 Given that $a=bx+c$, make b the subject of the formula.

5 Make a the subject of each formula.

> **Tip**
> Pay attention to the signs when you transform a formula.

(a) $a+b=c$	**(b)** $a-3b=2c$	**(c)** $ab-c=d$	**(d)** $ab+c=d$
(e) $bc-a=d$	**(f)** $bc-a=-d$	**(g)** $\dfrac{2a+b}{c}=d$	**(h)** $\dfrac{c+ba}{d}=e$
(i) $abc-d=e$	**(j)** $cab+d=ef$	**(k)** $\dfrac{ab}{c}+de=f$	**(l)** $c+\dfrac{ab}{d}=e$
(m) $c(a-b)=d$	**(n)** $d(a+2b)=c$		

Exercise 6.4 B

1 The perimeter of a rectangle can be given as $P=2(l+b)$, where P is the perimeter, l is the length and b is the breadth.

    (a) Make b the subject of the formula.

    (b) Find b if the rectangle has a length of 45 cm and a perimeter of 161 cm.

> **Tip**
> If you are given a value for π, you must use the given value to avoid calculator and rounding errors.

2 The circumference of a circle can be found using the formula $C=2\pi r$, where r is the radius of the circle.

    (a) Make r the subject of the formula.

    (b) Find the radius of a circle of circumference 56.52 cm. Use $\pi=3.14$.

    (c) Find the diameter of a circle of circumference 144.44 cm. Use $\pi=3.14$.

> **Tip**
> In questions such as question 3, it may be helpful to draw a diagram to show what the parts of the formula represent.

3 The area of a trapezium can be found using the formula $A=\dfrac{h(a+b)}{2}$, where h is the distance between the parallel sides and a and b are the lengths of the parallel sides. By transforming the formula and substitution, find the length of b, in a trapezium of area 9.45 cm^2 with $a=2.5$ cm and $h=3$ cm.

4 An airline uses the formula $T=70P+12B$ to roughly estimate the total mass of passengers and checked bags per flight in kilograms. T is the total mass, P is the number of passengers and B is the number of bags.

    (a) What mass does the airline assume for:

        (i) a passenger? **(ii)** a checked bag?

(b) Estimate the total mass for 124 passengers each with two checked bags.

(c) Make B the subject of the formula.

(d) Calculate the total mass of the bags if the total mass of 124 passengers and checked bags on a flight is 9.64 tonnes.

5 When an object is dropped from a height, the distance (m) in metres that it has fallen can be related to the time it takes for it to fall (t) in seconds by the formula $m = 5t^2$.

(a) Make t the subject of the formula.

(b) Calculate the time it takes for an object to fall from a distance of 180 m.

Mixed exercise

1 Solve for x.

(a) $4x-9=-21$ (b) $5x+4=-26$ (c) $\dfrac{2x-4}{7}=2$ (d) $5=\dfrac{1-4x}{5}$

(e) $4x-6=12-5x$ (f) $4x-8=3(2x+6)$ (g) $\dfrac{3x-7}{4}=\dfrac{1-4x}{8}$ (h) $\dfrac{3(2x-5)}{5}=\dfrac{x+1}{2}$

2 Make x the subject of each formula.

(a) $m=nxp-r$ (b) $m=\dfrac{nx+p}{q}$

3 Expand and simplify where possible.

> Remember to inspect your answer to see if there are any like terms. If there are, add and/or subtract them to simplify the expression.

(a) $3(x-1)+5$ (b) $-4x(3x-2)$ (c) $-2(4x-2y+3)$

(d) $-2y(7-y)-2y$ (e) $4(2x-1)+3(x+3)$ (f) $x(5x-1)+2(4x-2)$

(g) $-2x(x-4)+3x$ (h) $6x(2x+3)-2x(x-3)$

4 Factorise fully.

(a) $4x-8$ (b) $12x-3y$ (c) $-2x-4$

(d) $3xy-24x$ (e) $14x^2y^2+7xy$ (f) $2(x-y)+x(x-y)$

(g) $x(4+3x)-3(3x+4)$ (h) $4x^2(x+y)-8x(x+y)$

5 Given that, for a rectangle, area = length × breadth, write an expression for the area of each rectangle. Expand each expression fully.

(a)

(b)

(c)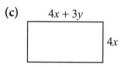

(d)

> **◄ REWIND**
>
> Use geometric properties to make the equations (see chapter 3). ◄

6 Use the information in each diagram to make an equation and solve it to find the size of each angle.

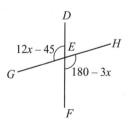

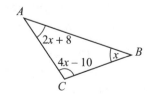

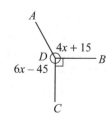

7 Perimeter, area and volume

7.1 Perimeter and area in two dimensions

- Perimeter is the total distance around the outside of a shape. You can find the perimeter of any shape by adding up the lengths of the sides.
- The perimeter of a circle is called the circumference. Use the formula $C=\pi d$ or $C=2\pi r$ to find the circumference of a circle.
- Area is the total space contained within a shape. Use these formulae to calculate the area of different shapes:
  - triangle: $A = \dfrac{bh}{2}$
  - square: $A=s^2$
  - rectangle: $A=bh$
  - parallelogram: $A=bh$
  - rhombus: $A=bh$
  - kite: $A=\dfrac{1}{2}$(product of diagonals)
  - trapezium: $A = \dfrac{(\text{sum of parallel sides})h}{2}$
  - circle: $A=\pi r^2$
- You can work out the area of complex shapes in a few steps. Divide complex shapes into known shapes. Work out the area of each part and then add the areas together to find the total area.

Exercise 7.1 A

1 Find the perimeter of each shape.

(a)
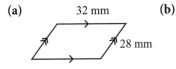
32 mm
28 mm

(b)
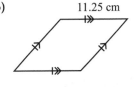
11.25 cm

(c)
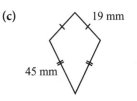
19 mm
45 mm

(d)
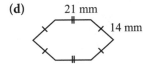
21 mm
14 mm

(e)
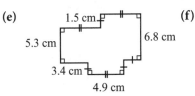
1.5 cm
5.3 cm
6.8 cm
3.4 cm
4.9 cm

(f)
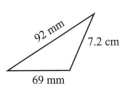
92 mm
7.2 cm
69 mm

> **! Tip**
> For a semi-circle, the perimeter includes half the circumference plus the length of the diameter. If you are not given the value of π, use the π key on your calculator. Round your answers to three significant figures.

2 Find the perimeter of the shaded area in each of these shapes. Use π=3.14 in your calculations.

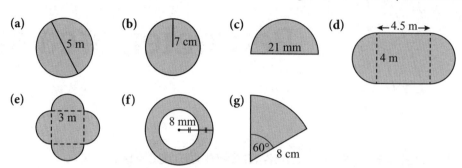

3 A square field has a perimeter of 360 m. What is the length of one of its sides?

4 Find the cost of fencing a rectangular plot 45 m long and 37 m wide if the cost of fencing is $45.50 per metre.

5 An isosceles triangle has a perimeter of 28 cm. Calculate the length of each of the equal sides if the remaining side is 100 mm long.

6 How much string would you need to form a circular loop with a diameter of 28 cm?

7 The rim of a bicycle wheel has a radius of 31.5 cm.

   (a) What is the circumference of the rim?

   (b) The tyre that goes onto the rim is 3.5 cm thick. Calculate the circumference of the wheel when the tyre is fitted to it.

> **! Tip**
> Make sure all measurements are in the same units before you do any calculations.

Remember, give your answer in square units.

Exercise 7.1 B

1 Find the area of each of these shapes.

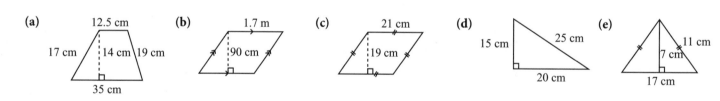

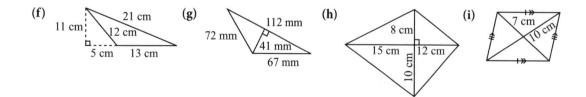

2 Find the area of each shape. Use π=3.14 in your calculations. Give your answers correct to two decimal places.

(a)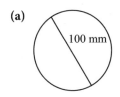
100 mm

(b)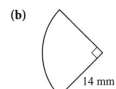
14 mm

(c)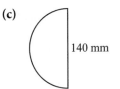
140 mm

(d)
20° 10 cm

(e)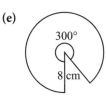
300°
8 cm

> **Tip**
> Work out any missing dimensions on the figure using the given dimensions and the properties of shapes.

3 Find the area of the shaded part in each of these figures. Show your working clearly in each case. All dimensions are given in centimetres.

(a)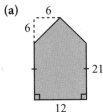
6
6
21
12

(b)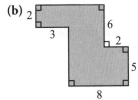
2
3
6
2
5
8

(c)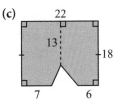
22
13
18
7   6

(d)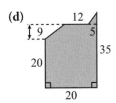
12
9   5
20   35
20

(e)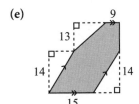
9
13
14   14
15

(f)
1
3 6
3
6
2

(g)
14

(h)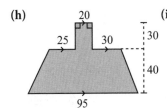
20
25   30
30
40
95

(i)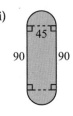
45
90   90

> **Tip**
> Divide irregular shapes into known shapes and combine the areas to get the total area.

4 Find the area of the following figures giving your answers correct to two decimal places. (Use π=3.14 for part **(f)**.)

(a)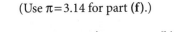
2.5 cm
6 cm

(b)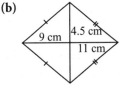
9 cm   4.5 cm
11 cm

(c)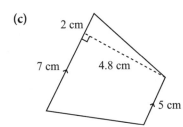
2 cm
7 cm   4.8 cm
5 cm

(d)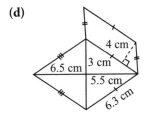
4 cm
6.5 cm   3 cm
5.5 cm
6.3 cm

(e)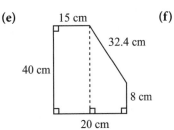
15 cm
32.4 cm
40 cm
8 cm
20 cm

(f)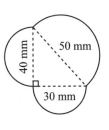
40 mm   50 mm
30 mm

5 A 1.5 m×2.4 m rectangular rug is placed on the floor in a 3.5 m×4.2 m rectangular room. How much of the floor is not covered by the rug?

6 The area of a rhombus of side 8 cm is 5600 mm². Determine the height of the rhombus.

Exercise 7.1 C

(Use π = 3.14 for these questions.)

1 Calculate the length of the arc *AB*, subtended by the given angle, in each of these circles.

(a)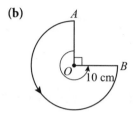

(b)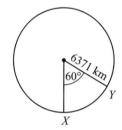

(c)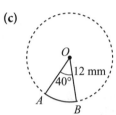

2 The diagram shows a cross-section of the Earth. Two cities, *X* and *Y*, lie on the same longitude. Given that the radius of the Earth is 6371 km, calculate the distance, *XY*, between the two cities.

3 Calculate the shaded area of each circle.

(a)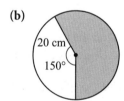

(b)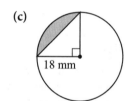

(c)

4 A large circular pizza has a diameter of 25 cm. The pizza restaurant cuts its pizzas into eight equal slices. Calculate the size of each slice in cm².

7.2 Three-dimensional objects

- Any solid object is three-dimensional. The three dimensions of a solid are length, breadth and height.
- The net of a solid is a two-dimensional diagram. It shows the shape of all faces of the solid and how they are attached to each other. If you fold up a net, you get a model of the solid.

Exercise 7.2

1 Which solids would be made from the following faces?

(a)
× 6

(b)
× 2   × 2   × 2

(c)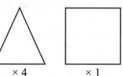
× 4   × 1

(d)
× 8

2 Describe the solid you could produce using each of the following nets.

(a)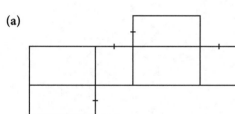

(b)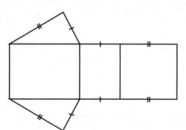

(c)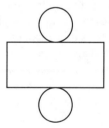

3 Sketch a possible net for each of the following solids.

(a)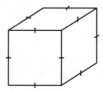

(b)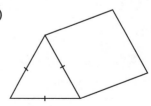

(c)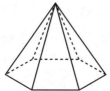

(d)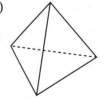

7.3 Surface areas and volumes of solids

- The surface area of a three-dimensional object is the total area of all its faces.
- The volume of a three-dimensional object is the amount of space it occupies.
- You can find the volume of a cube or cuboid using the formula, $V = l \times b \times h$, where l is the length, b is the breadth and h is the height of the object.
- A prism is a three-dimensional object with a uniform cross-section (the end faces of the solid are identical and parallel). If you slice through the prism anywhere along its length (and parallel to the end faces), you will get a section the same shape and size as the end faces. Cubes, cuboids and cylinders are examples of prisms.
- You can find the volume of any prism (including a cylinder) by multiplying the area of its cross-section by the distance between the parallel faces. This is expressed in the formula, $V = al$, where a is the area of the base and l is the length of the prism. You need to use the appropriate area formula for the shape of the cross-section.
- Find the volume of a cone using the formula, $V = \frac{1}{3}\pi r^2 h$, where h is the perpendicular height. To find the curved surface area use the formula, surface area $= \pi r l$, where l is the slant height of the cone.
- Find the volume of a pyramid using the formula, $V = \dfrac{\text{area of base} \times h}{3}$, where h is the perpendicular height.
- Find the volume of a sphere using the formula, $V = \frac{4}{3}\pi r^3$. To find the surface area use the formula, surface area $= 4\pi r^2$.

Exercise 7.3 A

(Use $\pi = 3.14$ for any shapes involving circles in this exercise.)

> **! Tip**
>
> Drawing the nets of the solids may help you work out the surface area of each shape.

1 Calculate the surface area of each shape.

(a)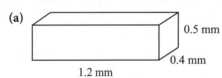
0.5 mm
0.4 mm
1.2 mm

(b)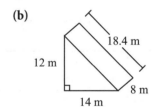
18.4 m
12 m
8 m
14 m

(c)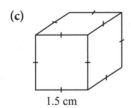
1.5 cm

(d)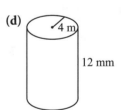
4 m
12 mm

2 A wooden cube has six identical square faces, each of area 64 cm².

    (a) What is the surface area of the cube?

    (b) What is the height of the cube?

3 Mrs Nini is ordering wooden blocks to use in her maths classroom.
The blocks are cuboids with dimensions 10 cm × 8 cm × 5 cm.

> Remember,
> 1 m² = 10 000 cm²

    (a) Calculate the surface area of one block.

    (b) Mrs Nini needs 450 blocks. What is the total surface area of all the blocks?

    (c) She decides to varnish the blocks. A tin of varnish covers an area of 4 m².
How many tins will she need to varnish all the blocks?

> **Tip**
>
> The length of the prism is the distance between the two parallel faces. When a prism is turned onto its face, the length may look like a height. Work out the area of the cross-section (end face) before you apply the volume formula.

4 Calculate the volume of each prism.

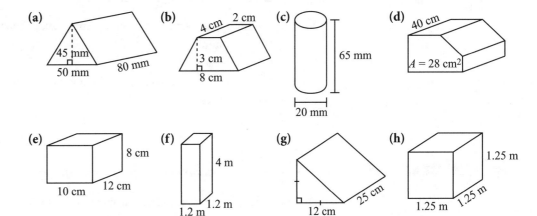

5 A pocket dictionary is 14 cm long, 9.5 cm wide and 2.5 cm thick. Calculate the volume of space it takes up.

6 **(a)** Find the volume of a lecture room that is 8 m long, 8 m wide and 3.5 m high.

(b) Safety regulations state that during an hour long lecture each person in the room must have 5 m³ of air. Calculate the maximum number of people who can attend an hour long lecture.

7 A cylindrical tank is 30 m high with an inner radius of 150 cm. Calculate how much water the tank will hold when full.

8 A machine shop has four different rectangular prisms of volume 64 000 mm³. Copy and fill in the possible dimensions for each prism to complete the table.

Volume (mm³)	64 000	64 000	64 000	64 000
Length (mm)	80	50		
Breadth (mm)	40		80	
Height (mm)				16

Exercise 7.3 B

(Use π = 3.14 for any shapes involving circles in this exercise.)

1 Find the volume of the following solids. Give your answers correct to two decimal places.

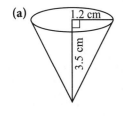

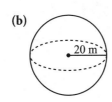

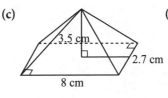

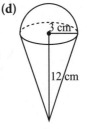

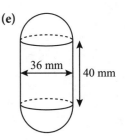

2 Give your answers to this question in standard form to three significant figures.
The Earth has an average radius of 6371 km.

(a) Assuming the Earth is more or less spherical, calculate:
(i) its volume.
(ii) its surface area.
(b) If 71% of the surface area of the Earth is covered by the oceans, calculate the area of land on the surface.

Mixed exercise

(Use $\pi = 3.14$ for any shapes involving circles in this exercise.)

1 A circular plate on a stove has a diameter of 21 cm. There is a metal strip around the outside of the plate.

(a) Calculate the surface area of the top of the plate.
(b) Calculate the length of the metal strip.

2 What is the radius of a circle with an area of 65 cm²?

3 Calculate the shaded area in each figure.

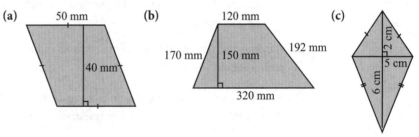

(a) 50 mm, 40 mm

(b) 120 mm, 170 mm, 150 mm, 192 mm, 320 mm

(c) 2 cm, 5 cm, 6 cm

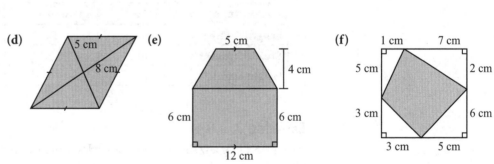

(d) 5 cm, 8 cm

(e) 5 cm, 4 cm, 6 cm, 6 cm, 12 cm

(f) 1 cm, 7 cm, 5 cm, 2 cm, 3 cm, 6 cm, 3 cm, 5 cm

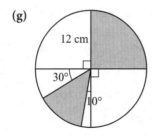

(g) 12 cm, 30°, 10°

4 *MNOP* is a trapezium with an area of 150 cm². Calculate the length of *NO*.

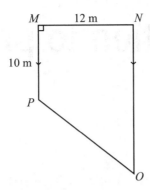

5 Study the two prisms.

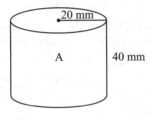
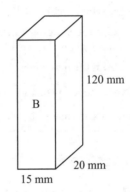

   (a) Which of the two prisms has the smaller volume?
   (b) What is the difference in volume?
   (c) Sketch a net of the cuboid. Your net does not need to be to scale, but you must indicate the dimensions of each face on the net.
   (d) Calculate the surface area of each prism.

6 How many cubes of side 4.48 cm can be packed into a wooden box measuring 32 cm by 16 cm by 9 cm?

7 Find the difference between the volume of a 10 cm high cone which has a 3 cm wide base and a square-based pyramid that is 3 cm wide at its base and 10 cm high.

8 Tennis balls of diameter 9 cm are packed into cylindrical metal tubes that are sealed at both ends. The inside of the tube has an internal diameter of 9.2 cm and the tube is 28 cm long. Calculate the volume of space left in the tube if three tennis balls are packed into it.

Introduction to probability

8.1 Basic probability

- Probability is a measure of the chance that something will happen. It is measured on a scale of 0 to 1:
  - outcomes with a probability of 0 are impossible
  - outcomes with a probability of 1 are certain
  - an outcome with a probability of 0.5 or $\frac{1}{2}$ has an even chance of occurring.
- Probabilities can be found through doing an experiment, such as tossing a coin. Each time you perform the experiment is called a trial. If you want to get heads, then heads is your desired outcome or successful outcome.
- To calculate probability from the outcomes of experiments, use the formula:

$$\text{Experimental probability of outcome} = \frac{\text{number of successful outcomes}}{\text{number of trials}}$$

- Experimental probability is also called the relative frequency.

Exercise 8.1

1 Salma has a bag containing one red, one white and one green ball. She draws a ball at random and replaces it before drawing again. She repeats this 50 times. She uses a tally table to record the outcomes of her experiment.

Red	卌 卌 卌
White	卌 卌 卌 |||
Green	卌 卌 卌 ||

   (a) Calculate the relative frequency of drawing each colour.
   (b) Express her chance of drawing a red ball as a percentage.
   (c) What is the sum of the three relative frequencies?
   (d) What should your chances be in theory of drawing each colour?

2 It is Josh's job to call customers who have had their car serviced at the dealer to check whether they are happy with the service they received. He kept this record of what happened for 200 calls made one month.

Result	Frequency
Spoke to customer	122
Phone not answered	44
Left message on answering machine	22
Phone engaged or out of order	10
Wrong number	2

(a) Calculate the relative frequency of each event as a decimal fraction.
(b) Is it highly likely, likely, unlikely or highly unlikely that the following outcomes will occur when Josh makes a call?

  (i) The call will be answered by the customer.
  (ii) The call will be answered by a machine.
  (iii) He will dial the wrong number.

8.2 Theoretical probability

● You can calculate the theoretical probability of an event without doing experiments if the outcomes are equally likely. Use the formula:

$$P(\text{outcome}) = \frac{\text{number of favourable outcomes}}{\text{number of possible outcomes}}$$

For example, when you toss a coin you can get heads or tails (two possible outcomes). The probability of heads is $P(H) = \frac{1}{2}$.

● You need to work out what *all* the possible outcomes are before you can calculate theoretical probability.

Tip
It is helpful to list the possible outcomes so that you know what to substitute in the formula.

Exercise 8.2

1 Sally has ten identical cards numbered one to ten. She draws a card at random and records the number on it.

(a) What are the possible outcomes for this event?
(b) Calculate the probability that Sally will draw:
  (i) the number five   (ii) any one of the ten numbers
  (iii) a multiple of three (iv) a number < 4
  (v) a number < 5   (vi) a number < 6
  (vii) a square number   (viii) a number < 10
  (ix) a number > 10

2 There are five cups of coffee on a tray. Two of them contain sugar.

(a) What are your chances of choosing a cup with sugar in it?
(b) Which choice is most likely? Why?

3 Mike has four cards numbered one to four. He draws one card and records the number. Calculate the probability that the result will be:

(a) a multiple of three   (b) a multiple of two   (c) a factor of three.

4 For a fly-fishing competition, the organisers place 45 trout, 30 salmon and 15 pike in a small dam.

(a) What is an angler's chance of catching a salmon on her first attempt?
(b) What is the probability the angler catches a trout?
(c) What is the probability of catching a pike?

5 A dartboard is divided into 20 sectors numbered from one to 20. If a dart is equally likely to land in any of these sectors, calculate:

(a) P(<8)   (b) P(odd)   (c) P(prime)
(d) P(multiple of 3)   (e) P(multiple of 5).

6 A school has forty classrooms numbered from one to 40. Work out the probability that a classroom number has the numeral '1' in it.

8.3 The probability that an event does not happen

- An event may happen or it may not happen. For example, you may throw a six when you roll a die, but you may not.
- The probability of an event happening may be different from the probability of the event not happening, but the two combined probabilities will always add up to one.
- If A is an event happening, then A′ (or $\overline{A}$) represents the event A not happening and P(A′) = 1 – P(A).

Exercise 8.3

1 The probability that a driver is speeding on a stretch of road is 0.27. What is the probability that a driver is not speeding?

2 The probability of drawing a green ball in an experiment is $\frac{3}{8}$. What is the probability of not drawing a green ball?

3 A container holds 300 sweets in five different flavours. The probability of choosing a particular flavour is given in the table.

Flavour	Strawberry	Lime	Lemon	Blackberry	Apple
P(flavour)	0.21	0.22	0.18	0.23	

(a) Calculate P(apple).
(b) What is P(not apple)?
(c) Calculate the probability of choosing P(neither lemon nor lime)?
(d) Calculate the number of each flavoured sweet in the container.

4 Students in a school have five after school clubs to choose from. The probability that a student will choose each club is given in the table.

Club	Computers	Sewing	Woodwork	Choir	Chess
P(Club)	0.57	0.2	0.2	0.02	0.01

(a) Calculate P(not sewing nor woodwork).
(b) Calculate P(not chess nor choir).
(c) If 55 students have to choose a club, how many would you expect to choose sewing?
(d) If four students chose choir, calculate how many students chose computers.

8.4 Possibility diagrams

- The set of all possible outcomes is called the sample space (or probability space) of an event.
- Possibility diagrams can be used to show all outcomes clearly.
- When you are dealing with combined events, it is much easier to find a probability if you represent the sample space in a diagram: possibility diagrams are useful for doing this.

Tip

Think of the probability space diagram as a map of all the possible outcomes in an experiment.

FAST FORWARD

Tree diagrams are also probability space diagrams. These are dealt with in detail in chapter 24. ▶

Exercise 8.4

1 Draw a possibility diagram to show all possible outcomes when you toss two coins at the same time. Use your diagram to help you answer the following.

(a) What is P(at least one tail)?

(b) What is P(no tails)?

2 Jess has three green cards numbered one to three and three yellow cards also numbered one to three.

(a) Draw a possibility diagram to show all possible outcomes when one green and one yellow card is chosen at random.

(b) How many possible outcomes are there?

(c) What is the probability that the number on both the cards will be the same?

(d) What is the probability of getting a total < 4 if the scores on the cards are added?

3 On a school outing, the students are allowed to choose one drink and one snack from this menu:

Drinks: cola, fruit juice, water
Snacks: biscuit, cake, muffin

(a) Draw a possibility diagram to show the possible choices that a student can make.

(b) What is the probability a student will choose cola and a biscuit?

(c) What is the probability that the drink chosen is not water?

8.5 Combining independent and mutually exclusive events

- When one outcome in a trial has no effect on the next outcome we say the events are independent.
  - Drawing a counter at random from a bag, replacing it and then drawing another counter is an example of independent events. Because you replace the counter, the first draw does not affect the second draw.
- If A and B *are* independent events then: P(A happens and then B happens) = P(A) × P(B) or
  P(A and B) = P(A) × P (B)
- Mutually exclusive events cannot happen at the same time.
  - For example, you cannot throw an odd number and an even number at the same time when you roll a die.
- If A and B *are* mutually exclusive events then: P(A or B) = P(A) + P(B).
- When the outcome of the first event affects the outcome of the next event, the events are said to be dependent.
  - For example, if you have two red counters and three white counters, draw a counter without replacing it and then draw a second counter, the probability of drawing a red or a white on the second draw depends on what you drew first time round. You can find P(A then B) by calculating P(A) × P(B given that A has already happened).

Exercise 8.5

1 Nico is on a bus and he is bored, so he amuses himself by choosing a consonant and a vowel at random from the names of towns on road signs. The next road sign is CALCUTTA.

   (a) Draw up a sample space diagram to show all the options that Nico has.
   (b) Calculate P(T and A).
   (c) Calculate P(C or L and U).
   (d) Calculate P(not L and U).

2 A bag contains three red counters, four green counters, two yellow counters and one white counter. Two counters are drawn from the bag one after the other, without being replaced. Calculate:

   (a) P(two red counters)
   (b) P(two green counters)
   (c) P(two yellow counters)
   (d) P(white and then red)
   (e) P(white or yellow, in either order but not both)
   (f) P(white or red, in either order but not both).
   (g) What is the probability of drawing a white or yellow counter first and then any colour second?

3 Maria has a bag containing 18 fruit drop sweets. 10 are apple flavoured and 8 are blackberry flavoured. She chooses a sweet at random and eats it. Then she chooses another sweet at random. Calculate the probability that:

   (a) both sweets were apple flavoured
   (b) both sweets were blackberry flavoured
   (c) the first was apple and the second was blackberry
   (d) the first was blackberry and the second was apple.
   (e) Your answers to (a), (b), (c) and (d) should add up to one. Explain why this is the case.

Mixed exercise

1 A coin is tossed a number of times giving the following results.

       Heads: 4083   Tails: 5917

  (a) How many times was the coin tossed?

  (b) Calculate the relative frequency of each outcome.

  (c) What is the probability that the next toss will result in heads?

  (d) Jess says she thinks the results show that the coin is biased. Do you agree? Give a reason for your answer.

2 A bag contains 10 red, eight green and two white balls. Each ball has an equal chance of being chosen. Calculate the probability of:

  (a) choosing a red ball

  (b) choosing a green ball

  (c) choosing a white ball

  (d) choosing a blue ball

  (e) choosing a red or a green ball

  (f) not choosing a white ball

  (g) choosing a ball that is not red.

3 Two normal unbiased dice are rolled and the sum of the numbers on their faces is recorded.

  (a) Calculate P(12).

  (b) Which sum has the greatest probability? What is the probability of rolling this sum?

  (c) What is P(not even)?

  (d) What is P(sum < 5)?

4 Josh and Carlos each take a coin at random out of their pockets and add the totals together to get an amount. Josh has three $1 coins, two 50c coins, a $5 coin and two 20c coins in his pocket. Carlos has four $5 coins, a $2 coin and two 50c pieces.

  (a) Draw up a probability space diagram to show all the possible outcomes for the sum of the two coins.

  (b) What is the probability that the coins will add up to $6?

  (c) What is the probability that the coins will add up to less than $2?

  (d) What is the probability that the coins will add up to $5 or more?

5 A fair die is rolled three times and the number revealed written down. What is the probability that a prime number will be written down three times?

6 Patrick keeps his socks loose in a drawer. He has six dark ones, four white ones and two striped ones. What is the probability that he takes out two socks and they are a pair?

Sequences and sets

9.1 Sequences

- A number sequence is a list of numbers that follows a set pattern. Each number in the sequence is called a term. T_1 is the first term, T_{10} is the tenth term and T_n is the nth term, or general term.
- A linear sequence has a constant difference (d) between the terms. The general rule for finding the nth term of any linear sequence is $T_n = a + (n - 1)d$, where a is the first value in the sequence.
- When you know the rule for making a sequence, you can find the value of any term. Substitute the term number into the rule and solve it.

> You should recognise these sequences of numbers:
>
> square numbers: 1, 4, 9, 16 . . .
> cube numbers: 1, 8, 27, 64 . . .
> triangular numbers: 1, 3, 6, 10 . . .
> Fibonacci numbers: 1, 1, 2, 3, 5, 8 . . .

Exercise 9.1

1 Find the next three terms in each sequence and describe the rule you used to find them.

   (a) 11, 13, 15 . . .   **(b)** 88, 99, 110 . . .   **(c)** 64, 32, 16 . . .   **(d)** 8, 16, 24, 32 . . .

   (e) $-2, -4, -6, -8$ . . . **(f)** $\frac{1}{4}, \frac{1}{2}, 1$ . . .   **(g)** 1, 2, 4, 7 . . .   **(h)** 1, 6, 11, 16 . . .

2 List the first four terms of the sequences that follow these rules.

   (a) Start with seven and add two each time.

   (b) Start with 37 and subtract five each time.

   (c) Start with one and multiply by $\frac{1}{2}$ each time.

   (d) Start with five then multiply by two and add one each time.

   (e) Start with 100, divide by two and subtract three each time.

3 Write down the first three terms of each of these sequences. Then find the 35th term.

   (a) $T_n = 2n + 3$

   (b) $T_n = n^2$

   (c) $T_n = 6n - 1$

   (d) $T_n = n^3 - 1$

   (e) $T_n = n^2 - n$

   (f) $T_n = 3 - 2n$

4 Consider the sequence:

      2, 10, 18, 26, 34, 42, 50 . . .

   (a) Find the nth term of the sequence.

   (b) Find the 200th term.

   (c) Which term of this sequence has the value 234? Show full working.

   (d) Show that 139 is not a term in the sequence.

5 For each sequence below find the general term and the 50th term.

  (a) 7, 9, 11, 13 . . .
  (b) −5, − 13, − 21, − 29 . . .
  (c) 2, 8, 14, 20, 26 . . .
  (d) 4, 9, 16, 25 . . .
  (e) 2.3, 3.5, 4.7, 5.9 . . .

6 The diagram shows a pattern made using matchsticks:

$n = 1$ $n = 2$ 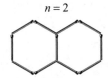 $n = 3$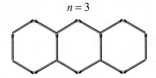

  (a) Draw a sequence table for the number of matchsticks in the first six patterns.
  (b) Find a formula for the nth pattern.
  (c) How many matches are needed for the 99th pattern?
  (d) Which pattern will need 276 matches?

9.2 Rational and irrational numbers

- You can express any rational number as a fraction in the form of $\frac{a}{b}$ where a and b are integers and $b \neq 0$.
- Whole numbers, integers, common fractions, mixed numbers, terminating decimal fractions and recurring decimals are all rational.
- You can convert recurring decimal fractions into the form $\frac{a}{b}$.
- Irrational numbers cannot be written in the form $\frac{a}{b}$. Irrational numbers are all non-recurring, non-terminating decimals.
- The set of real numbers is made up of rational and irrational numbers.

In $1.\dot{2}$, the dot above the two in the decimal part means it is recurring (the '2' repeats forever). If a set of numbers recurs, e.g. 0.273273273..., there will be a dot at the start and end of the recurring set: $0.\dot{2}7\dot{3}$.

Exercise 9.2

1 Write down all the irrational numbers in each set of real numbers.

  (a) $\frac{3}{8}$, $\sqrt{16}$, $\sqrt[3]{16}$, $\frac{22}{7}$, $\sqrt{12}$, $0.090090009...$, $\frac{31}{3}$, $0.020202...$,

  (b) 23, $\sqrt{45}$, $0.\dot{6}$, $\frac{3}{4}$, $\sqrt[3]{90}$, π, $5\frac{1}{2}$, $\sqrt{8}$, 0.834

2 Convert each of the following recurring decimals to a fraction in its simplest form.

  (a) $0.\dot{4}$ (b) $0.\dot{7}\dot{4}$ (c) $0.8\dot{7}$
  (d) $0.11\dot{4}$ (e) $0.\dot{9}4\dot{3}$ (f) $0.1\dot{8}5\dot{7}$

9.3 Sets

- A set is a list or collection of objects that share a characteristic.
- An element (∈) is a member of a set.
- A set that contains no elements is called the empty set ({} or Ø).
- A universal set (ℰ) contains all the possible elements appropriate to a particular problem.
- The elements of a subset (⊂) are all contained in a larger set.
- The elements of two sets can be combined (without repeats) to form the union (∪) of the two sets.
- The elements that two sets have in common is called the intersection (∩) of the two sets.
- The complement of set A (A′) is the elements that are in the universal set for that problem but not in set A.
- A Venn diagram is a pictorial method of showing sets.
- A shorthand way of describing the elements of a set is called set builder notation. For example $\{x : x$ is an integer, $40 < x < 50\}$.

Exercise 9.3 A

Tip
Make sure you know the meaning of the symbols used to describe sets and parts of sets.

1 Say whether each of the following statements is true or false.

(a) $2 \in \{$odd numbers$\}$.
(b) $8 \in \{$cubed numbers$\}$.
(c) $\{1, 2, 3\} \subset \{$prime numbers$\}$.
(d) $\{1\} \not\subset \{$prime numbers$\}$.
(e) $\{1, 2, 3\} \cap \{3, 6, 9\} = \{1, 2, 3, 6, 9\}$.
(f) $\{1, 2, 3\} \cup \{3, 6, 9\} = \{1, 2, 3, 6, 9\}$.
(g) $A = \{1, 2, 3\}$, $B = \{3, 6, 9\}$, so $A = B$.
(h) If $ℰ = \{$letters of the alphabet$\}$ and $A = \{$consonants$\}$, then $A′ = \{$a, e, i, o, u$\}$.

2 A is the set $\{2, 4, 6, 8, 10, 12\}$.

(a) Describe set A in words.
(b) What is n(A)?
(c) List set B which is the prime numbers in A.
(d) List set C which is the single digit numbers in A.
(e) List $B \cap C$.
(f) List $C′$.

Sometimes listing the elements of each set will make it easier to answer the questions.

3 $ℰ = \{$whole numbers from 1 to 20$\}$, $A = \{$even numbers from 1 to 12$\}$, $B = \{$odd numbers from 1 to 15$\}$ and $C = \{$multiples of 3 from 1 to 20$\}$.
List the elements of the following sets.

(a) $A \cap B$
(b) $B \cup C$
(c) $A′ \cap B$
(d) $(B \cap C)′$
(e) $A \cap B′$
(f) $A \cup B \cup C$

4 List the elements of the following sets.

(a) $\{x : x \in \text{integers}, -2 \leq x < 3\}$

(b) $\{x : x \in \text{natural numbers}, x \leq 5\}$

5 Write in set builder notation.

(a) $\{2, 4, 6, 8, 10\}$

(b) $\{1, 4, 9, 16, 25\}$

Exercise 9.3 B

1 Draw a Venn diagram to show the following sets and write each element in its correct space.

$\mathscr{E} = \{\text{letters in the alphabet}\}$

$P = \{\text{letters in the word physics}\}$

$C = \{\text{letters in the word chemistry}\}$

2 Use the Venn diagram you drew in question 1 to find:

(a) $n(C)$

(b) $n(P')$

(c) $C \cap P$

(d) $P \cup C$

(e) $(P \cup C)'$

(f) $P \subset C$.

3 In a survey of 100 students, seven did not like maths or science. Of the rest, 78 said they liked maths and 36 said they liked science.

(a) Draw a Venn diagram to show this information.

(b) Find the number of students who liked both maths and science.

(c) A student is chosen at random. Find the probability that the student likes maths but not science.

> **Tip**
> You can use any shapes to draw a Venn diagram but usually the universal set is drawn as a rectangle and circles within it show the sets.

> **REWIND**
> Exam questions often combine probability with Venn diagrams. Revise chapter 8 if you've forgotten how to work this out. ◄

Mixed exercise

1 For each of the following sequences, find the nth term and the 120th term.

(a) $1, 6, 11, 16 \ldots$

(b) $20, 14, 8, 2 \ldots$

(c) $2, 5, 8, 11 \ldots$

2 $T_n = 2(n - 3)$

(a) Give the first six terms of the sequence.

(b) What is the 90th term?

(c) Which term is equal to 86?

3 Which of the following numbers are irrational?

$$1\frac{5}{8}, 0.213231234\ldots, \sqrt{25}, \frac{7}{17}, 0.1, -0.654, \sqrt{2}, \frac{22}{5}, 4\pi$$

4 Write each recurring decimal as a fraction in simplest form.

(a) $0.\dot{2}\dot{3}$ (b) $0.\dot{2}8\dot{6}$

5 In a group of 80 students, 41 study biology and 34 study chemistry. 16 students study both subjects.

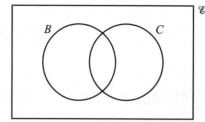

B = biology
C = chemistry

(a) Make a copy of the Venn diagram and complete it show the information about the students.

(b) How many students in the group study neither biology nor chemistry?

(c) What is $n(B \cap C)$?

(d) If a student is chosen at random from the group, what is the probability that he or she studies:

    (i)   chemistry

    (ii) biology

    (iii) chemistry and biology

    (iv) chemistry or biology (or both)

    (v) neither chemistry nor biology?

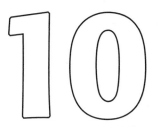

10 Straight lines and quadratic equations

10.1 Straight lines

- The position of a point can be uniquely described on the Cartesian plane using ordered pairs (x, y) of coordinates.
- You can use equations in terms of x and y to generate a table of paired values for x and y. You can plot these on the Cartesian plane and join them to draw a graph. To find y-values in a table of values, substitute the given (or chosen) x-values into the equation and solve for y.
- The gradient of a line describes its slope or steepness. Gradient can be defined as:

$$m = \frac{\text{change in } y}{\text{change in } x}$$

  - lines that slope up to the right have a positive gradient
  - lines that slope down to the right have a negative gradient
  - lines parallel to the x-axis (horizontal lines) have a gradient of 0
  - lines parallel to the y-axis (vertical lines) have an undefined gradient
  - lines parallel to each other have the same gradients.
- The equation of a straight line can be written in general terms as $y = mx + c$, where x and y are coordinates of points on the line, m is the gradient of the line and c is the y-intercept (the point where the graph crosses the y-axis).
- To find the equation of a given line you need to find the y-intercept and substitute this for c. Then you need to find the gradient of the line and substitute this for m.
- You can find the coordinates of the midpoint of a line segment by adding the x-coordinates of its end points and dividing by 2 to get the x-value of the midpoint and then doing the same with the y-coordinates to get the y-value of the midpoint.

> **Tip**
>
> Normally the x-values will be given. If not, choose three small values (for example, −2, 0 and 2). You need a minimum of three points to draw a graph. All graphs should be clearly labelled with their equation.

> Remember, parallel lines have the same gradient.

Exercise 10.1

1. For x-values of −1, 0, 1, 2 and 3, draw a table of values for each of the following equations.

   (a) $y = x + 5$ (b) $y = -2x - 1$ (c) $y = 7 - 2x$ (d) $y = -x - 2$

   (e) $x = 4$ (f) $y = -2$ (g) $y = -2x - \frac{1}{2}$ (h) $4 = 2x - 5y$

   (i) $0 = x - 2y - 1$ (j) $x + y = -\frac{1}{2}$

2. Draw and label graphs (a) to (e) in question 1 on one set of axes and graphs (f) to (j) on another.

3. Find the equation of a line parallel to graph (a) in question 1 and passing through point (0, −2).

4. Are the following pairs of lines parallel?

   (a) $y = 3x + 3$ and $y = x + 3$

   (b) $y = \frac{1}{2}x - 4$ and $y = \frac{1}{2}x - 8$

   (c) $y = -3x$ and $y = -3x + 7$

   (d) $y = 0.8x - 7$ and $y = 8x + 2$

   (e) $2y = -3x + 2$ and $y = \frac{3}{2}x + 2$

   (f) $2y - 3x = 2$ and $y = -1.5x + 2$

   (g) $y = 8$ and $y = -9$

   (h) $x = -3$ and $x = \frac{1}{2}$

5 Find the gradient of the following lines.

(a)

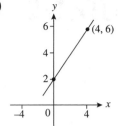

(b)

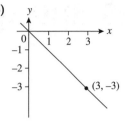

(c)

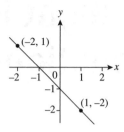

(d)

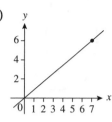

(e)

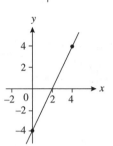

(f)

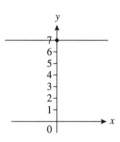

(g)

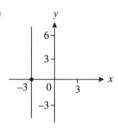

(h)

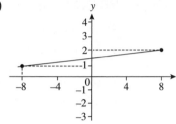

> **Tip**
>
> You may need to rewrite the equations in the form $y = mx + c$ before you can do this.

6 Determine the gradient (m) and the y-intercept (c) of each of the following graphs.

(a) $y = 3x - 4$ **(b)** $y = -x - 1$ **(c)** $y = -\frac{1}{2}x + 5$ **(d)** $y = x$

(e) $y = \frac{x}{2} + \frac{1}{4}$ **(f)** $y = \frac{4x}{5} - 2$ **(g)** $y = 7$ **(h)** $y = -3x$

(i) $x + 3y = 14$ **(j)** $x + y + 4 = 0$ **(k)** $x - 4 = y$ **(l)** $2x = 5 - y$

(m) $x + \frac{y}{2} = -10$

7 Determine the equation of each of the following graphs.

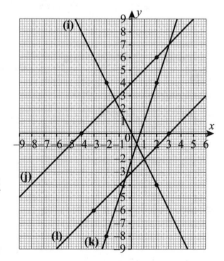

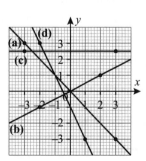

8 Find the x- and y-intercepts of the following lines.

(a) $y = 3x - 6$ **(b)** $y = -\frac{1}{2}x + 3$ **(c)** $2y - 3x = 12$

(d) $\frac{x + y}{2} = 5$ **(e)** $2x + y + 5 = 0$

9   Without drawing the graphs, calculate the gradient of the line that passes through each of these pairs of points.

(a) $(-2, -2)$ and $(2, 2)$
(b) $(-3, -1)$ and $(0, 2)$
(c) $(-4, 5)$ and $(0, 1)$
(d) $(2, 4)$ and $(8, 16)$
(e) $(-1, -3)$ and $(2, -3)$
(f) $(-2, 0)$ and $(4, 3)$

10   Using the same set of points as in question 9, find the coordinates of the midpoint of each line segment.

10.2 Quadratic expressions

- A quadratic expression has terms where the highest power of the variable is two (for example x^2).
- You can expand (multiply out) the product of two brackets by multiplying each term of the first bracket by each term of the second. You may then need to add or subtract any like terms.
- If the two brackets are the same (that is, the expressions a square), the following expansions can be applied:
  - $(x - y)^2 = x^2 - 2xy + y^2$
  - $(x + y)^2 = x^2 + 2xy + y^2$
- Factorising is the opposite of expanding, i.e. putting back into brackets.
- A trinomial is a quadratic expression with three terms. To factorise trinomials of the form $x^2 + 7x + 6$, look for two numbers whose sum is the coefficient of the x term (7 in this case) and whose product is the constant term (6 in this case). For example, $1 + 6 = 7$ and $1 \times 6 = 6$, so the two numbers are 1 and 6 and the factors are: $(x + 1)(x + 6)$.
- You can factorise the difference of two squares. The first and last terms in the brackets are the square roots of the terms in the difference of squares. The signs between the terms are different in each bracket. For example, $x^2 - 64 = (x + 8)(x - 8)$.
- You can use factorisation to solve some quadratic equations. For example, $x^2 - 6x = -8$:
  - first reorganise the equation so that the right-hand side equals 0, $x^2 - 6x + 8 = 0$
  - next factorise the trinomial, $(x - 2)(x - 4) = 0$
  - finally, use the fact that if $a \times b = 0$ then $a = 0$ or $b = 0$ to find the roots. Therefore $x - 2 = 0$, so $x = 2$, or $x - 4 = 0$, so $x = 4$. These are both solutions to the equation.

Exercise 10.2 A

> **Tip**
>
> The acronym, FOIL, may help you to systematically expand pairs of brackets:
>
> F – first × first
> O – outer × outer
> I – inner × inner
> L – last × last

1   Expand and simplify.

(a) $(x + 2)(x + 3)$ (b) $(x + 2)(x - 3)$

(c) $(x + 5)(x + 7)$ (d) $(x - 5)(x + 7)$

(e) $(x - 1)(x - 3)$ (f) $(2x - 1)(x + 1)$

(g) $(y - 7)(y - 2)$ (h) $(2x - y)(3x - 2y)$

(i) $(x^2 + 1)(2x^2 - 3)$ (j) $(x - 11)(x + 12)$

(k) $\left(\frac{1}{2}x + 1\right)\left(1 - \frac{1}{2}x\right)$ (l) $(x - 3)(2 - 3x)$

(m) $(3x - 2)(2 - 4x)$

2 Expand and simplify.

(a) $(x+4)^2$ (b) $(x-3)^2$ (c) $(x+5)^2$

(d) $(y-2)^2$ (e) $(x+y)^2$ (f) $(2x-y)^2$

(g) $(3x-2)^2$ (h) $(2x-3y)^2$ (i) $(2x+5)^2$

(j) $(4x-6)^2$ (k) $(3-x)^2$ (l) $(4-2x)^2$

(m) $(6-3y)^2$

3 Write in expanded form. Try to do this by inspection.

(a) $(x-5)(x+5)$ (b) $(2x+5)(2x-5)$

(c) $(3+7y)(7y-3)$ (d) $(x^2-y^2)(x^2+y^2)$

(e) $(4+3x)(3x-4)$ (f) $(x^3+2y^2)(x^3-2y^2)$

(g) $(4x^2y^2+2z^2)(4x^2y^2-2z^2)$

(h) $(2x^4-2y)(2x^4+2y)$

(i) $(5y+4xy^2)(4xy^2-5y)$

(j) $(8x^3y^2-7z^2)(8x^3y^2+7z^2)$

Exercise 10.2 B

1 Factorise fully.

(a) x^2+4x+4 (b) $x^2+7x+12$

(c) x^2+6x+9 (d) $4+5x+x^2$

(e) $15+8x+x^2$ (f) x^2-9x+8

(g) $x^2-8x+15$ (h) $3-4x+x^2$

(i) $26-27x+x^2$ (j) x^2-7x-8

(k) $x^2+3x-10$ (l) $x^2-4x-32$

(m) $12-7x+x^2$ (n) $-12+x+x^2$

(o) $-54+3x+x^2$

2 Factorise fully.

(a) $5x^2+15x+10$ (b) $3x^2-18x+24$

(c) $3x^3-12x^2+9x$ (d) $5x^2-15x+10$

(e) x^3+12x^2+20x (f) $x^4y+x^3y-2x^2y$

(g) x^3+5x^2-14x (h) $3x^2-15x+18$

(i) $-2x^2+4x+48$ (j) $2x^2-2x-112$

3 Factorise fully.

(a) x^2-9 (b) $16-x^2$ (c) x^2-25

(d) $49-x^2$ (e) $9x^2-4y^2$ (f) $81-4x^2$

(g) x^2-9y^2 (h) $121y^2-144x^2$ (i) $16x^2-49y^2$

(j) $2x^2-18$ (k) $200-2x^2$ (l) x^4-y^2

(m) $25-x^{16}$ (n) x^2y^2-100 (o) $\dfrac{25x^2}{y^4}-\dfrac{64w^2}{z^2}$

(p) $25x^{10}-1$ (q) $1-81x^4y^6$

Exercise 10.2 C

Remember to make the right-hand side equal to zero and to factorise before you try to solve the equation.

Quadratic equations always have two roots (although sometimes the two roots are the same).

1 Solve the following quadratic equations.

(a) $x^2 - 3x = 0$ (b) $8x^2 - 32 = 0$

(c) $6x^2 = 12x$ (d) $-16x - 24x^2 = 0$

(e) $x^2 - 1 = 0$ (f) $49 - 4x^2 = 0$

(g) $8x^2 = 2$ (h) $x^2 + 6x + 8 = 0$

(i) $x^2 + 5x + 4 = 0$ (j) $x^2 - 4x - 5 = 0$

(k) $x^2 - x - 20 = 0$ (l) $x^2 + 8x = 20$

(m) $x^2 + 15 = 8x$ (n) $-60 - 17x = -x^2$

(o) $x^2 + 56 = 15x$ (p) $x^2 - 20x + 100 = 0$

(q) $5x^2 - 20x + 20 = 0$

Mixed exercise

1 For each equation, copy and complete the table of values. Draw the graphs for all four equations on the same set of axes.

(a) $y = \dfrac{1}{2}x$

x	−1	0	2	3
y				

(b) $y = -\dfrac{1}{2}x + 3$

x	−1	0	2	3
y				

(c) $y = 2$

x	−1	0	2	3
y				

(d) $y - 2x - 4 = 0$

x	−1	0	2	3
y				

2 Determine the gradient and the y-intercept of each graph.

(a) $y = -2x - 1$ (b) $y + 6 = x$ (c) $x - y = -8$

(d) $y = -\dfrac{1}{2}$ (e) $2x + 3y = 6$ (f) $y = -x$

3 What equation defines each of these lines?

(a) a line with a gradient of 1 and a y-intercept of −3

(b) a line with a y-intercept of $\dfrac{1}{2}$ and a gradient of $-\dfrac{2}{3}$

(c) a line parallel to $y = -x + 8$ with a y-intercept of −2

(d) a line parallel to $y = -\dfrac{4}{5}x$ which passes through the point $(0, -3)$

(e) a line parallel to $2y - 4x + 2 = 0$ with a y-intercept of -3

(f) a line parallel to $x + y = 5$ which passes through $(1, 1)$

(g) a line parallel to the x-axis which passes through $(1, 2)$

(h) a line parallel to the y-axis which passes through $(-4, -5)$

4 Find the gradient of the following lines.

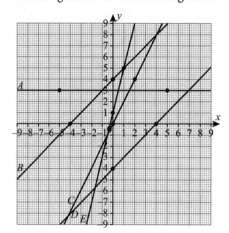

5 What is the equation of each of these lines?

(a)

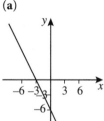

(b)

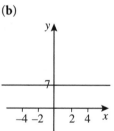

(c)

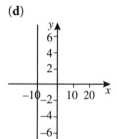

(d)

(e)

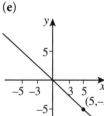

(f)

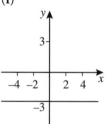

6 Caroline likes running. She averages a speed of 7 km/h when she runs. This relationship can be expressed as $D = 7t$, where D is the distance covered and t is the time (in hours) that she runs for.

(a) Use the formula $D = 7t$ to draw up a table of values for 0, 2, 4 and 6 hours of running.

(b) On a set of axes, draw a graph to show the relationship between D and t. Think carefully about how you will number the axes before you start.

(c) Write an equation in the form of $y = mx + c$ to describe this graph.

(d) What is the gradient of the line?

(e) Use your graph to find the time it takes Caroline to run:

(i) 21 km   (ii) 10 km   (iii) 5 km.

(f) Use your graph to find out how far she runs in:

  (i) 3 hours   **(ii)** $2\frac{1}{2}$ hours   **(iii)** $\frac{3}{4}$ of an hour.

(g) Caroline enters the Two Oceans Marathon. The route is 42 km long, but it is very hilly. She estimates her average speed will drop to around 6 km/h. How long will it take her to complete the race if she runs at 6 km/h?

7   For each pair of points, find:

 (a) the gradient of the line that passes through both points

 (b) the coordinates of the midpoint of a line segment joining each pair of points.

  (i) $(-1, 5)$ and $(2, 8)$

  (ii) $(-1, 3)$ and $(1, 7)$

  (iii) $(0, 4)$ and $(2, 2)$

  (iv) $(-2, 5)$ and $(1, 1)$

  (v) $(-1.5, -1.5)$ and $(-1.5, 2)$

8   Remove the brackets and simplify if possible.

 (a) $(x-8)^2$ **(b)** $(2x+2)(x-1)$

 (c) $(3x-2y)^2$ **(d)** $(1-6y)^2$

 (e) $(2+3x)(3x-2)$ **(f)** $(2x+5)^2$

 (g) $(3x^2y+1)^2$ **(h)** $\left(x+\frac{1}{2}y\right)^2$

 (i) $\left(x+\frac{1}{2}\right)\left(x-\frac{1}{2}\right)$ **(j)** $\left(\frac{1}{x}-2\right)\left(\frac{1}{x}+2\right)$

 (k) $(x-2)^2-(x-7)^2$ **(l)** $-2x(x-2)^2+8x^2$

 (m) $2x(x+1)^2-(7+2x)(-2x)$

9   Factorise fully.

 (a) a^3-4a **(b)** x^4-1

 (c) x^2-x-2 **(d)** x^2-2x+1

 (e) $(2x-3y)^2-4z^2$ **(f)** $x^2+16x+48$

 (g) $x^4-\frac{x^2}{4}$ **(h)** x^2-5x-6

 (i) $4x^2-4x-48$ **(j)** $2x^2-14x+24$

 (k) $5-20x^{16}$ **(l)** $3x^2+15x+18$

10   Solve for x.

 (a) $7x^2+42x+35=0$

 (b) $2x^2-8=0$

 (c) $6x^2-18x=-12$

 (d) $3x^2+6x=-3$

 (e) $4x^2-16x-20=0$

 (f) $5x^2-20x+20=0$

11 Pythagoras' theorem and similar shapes

11.1 Pythagoras' theorem

- In a right-angled triangle, the square of the length of the hypotenuse (the longest side) is equal to the sum of the squares of the lengths of the other two sides. This can be expressed as $c^2 = a^2 + b^2$, where c is the hypotenuse and a and b are the two shorter sides of the triangle.
- Conversely, If $c^2 = a^2 + b^2$ then the triangle will be right-angled.
- To find the length of an unknown side in a right-angled triangle you need to know two of the sides. Then you can substitute the two known lengths into the formula and solve for the unknown length.
- You can find the length of a line joining two points using Pythagoras' theorem.

Exercise 11.1 A

! Tip

The *hypotenuse* is the longest side. It is always opposite the right angle.

1 Calculate the length of the unknown side in each of these triangles.

(a)

(b)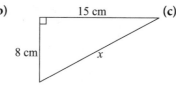

(c)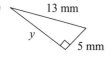

(d)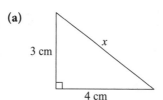

(e)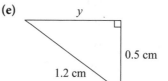

(f)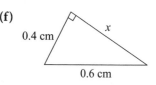

(g)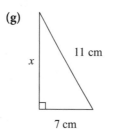

(h)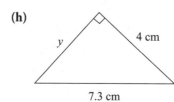

Tip

If you get an answer that is an irrational number, round your answer to three significant figures unless the instruction tells you otherwise.

2 Find the length of the side marked with a letter in each figure.

(a)

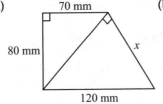

(b)

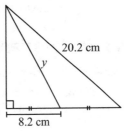

(c)

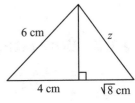

(d)

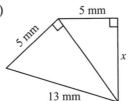

(e)

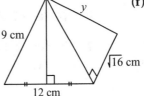

(f)

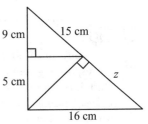

3 Determine whether each of the following triangles is right-angled. Side lengths are all in centimetres.

(a)

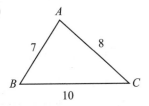

(b)

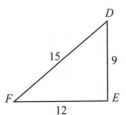

(c)

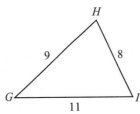

(d)

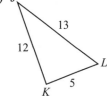

4 Calculate the length of the line segment joining each of the following pairs of points.

    (a) $(-2, -2)$ and $(2, 2)$ **(b)** $(-3, -1)$ and $(0, 2)$

    (c) $(-4, 5)$ and $(0, 1)$ **(d)** $(2, 4)$ and $(8, 16)$

    (e) $(-1, -3)$ and $(2, -3)$ **(f)** $(-2, 0)$ and $(4, 3)$

Tip

With worded problems, do a rough sketch of the situation, fill in the known lengths and mark the unknown lengths with letters.

Exercise 11.1 B

1 A rectangle has sides of 12 mm and 16 mm. Calculate the length of one of the diagonals.

2 The size of a rectangular computer screen is determined by the length of the diagonal. Nick buys a 55 cm screen that is 33 cm high. How long is the base of the screen?

3 The sides of an equilateral triangle are 100 mm long. Calculate the perpendicular height of the triangle and hence find its area.

4 A vertical pole is 12 m long. It is supported by two wire stays. The stays are attached to the top of the pole and fixed to the ground. One stay is fixed to the ground 5 m from the base of the pole and the other is fixed to the ground 9 m from the base of the pole. Calculate the length of each wire stay.

5 Nick has a 2.5 m ladder that he uses to reach shelves fixed to the wall of his garage. He wants to reach a shelf that is 2.4 metres above the ground. What is the furthest distance he can place the foot of his ladder from the wall?

11.2 Understanding similar triangles

- Triangles are similar when the corresponding sides are proportional and the corresponding angles are equal in size.
- In similar figures, if the length of each side is divided by the length of its corresponding side, all the answers will be same. You can use this property to find the lengths of unknown sides in similar figures.

> **Tip**
> Work out which sides are corresponding before you start. It is helpful to mark corresponding sides in the same colour or with a symbol.

Exercise 11.2

1 The pairs of triangles in this question are similar. Calculate the unknown (lettered) length in each case.

(a)

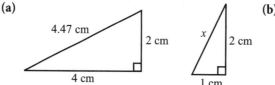

(b)

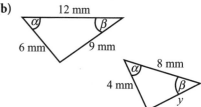

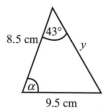

(c)

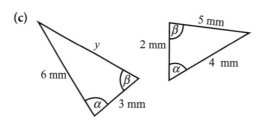

(d)

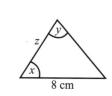

(e)

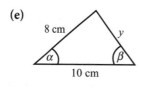

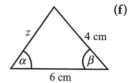

(f)

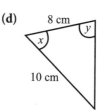

(g)

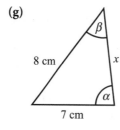

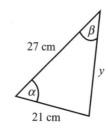

(h)

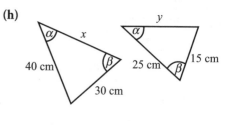

2 Explain fully why $\triangle ABC$ is similar to $\triangle ADE$.

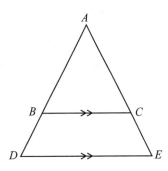

3 Nancy is lying on a blanket on the ground, 4 m away from a 3 m tall tree. When she looks up past the tree she can see the roof of a building which is 30 m beyond the tree. Work out the height of the building.

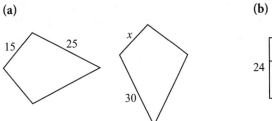

11.3 Understanding similar shapes

- The ratio of corresponding sides in similar shapes is equal. The lengths of unknown sides can be found by the same method used for similar triangles.
- There is a relationship between the sides of similar figures and the areas of the figures. In similar figures, where the ratio of sides is $a : b$, the ratio of areas is $a^2 : b^2$. In other words, the (scale factor)^2 = area factor.
- Similar solids have the same shape, their corresponding angles are equal and all corresponding linear measures (edges, diameters, radii, heights and slant heights) are in the same ratio.
- If two solids (A and B) are similar then the ratio of their volumes is equal to the cube of the ratio of corresponding linear measures. In other words: $\dfrac{\text{volume } A}{\text{volume } B} = \left(\dfrac{a}{b}\right)^3$. In addition, the ratio of their surface areas is equal to the square of the ratio of corresponding linear measures. In other words: $\dfrac{\text{surface area } A}{\text{surface area } B} = \left(\dfrac{a}{b}\right)^2$.

Exercise 11.3

1 Find the length of each side marked with a letter in these pairs of similar shapes. All dimensions are in centimetres.

(a)

(b)

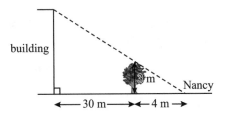

2 If the areas of two similar quadrilaterals are in the ratio 81 : 16, what is the ratio of matching sides?

3 The two shapes in each pair below are similar. The area of the shape on the left of each pair is given. Find the area of the other shape.

(a)

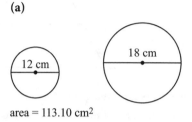

area = 113.10 cm²

(b)

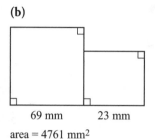

69 mm   23 mm

area = 4761 mm²

4 The two shapes in each pair below are similar. The area of both shapes is given. Use this to calculate the length of the missing side in each figure.

(a)

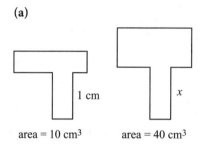

area = 10 cm³   area = 40 cm³

(b)

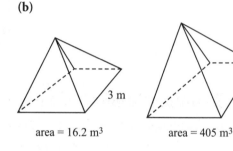

area = 16.2 m³   area = 405 m³

5 A shipping crate has a volume of 3500 cm³. If the dimensions of the crate are doubled, what will its new volume be?

6 Two similar cubes, A and B, have sides of 15 cm and 3 cm respectively.

    (a) What is the linear scale factor of A to B?
    (b) What is the ratio of their surface areas?
    (c) What is the ratio of their volumes?

11.4 Understanding congruence

- Congruent shapes are identical in shape and size. Two shapes are congruent if the corresponding sides are equal in length and the corresponding angles are equal in size.
- Triangles are congruent if any of the following four conditions are met:
  - three sides of one triangle are equal to three corresponding sides of the other (SSS)
  - two sides and the included angle of one triangle are equal to the same two sides and included angle of the other (SAS)
  - two angles and the included side (side between the angles) of one triangle are equal to the corresponding angles and included side of the other (ASA)
  - the hypotenuse and one other side of one right-angled triangle are equal to the hypotenuse and corresponding side of the other right-angled triangle (RHS).

Remember, the order in which you name a triangle is important if you are stating congruency. If △*ABC* is congruent to △*XYZ* then:

AB=XY

BC=YZ

AC=XZ

Exercise 11.4

1 State whether each pair of triangles is congruent or not. If they are congruent, state the condition of congruency.

(a)
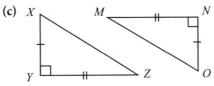

(b)
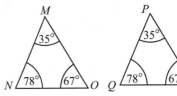

(c)
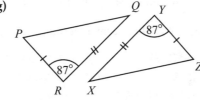

(d)
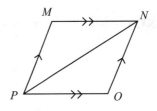

(e)
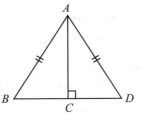

(f)
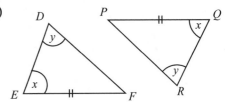

(g)

(h)
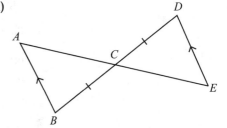

2 *MNOP* is a trapezium. *MP=NO* and *PN=MO*. Show that △ *MPO* is congruent to △ *NOP* giving reasons.

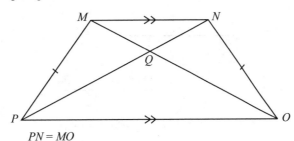

PN = MO

Tip

When you are asked to show triangles are congruent you must always state the condition that you are using.

3 In the following figure, show that *AB* is half the length of *AC* giving reasons for each statement you make.

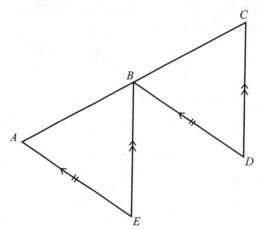

Mixed exercise

1 A school caretaker wants to mark out a sports field 50 m wide and 120 m long. To make sure that the field is rectangular, he needs to know how long each diagonal should be.

(a) Draw a rough sketch of the field.

(b) Calculate the required lengths of the diagonals.

2 In △*ABC*, *AB* = 10 cm, *BC* = 8 cm and *AC* = 6 cm. Determine whether the triangle is right-angled or not and give reasons for your answer.

3 Find the length of the line segment joining each of the following pairs of points.

(a) (−1, 5) and (2, 8)   (b) (−1, 3) and (1, 7)

(c) (0, 4) and (2, 2)   (d) (−2, 5) and (1, 1)

(e) (−1.5, −1.5) and (−1.5, 2)

4 A triangle with sides of 25 mm, 65 mm and 60 mm is similar to another triangle with its longest side 975 mm. Calculate the perimeter of the larger triangle.

5 Calculate the missing dimensions or angles in each of these pairs of similar triangles.

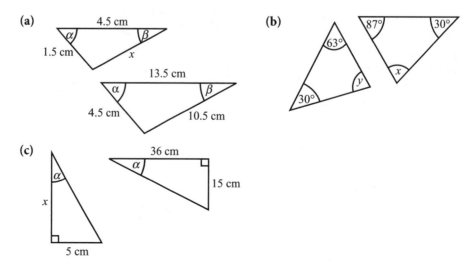

6 Calculate the ratio of the areas of each pair of similar shapes.

(a)   **(b)**

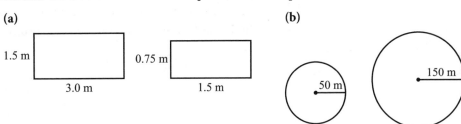

7 The two parallelograms below are similar. The area of the larger is 288 cm². Find the area of the smaller parallelogram.

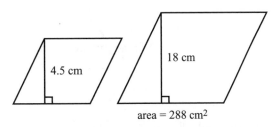

8 The two cuboids, *A* and *B*, are similar. The larger has a surface area of 60 800 mm². What is the surface area of the smaller?

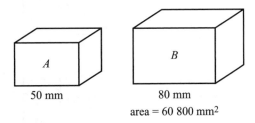

9 A square-based pyramid has a base of area 16 cm² and a volume of 16 cm³. Calculate:

(a) The perpendicular height of the pyramid.

(b) The height and area of the base of a similar pyramid with a volume of 1024 cm³.

10 Two of the triangles in each set of three are congruent. State which two are congruent and give the conditions that you used to prove them congruent.

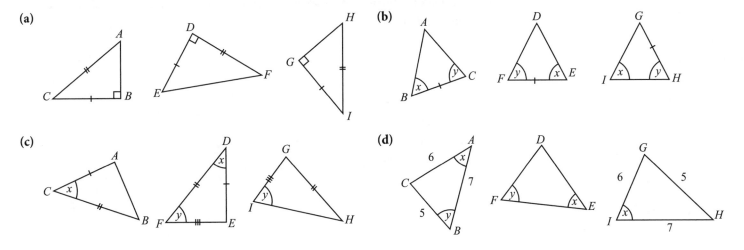

11 An 8.6 m long wire cable is used to secure a mast of height x m. The cable is attached to the top of the mast and secured on the ground 6.5 m away from the base of the mast. How tall is the mast? Give your answer correct to two decimal places.

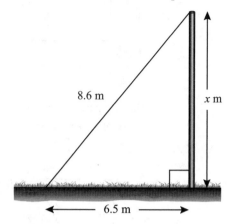

12 Nadia wants to have a metal number 1 made for her gate. She has found a sample brass numeral and noted its dimensions. She decides that her numeral should be similar to this one, but that it should be four times larger.

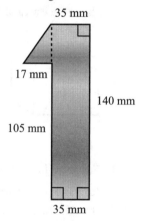

(a) Draw a rough sketch of the numeral that Nadia wants to make with the correct dimensions written on it in millimetres.

(b) Calculate the length of the sloping edge at the top of the full size numeral to the nearest whole millimetre.

Averages and measures of spread

12.1 Different types of average

- Statistical data can be summarised using an average (measure of central tendency) and a measure of spread (dispersion).
- There are three types of average: mean, median and mode.
- A measure of spread is the range (largest value minus smallest value).
- The mean is the sum of the data items divided by the number of items in the data set. The mean does not have to be one of the numbers in the data set.
  - The mean can be affected by extreme values in the data set. When one value is much lower or higher than the rest of the data it is called an outlier. Outliers skew the mean and make it less representative of the data set.
- The median is the middle value in a set of data when the data is arranged in increasing order.
  - When there is an even number of data items, the median is the mean of the two middle values.
- The mode is the number (or item) that appears most often in a data set.
  - When two numbers appear most often the data has two modes and is said to be bimodal. When more than two numbers appear equally often the mode has no real value as a statistic.

Exercise 12.1

1 Determine the mean, median and mode of the following sets of data.

   (a) 5, 9, 6, 4, 7, 6, 6
   (b) 23, 38, 15, 27, 18, 38, 21, 40, 27
   (c) 12, 13, 14, 12, 12, 13, 15, 16, 14, 13, 12, 11
   (d) 4, 4, 4, 5, 5, 5, 6, 6, 6
   (e) 4, 4, 4, 4, 5, 5, 6, 6, 6
   (f) 4, 4, 5, 5, 5, 6, 6, 6, 6

2 Five students scored a mean mark of 14.8 out of 20 for a maths test.

   (a) Which of these sets of marks fit this average?
(i) 14, 16, 17, 15, 17	(ii) 12, 13, 12, 19, 19	(iii) 12, 19, 12, 18, 13
(iv) 13, 17, 15, 16, 17	(v) 19, 19, 12, 0, 19	(vi) 15, 15, 15, 15, 14

   (b) Compare the sets of numbers in your answer above. Explain why you can get the same mean from different sets of numbers.

3 The mean of 15 numbers is 17. What is the sum of the numbers?

4 The sum of 21 numbers is 312.8. Which of the following numbers is closest to the mean of the 21 numbers? 14, 15, 16 or 17.

> **Tip**
> If you multiply the mean by the number of items in the data set, you get the total of the scores. This will help you solve problems like question 2.

5 An agricultural worker wants to know which of two dairy farmers have the best milk producing cows. Farmer Singh says his cows produce 2490 litres of milk per day. Farmer Naidoo says her cows produce 1890 litres of milk per day.

There is not enough information to decide which cows are the better producers of milk. What other information would you need to answer the question?

6 In a group of students, six had four siblings, seven had five siblings, eight had three siblings, nine had two siblings and ten had one sibling. (Siblings are brothers and sisters.)

> **Tip**
> It may help to draw a rough frequency table to solve problems like this one.

  (a) What is the mean number of siblings?

  (b) What is the modal number of siblings?

7 The management of a factory announced salary increases and said that workers would receive an average increase of $20 to $40.

The table shows the old and new salaries of the workers in the factory.

	Previous salary	Salary with increase
Four workers in Category A	$180	$240
Two workers in Category B	$170	$200
Six workers in Category C	$160	$170
Eight workers in Category D	$150	$156

  (a) Calculate the mean increase for all workers.

  (b) Calculate the modal increase.

  (c) What is the median increase?

  (d) How many workers received an increase of between $20 and $40?

  (e) Was the management announcement true? Say why or why not.

12.2 Making comparisons using averages and ranges

- You can use averages to compare two or more sets of data. However, averages on their own may be misleading, so it is useful to work with other summary statistics as well.
- The range is a measure of how spread out (dispersed) the data is. Range = largest value – smallest value.
- A large range means that the data is spread out, so the measures of central tendency (averages) may not be representative of the whole data set.

> **Tip**
> When the mean is affected by extreme values the median is more representative of the data.

Exercise 12.2

1 For the following sets of data, one of the three averages is not representative. State which one is not representative in each case.

  (a) 6, 2, 5, 1, 5, 7, 2, 3, 8

  (b) 2, 0, 1, 3, 1, 6, 2, 9, 10, 3, 2, 2, 0

  (c) 21, 29, 30, 14, 5, 16, 3, 24, 17

2 Twenty students scored the following results in a test (out of 20).

17	18	17	14	8	3	15	18	3	15
0	17	16	17	14	7	18	19	5	15

(a) Calculate the mean, median, mode and range of the marks.

(b) Why is the median the best summary statistic for this particular set of data?

3 The table shows the times (in minutes and seconds) that two runners achieved over 800 m during one season.

Runner A	2 m 2.5 s	2 m 1.7 s	2 m 2.2 s	2 m 3.7 s	2 m 1.7 s	2 m 2.9 s	2 m 2.6 s
Runner B	2 m 2.4 s	2 m 1.8 s	2 m 2.3 s	2 m 4.4 s	2 m 0.6 s	2 m 2.2 s	2 m 1.2 s

(a) Which runner is the better of the two? Why?

(b) Which runner is most consistent? Why?

12.3 Calculating averages and ranges for frequency data

- The mean can be calculated from a frequency table. To calculate the mean you add a column to the table and calculate the score × frequency (fx). $\text{Mean} = \dfrac{\text{total of (score} \times \text{frequency) column}}{\text{total of frequency column}}$.

- Find the mode in a table by looking at the frequency column. The data item with the highest frequency is the mode.

- In a frequency table, the data is already ordered by size. To find the median, work out its position in the data and then add the frequencies till you equal or exceed this value. The score in this category will be the median.

Exercise 12.3

1 Construct a frequency table for the data below and then calculate:

(a) the mean   (b) the mode   (c) the median   (d) the range.

0	3	4	3	3	2	2	2	2	1
3	3	4	3	6	2	2	2	0	0
5	4	3	2	4	3	3	3	2	1
3	1	1	1	1	0	0	0	2	4

2 For each of the following frequency distributions calculate:

(a) the mean score   (b) the median score   (c) the modal score.

Data set A

Score	1	2	3	4	5	6
Frequency	12	14	15	12	15	12

Data set B

Score	10	20	30	40	50	60	70	80
Frequency	13	25	22	31	16	23	27	19

Data set C

Score	1.5	2.5	3.5	4.5	5.5	6.5
Frequency	15	12	15	12	10	21

12.4 Calculating averages and ranges for grouped continuous data

- Continuous data can take any value between two given values.
- When given a frequency table containing grouped data (in class intervals) you don't know the exact values of the data items; you only know into which class they fall. This means you cannot work out the exact mean, median or mode, but you can estimate them.
- To estimate the mean you need to use the midpoints of the class intervals in the table.
  - The midpoint is the mean of the smallest and largest scores in the interval.
  - The lowest and highest scores in a class interval are called the lower and upper class limits.
  - Once you have found the midpoints you can estimate the mean: $\text{Estimated mean} = \dfrac{\text{sum of (midpoint} \times \text{frequency)}}{\text{sum of frequencies}}$
- The modal class is the class interval with the highest frequency.
- The median class is the class interval into which the middle value in the data set falls. Work out the position of the median (total frequency ÷ two) and then add the totals in the frequency column until you reach that position to find the median class.

Exercise 12.4

Tip

Class intervals are often given using inequality symbols. $0 \le m < 10$, means values greater or equal to 0 up to values that are less than 10. The next class interval has values equal to or greater than 10, so a value of 10 would go into the second class interval.

1 The table shows the marks (m) obtained by a group of students for an assignment.

Marks (m)	Midpoint	Frequency (f)	Frequency × midpoint
$0 \le m < 10$		2	
$10 \le m < 20$		5	
$20 \le m < 30$		13	
$30 \le m < 40$		16	
$40 \le m < 50$		14	
$50 \le m < 60$		13	
Total			

(a) Copy and complete the table.

(b) Calculate an estimate for the mean mark.

(c) Into which class does the modal mark fall?

(d) What is the median class?

Tip

In some texts, the midpoint is called the class centre.

2 The table shows the number of words per minutes typed by a group of computer programmers.

Words per minute (w)	Frequency
$31 \le w < 36$	40
$36 \le w < 41$	70
$41 \le w < 46$	80
$46 \le w < 51$	90
$51 \le w < 55$	60
$55 \le w < 60$	20
Total	

(a) Determine an estimate for the mean number of words typed per minute.

(b) How many words do most of the programmers manage to type per minute?

(c) What is the median class?

(d) What is the range of words typed per minute?

12.5 Percentiles and quartiles

- Percentiles are used to divide a data set into 100 equal groups. If you score in the 80th percentile in a test, it means that 80% of the other marks are lower than yours.
- Quartiles are used to divide a set of data into four equal groups (quarters).
  - The lower quartile (Q_1) is the value below which one-quarter of the data lie.
  - The second quartile is also the median of the data set (Q_2).
  - The upper quartile (Q_3) is the value below which three-quarters of the data lie (obviously the other quarter lie above this).
- The interquartile range, IQR = $Q_3 - Q_1$.

Tip

You can find the position of the quartiles using these rules:

$Q_1 = \frac{1}{4}(n+1)$

$Q_2 = \frac{1}{2}(n+1)$

$Q_3 = \frac{3}{4}(n+1)$

When the quartile falls between two values, find the mean of the two scores.

Exercise 12.5

1 For each of the following sets of data calculate the median, upper and lower quartiles. In each case calculate the interquartile range.

(a) | 67 | 44 | 63 | 56 | 46 | 48 | 55 | 63 |

(b) | 17 | 18 | 17 | 14 | 8 | 3 | 15 | 18 | 3 | 15 |

(c) | 0.8 | 1.3 | 0.7 | 1.4 | 2.3 | 0.4 |

(d) | 1 | 0 | 2 | 2 | 0 | 4 | 1 | 3 |
     | 3 | 4 | 5 | 4 | 5 | 5 | 1 | 2 |

Mixed exercise

1 Find the mean, median, mode and range of the following sets of data.

(a) | 6 | 5 | 6 | 7 | 4 | 5 | 8 | 6 | 7 | 10 |

(b) | 6 | 3 | 2 | 4 | 2 | 1 | 2 | 2 | 1 |

(c) | 12.5 | 13.2 | 19.4 | 12.8 | 7.5 | 18.6 | 12.6 |

2 The mean of two consecutive numbers is 9.5. The mean of eight different numbers is 4.7.

(a) Calculate the total of the first two numbers.
(b) What are these two numbers?
(c) Calculate the mean of the ten numbers together.

3 Three suppliers sell specialised remote controllers for access systems. A sample of 100 remote controllers is taken from each supplier and the working life of each controller is measured in weeks. The following table shows the mean time and range for each supplier.

Supplier	Mean (weeks)	Range (weeks)
A	137	16
B	145	39
C	141	16

Which supplier would you recommend to someone who is looking to buy a remote controller? Why?

4 A box contains 50 plastic blocks of different volume as shown in the frequency table.

Volume (cm^3)	2	3	4	5	6	7
Frequency	4	7	9	12	10	8

(a) Find the mean volume of the blocks.

(b) What volume is most common?

(c) What is the median volume?

5 The ages of people who visited an art exhibition are recorded and organised in the grouped frequency table below.

Age in years (a)	Frequency
$0 \leq a < 10$	13
$10 \leq a < 20$	28
$20 \leq a < 30$	39
$30 \leq a < 40$	46
$40 \leq a < 50$	48
$50 \leq a < 60$	31
$60 \leq a < 70$	19
Total	

(a) Estimate the mean age of people attending the exhibition.

(b) Into what age group did most visitors fall?

(c) What is the median age of visitors to the exhibition?

(d) Why can you not calculate an exact mean for this data set?

6 The number of students attending a chess club on various days was recorded:

18, 19, 18, 19, 21, 18, 21, 23, 18, 23, 23

(a) Find the median of the data.

(b) What is the range of the data?

(c) Find Q_1 and Q_3 and hence calculate the IQR.

(d) Compare the range and the IQR. What does this tell you about the data?

7 A teacher announces that all students who score below the 60th percentile in a test will have to rewrite it. When the results are out, 15 out of the 26 students have to rewrite the test.

(a) What does this tell you about the scores?

(b) What does this tell you about the performance of the class overall?

13 Understanding measurement

13.1 Understanding units

- Units of measure in the metric system are metres (m), grams (g) and litres (l). Sub-divisions have prefixes such as milli- and centi-; the prefix kilo- is a multiple.
- To convert from a larger unit to a smaller unit you multiply the measurement by the correct multiple of ten.
- To convert from a smaller unit to a larger unit you divide the measurement by the correct multiple of ten.

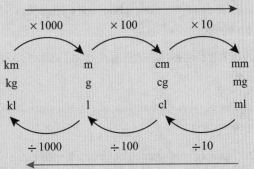

- Area is always measured in square units. To convert areas from one unit to another you need to square the appropriate length conversion factor.
- Volume is measured in cubic units. To convert volumes from one unit to another you need to cube the appropriate length conversion factor.

Exercise 13.1

Tip
Memorise these conversions:
10 mm = 1 cm
100 cm = 1 m
1000 m = 1 km
1000 mg = 1 g
1000 g = 1 kg
1000 kg = 1 t
1000 ml = 1 litre
1 cm³ = 1 ml

Tip
Memorise these conversions:
10 mm = 1 cm
100 cm = 1 m
1000 m = 1 km
1000 mg = 1 g
1000 g = 1 kg
1000 kg = 1 t
1000 ml = 1 litre
$1 \text{ cm}^3 = 1 \text{ ml}$

1 Use the conversion diagram in the box above as a basis to draw your own diagrams to show how to convert:

   (a) units of area   **(b)** units of volume.

2 Convert the following length measurements to the units given:

   (a) 2.6 km = _____ m   **(b)** 23 cm = _____ mm

   (c) 8.2 m = _____ cm   **(d)** 2 450 809 m = _____ km

   (e) 0.02 m = _____ mm   **(f)** 15.7 cm = _____ m.

3 Convert the following measurements of mass to the units given:

   (a) 9.08 kg = _____ g   **(b)** 49.34 kg = _____ g

   (c) 0.5 kg = _____ g   **(d)** 68 g = _____ kg

   (e) 15.2 g = _____ kg   **(f)** 2 300 000 g = _____ tonne.

4 Identify the greater length in each of these pairs of lengths. Then calculate the difference between the two lengths. Give your answer in the most appropriate units.

(a)	19 km	18 900 m	**(b)**	90 m	9015 cm
(c)	43.3 cm	435 mm	**(d)**	492 cm	4.29 m
(e)	635 m	0.6 km	**(f)**	5.8 km	580 500 cm

5 Convert the following area measurements to the units given:

(a) $12\,cm^2 = $ _____ mm^2 **(b)** $9\,cm^2 = $ _____ mm^2

(c) $164.2\,cm^2 = $ _____ mm^2 **(d)** $0.37\,km^2 = $ _____ m^2

(e) $9441\,m^2 = $ _____ km^2 **(f)** $0.423\,m^2 = $ _____ mm^2.

6 Convert the following volume measurements to the units given:

Cubic centimetres or cm^3 is sometimes written as cc. For example, a scooter may have a 50 cc engine. That means the total volume of all cylinders in the engine is $50\,cm^3$.

(a) $69\,cm^3 = $ _____ mm^3 **(b)** $19\,cm^3 = $ _____ mm^3

(c) $30.04\,cm^3 = $ _____ mm^3 **(d)** $4.815\,m^3 = $ _____ cm^3

(e) $103\,mm^3 = $ _____ cm^3 **(f)** $46\,900\,mm^3 = $ _____ m^3.

7 Naeem lives 1.2 km from school and Sadiqa lives 980 m from school. How much closer to the school does Sadiqa live?

8 A coin has a diameter of 22 mm. If you placed 50 coins in a row, how long would the row be in cm?

9 A square of fabric has an area of $176\,400\,mm^2$. What are the lengths of the sides of the square in cm?

10 How many cuboid-shaped boxes, each with dimensions $50\,cm \times 90\,cm \times 120\,cm$, can you fit into a volume of $48\,m^3$?

13.2 Time

- Time is not decimal. 1 h 15 means one hour and $\frac{15}{60}$ (or $\frac{1}{4}$) of an hour, not 1.15 h.
- One hour and 15 minutes is written as 1:15.
- Time can be written using a.m. and p.m. notation or as a 24-hour time using the numbers from 0 to 24 to give the times from 12 midnight on one day (00:00 h) to one second before midnight (23:59:59). Even in the 24-hour clock system, time is not decimal. The time one minute after 15:59 is 16:00.

Tip

You can express parts of an hour as a decimal. Divide the number of minutes by 60.

For example 12 minutes $= \frac{12}{60} = \frac{1}{5} = 0.2$ hours. This can make your calculations easier.

Exercise 13.2

1 Five people record the time they start work, the time they finish and the length of their lunch break.

(a) Copy and complete this table to show how much time each person spent at work on this particular day.

Name	Time in	Time out	Lunch	Hours worked
Dawoot	$\frac{1}{4}$ past 9	Half past five	$\frac{3}{4}$ hour	
Nadira	8:17 a.m.	5:30 p.m.	$\frac{1}{2}$ hour	
John	08:23	17:50	45 min	
Robyn	7:22 a.m.	4:30 p.m.	1 hour	
Mari	08:08	18:30	45 min	

(b) Calculate each person's daily earnings to the nearest whole cent if they are paid $7.45 per hour.

2 On a particular day, the low tide in Hong Kong harbour is at 09:15. The high tide is at 15:40 the same day. How much time passes between low tide and high tide?

3 Sarah's plane was due to land at 2:45 p.m. However, it was delayed and it landed at 15:05. How much later did the plane arrive than it was meant to?

4 How much time passes between:

(a) 2:25 p.m. and 8:12 p.m. on the same day?
(b) 1:43 a.m. and 12:09 p.m. on the same day?
(c) 6:33 p.m. and 6:45 a.m. the next day?
(d) 1:09 a.m. and 15:39 on the same day?

5 Use this section from a bus timetable to answer the questions that follow.

Chavez Street	09:00	09:30	10:00
Castro Avenue	09:18	09:48	10:18
Peron Place	09:35	10:05	10:35
Marquez Lane	10:00	10:30	11:00

(a) What is the earliest bus from Chavez Street?
(b) How long does the journey from Chavez Street to Marquez Lane take?
(c) A bus arrives at Peron Place at quarter past ten. The bus is 10 minutes late. At what time did it leave Chavez Street?
(d) Sanchez misses the 09:48 bus from Castro Avenue. How long will have to wait before the next scheduled bus arrives?
(e) The 10:00 bus from Chavez Street is delayed in roadworks between Castro Avenue and Peron Place for 19 minutes. How will this affect the rest of the timetable?

13.3 Upper and lower bounds

- All measurements we make are rounded to some degree of accuracy. The degree of accuracy (for example the nearest metre or to two decimal places) allows you to work out the highest and lowest possible value of the measurements. The highest possible value is called the upper bound and the lowest possible value is called the lower bound.
- When you work with more than one rounded value you need to use the upper and lower bounds of each.

dp means decimal places
sf means significant figures

Exercise 13.3

1 Each of the numbers below has been rounded to the degree of accuracy shown in the brackets. Find the upper and lower bounds in each case.

   (a) 42 (nearest whole number)
   (b) 13 325 (nearest whole number)
   (c) 400 (1sf)
   (d) 12.24 (2dp)
   (e) 11.49 (2dp)
   (f) 2.5 (to nearest tenth)
   (g) 390 (nearest ten)
   (h) 1.132 (4sf)

2 A building is 72 m tall measured to the nearest metre.

   (a) What are the upper and lower bounds of the building's height?
   (b) Is 72.499999999999999999 metres a possible height for the building? Explain why or why not.

3 The dimensions of a rectangular piece of land are 4.3 m by 6.4 m. The measurements are each correct to one decimal place.

   (a) Find the area of the piece of land.
   (b) Calculate the upper and lower bounds of the area of the land.

4 Usain Bolt holds the world records for the 100 m and 200 m sprints (2011). He was also a member of the Jamaican four by 100 m relay team that set a new world record of 36.84 seconds in August 2012.

   (a) Usain Bolt is 196 cm tall, correct to the nearest centimetre, and his mass is 94 kg, correct to the nearest kilogram. Find the upper and lower bounds of his height and mass.
   (b) The Jamaican coach says his team can run the 400 m relay in 34 seconds. Both these measurements are given to two significant figures. What is the maximum speed (in metres per second) at which they can run the relay? Give your answer correct to two decimal places.

5 The two short sides of a right-angled triangle are 4.7 cm (to the nearest mm) and 6.5 cm (to the nearest mm). Calculate upper and lower bounds for:

   (a) the area of the rectangle
   (b) the length of the hypotenuse.
   Give your answers in centimetres to four decimal places.

13.4 Conversion graphs

- Conversion graphs allow you to convert from one unit of measure to another by providing the values of both units on different axes. To find one value (*x*) when the other (*y*) is given, you need to find the *y*-value against the graph and then read off the corresponding value on the other axis.

Exercise 13.4

1 Sheila, an Australian, is going on holiday to the island of Bali in Indonesia. She finds this conversion graph to show the value of rupiah (the currency of Indonesia) against the Australian dollar.

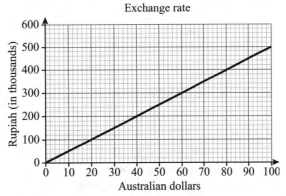

   (a) What is the scale on the vertical axis?
   (b) How many rupiah will Sheila get for:
       (i) Aus $50   (ii) Aus $100   (iii) Aus $500?
   (c) The hotel she plans to stay at charges 400 000 rupiah a night.
       (i) What is this amount in Australian dollars?
       (ii) How much will Sheila pay in Australian dollars for an eight night stay?

2 Study the conversion graph and answer the questions.

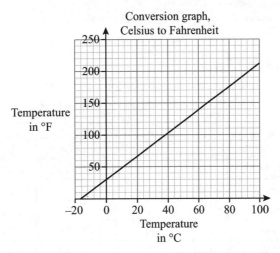

   (a) What is shown on the graph?
   (b) What is the temperature in Fahrenheit when it is:
       (i) 0 °C   (ii) 10 °C   (iii) 100 °C?

(c) Sarah finds a recipe for chocolate brownies that says she needs to cook the mixture at 210 °C for one hour. After an hour she finds that it has hardly cooked at all. What could the problem be?

(d) Jess is American. When she calls her friend Nick in England she says, 'It's really cold here, must be about 50 degrees out.' What temperature scale is she using? How do you know this?

3 This graph shows the conversion factor for pounds (imperial measurement of mass) and kilograms.

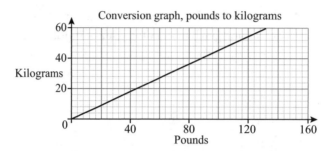

(a) Nettie says she needs to lose about 20 pounds. How much is this in kilograms?

(b) John says he's a weakling. He weighs 98 pounds. How much does he weigh in kilograms?

(c) Which is the greater mass in each of these cases:

    (i) 30 pounds or 20 kilograms

    (ii) 35 kilograms or 70 pounds

    (iii) 60 kilograms or 145 pounds?

13.5 More money

- When you change money from one currency to another you do so at a given rate of exchange. Changing to another currency is called buying foreign currency.

- Exchange rates can be worked out using conversion graphs (as in 13.4), but more often, they are worked out by doing calculations.

- Doing calculations with money is just like doing calculations with decimals but you need to remember to include the currency symbols in your answers.

Exercise 13.5

Use the exchange rate table below for these questions.

Tip

Currency rates change all the time. These rates were correct in 2011, but they may be very different today.

The inverse rows show the exchange rate of one unit of the currency in the column to the currency above the word inverse. For example, using the inverse row below US $ and the euro column, €1 will buy $1.39.

Currency exchange rates – October 2011

Currency	US $	Euro (€)	UK £	Indian rupee	Aus $	Can $	SA rand	NZ $	Yen (¥)
1 US $	1.00	0.72	0.63	49.81	0.97	1.01	9.08	1.25	76.16
inverse	1.00	1.39	1.59	0.02	1.03	0.99	0.12	0.80	0.01
1 Euro	1.39	1.00	0.87	69.10	1.34	1.40	11.21	1.73	105.64
inverse	0.72	1.00	1.15	0.01	0.74	0.71	0.09	0.58	0.01
1 UK £	1.59	1.15	1.00	79.37	1.54	1.61	12.88	1.99	121.36
inverse	0.63	0.87	1.00	0.01	0.65	0.62	0.08	0.50	0.01

(a) What is the exchange rate for:
    (i) US$ to yen   (ii) UK£ to NZ$
    (iii) euro to Indian rupee   (iv) Canadian dollar to euro
    (v) yen to pound   (vi) South African rand to US$?

(b) How many Indian rupees will you get for:
    (i) US$50   (ii) 600 euros   (iii) £95?

(c) How many yen will you need to buy:
    (i) US$120   (ii) 500 euros   (iii) £1200?

Mixed exercise

1 Convert the following measurements to the units given.

  (a) 2.7 km to metres   (b) 69 cm to mm   (c) 6 tonnes to kilograms
  (d) 23.5 grams to kilograms   (e) 263 grams to milligrams   (f) 29.25 litres to millilitres
  (g) 240 ml to litres   (h) $10\,\text{cm}^2$ to mm^2 (i) $6428\,\text{m}^2$ to km^2
  (j) $7.9\,\text{m}^3$ to cm^3 (k) $0.029\,\text{km}^3$ to m^3 (l) $168\,\text{mm}^3$ to cm^3

2 The average time taken to walk around a track is one minute and 35 seconds. How long will it take you to walk around the track 15 times at this rate?

3 A journey took 3 h 40 min and 10 s to complete. Of this, 1 h 20 min and 15 s was spent having lunch or stops for other reasons. The rest of the time was spent travelling. How much time was actually spent travelling?

4 Tayo's height is 1.62 m, correct to the nearest cm. Calculate the least possible and greatest possible height that he could be.

5 The number of people who attended a meeting was given as 50, correct to the nearest 10.

  (a) Is it possible that 44 people attended? Explain why or why not.
  (b) Is it possible that 54 people attended? Explain why or why not.

6 The dimensions of a rectangle are 3.61 cm and 2.57 cm, each correct to three significant figures.

  (a) Write down the range of possible values of each dimension.
  (b) Find the lower and upper bounds of the area of the rectangle.
  (c) Write down the lower and upper bounds of the area correct to three significant figures.

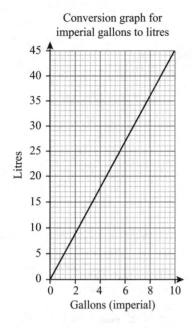

Conversion graph for
imperial gallons to litres

1 mile = 1.61 km

The US gallon is different from the
imperial gallon with a conversion
factor of 1 US gallon to 3.785 litres.

7 Study the graph and answer the questions.
  (a) What does the graph show?
  (b) Convert to litres:
    (i) 10 gallons   (ii) 25 gallons
  (c) Convert to gallons:
    (i) 15 litres   (ii) 120 litres
  (d) Naresh says he gets 30 mpg in the city and 42 mpg on the highway in his car.
    (i) Convert each rate to km per gallon.
    (ii) Given that one gallon is equivalent to 4.546 litres, convert both rates
          to kilometres per litre.

Use the exchange rate table below (repeated from Exercise 13.5) to answer the following
questions.

Currency exchange rates – October 2011

Currency	US$	Euro (€)	UK £	Indian rupee	Aus $	Can $	SA rand	NZ $	Yen (¥)
1 US $	1.00	0.72	0.63	49.81	0.97	1.01	9.08	1.25	76.16
inverse	.00	1.39	1.59	0.02	1.03	0.99	0.12	0.80	0.01
1 Euro	1.39	1.00	0.87	69.10	1.34	1.40	11.21	1.73	105.64
Inverse	0.72	1.00	1.15	0.01	0.74	0.71	0.09	0.58	0.01
1 UK £	1.59	1.15	1.00	79.37	1.54	1.61	12.88	1.99	121.36
inverse	0.63	0.87	1.00	0.01	0.65	0.62	0.08	0.50	0.01

8 Jan lives in South Africa and is going on holiday to Italy. He has R10 000 to exchange for
euros. How many Euros will he get?

9 Pete is an American who is travelling to India for business. He needs to exchange
$2000 for rupees.
  (a) What is the exchange rate?
  (b) How many rupees will he get at this rate?
  (c) At the end of the trip he has 12 450 rupees left over. What will he get if he changes these
      back to dollars at the given rate?

10 Jimmy is British and he is going to Spain on a package holiday. The cost of the holiday is
4875 euros. What is this amount in UK pounds?

14 Further solving of equations and inequalities

14.1 Simultaneous linear equations

- Simultaneous means 'at the same time'.
- There are two methods for solving simultaneous equations: graphically and algebraically.
- The graphical solution is the point where the two lines of the equations intersect. This point has an x- and a y-coordinate.
- There are two algebraic methods: by substitution and by elimination.
  - Sometimes you need to manipulate or rearrange one or both of the equations before you can solve them algebraically.
  - For the substitution method, one equation is substituted into the other.
  - For the elimination method you need either the same coefficient of x or the same coefficient of y in both equations.
  - If the variable with the same coefficient has the same sign in both equations, you should then subtract one equation from the other. If the signs are different then you should add the two equations.
  - If an equation contains fractions, you can make everything much easier by 'getting rid' of the fractions. Multiply each term by a suitable number (a common denominator) and 'clear' the denominators of the fractions.

Exercise 14.1 A

1 Draw the graphs for each pair of equations given. Then use the point of intersection to find the simultaneous solution. The limits of the x-axis that you should use are given in each case.

(a) $2x + 3 = y$
$x - y = 0$ $(-5 < x < 5)$

(b) $4x + 2 = y$
$x - 2y = 3$ $(-5 < x < 5)$

(c) $y = -2x + 2$
$2y + 3x - 1 = 0$ $(-5 < x < 10)$

(d) $y - x = 4$
$y = -x - 7$ $(-10 < x < 5)$

(e) $3x + 3y = 3$
$y = -2x + 3$ $(-5 < x < 5)$

2 The graph below shows lines corresponding to six equations.

(a) Find the equations of lines *A* to *F*

(b) Use the graphs to find the solutions to the following pairs of simultaneous equations.

(i) *A* and *C*   (ii) *D* and *F*   (iii) *A* and *E*

(c) Now check your solutions algebraically.

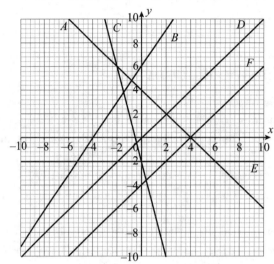

3 Solve for *x* and *y* by using the substitution method. Check each solution by substituting the values into one of the equations.

(a) $y = 2$
$x + y = 6$

(b) $y - x = 3$
$y - 3x = 5$

(c) $x + y = 4$
$2x + 3y = 12$

(d) $2x + y = 7$
$3x - y = 8$

4 Solve for *x* and *y* by using the elimination method. Check each solution.

(a) $x + y = 5$
$x - y = 7$

(b) $3x - y = 1$
$2x + y = 4$

(c) $2x + 3y = 12$
$3x + 3y = 30$

(d) $2x + 3y = 6$
$4x - 6y = -4$

(e) $2x - 5y = 11$
$3x + 2y = 7$

(f) $y - 2x = 1$
$2y - 3x = 5$

5 Solve simultaneously.

Remember that you might need to rearrange one or both equations before solving.

(a) $3x + y = 7$
$3x - y = 5$

(b) $\dfrac{2x + y}{2} = 3$
$\dfrac{x}{2} + y = 3$

(c) $3x + 2y = 4$
$2x + y = 3$

(d) $\dfrac{x}{3} + \dfrac{y}{2} = 2$
$x + 4y = 11$

(e) $\dfrac{5x}{2} + y = 10$
$\dfrac{x}{4} + y = 3\dfrac{1}{4}$

(f) $\dfrac{3x}{4} + \dfrac{y}{2} = 4$
$x + \dfrac{3y}{2} = 7$

(g) $7x - 6y = 17$
$\dfrac{2x}{3} + y = 6\dfrac{1}{3}$

(h) $\dfrac{3x + y}{2} = \dfrac{1}{2}$
$\dfrac{5x - 7y}{3} = 2$

(i) $2x = 9y$
$\dfrac{x}{3} = 6y + 9$

6 Sally bought two chocolate bars and one box of gums for $3.15 and Evan paid $2.70 for one chocolate and two boxes of gums. If they bought the same brands and sizes of products, what is the cost of a chocolate bar and the cost of a box of gums?

7 It costs $5 for an adult and $2 for a student to visit the National Botanical Gardens. Adults can be members of the Botanical Society and if you are a member, you can visit the gardens for free. A group of 30 adults and students visited the gardens. Five members of the group could go in for free and it cost the rest of the group $104 to go in. How many students were in the group?

8 Ephrahim has 12 coins in his pocket, consisting of quarters and dimes only. If he has $2.10 in his pocket, how many of each coin does he have?

Exercise 14.1 B

1 Form two equations using the information on each diagram and solve them simultaneously to find the values of x and y.

(a)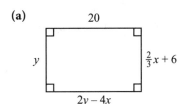

(b)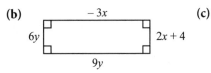

(c)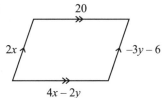

(d)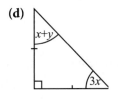

(e)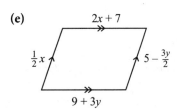

(f)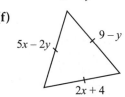

2 On a busy day, a shop sells a total of 15 desks and chairs for a total amount of $960. The desks sell for $120 each and the chairs sell for $50 each.

  (a) Express the information as two equations. Let d equal the number of desks and let c equal the number of chairs.

  (b) Solve the equations simultaneously to find how many of each were sold.

14.2 Linear inequalities

- The solution to a linear inequality is a range of values.
- The solution can be represented on a number line.
  - A solid circle on the number line means the value is included.
  - An open circle on the number line means the value is not included.

Exercise 14.2

1 Draw a number line to represent the possible values of the variable in each case.

(a) $x \le 4$ (b) $y \ge -2$ (c) $f > -3.5$

(d) $1.2 \le a \le 2.6$ (e) $-4 \ge n$ (f) $-m < 3$

(g) $-3.5 \le a \le -2$ (h) $0.25 < a \le 1.5$ (i) $4 \le a < 6$

2 Write down all integers that satisfy each of the following inequalities.

(a) $2 < x \le 4$ (b) $-2.5 \le h \le 3$ (c) $\sqrt{2} < a < 3$

(d) $-1.5 \le s \le 3.5$ (e) $-\dfrac{1}{3} \le e < 5$ (f) $\pi < b \le 3\pi$

3 Solve each of the following inequalities. Some of the answers will involve fractions. Leave your answers as fractions in their simplest form where appropriate.

(a) $2x \le -4$ (b) $x - 4 > 7$ (c) $3x - 5 \ge 7$ (d) $\dfrac{x}{4} \le 13$

(e) $\dfrac{x}{3} + 8 \ge 11$ (f) $\dfrac{x-5}{4} > 17$ (g) $4(x - 5) > 17$ (h) $\dfrac{2}{3}e \le e + 1$

(i) $\dfrac{r}{4} + \dfrac{1}{8} < 3$ (j) $5(2x - 13) \ge 7(x + 10)$ (k) $3g - 23 < 51 - 5g$

(l) $\dfrac{y+4}{12} \ge y - \dfrac{1}{2}$ (m) $\dfrac{3n-6}{3} - 8 > 21$ (n) $6(n - 1) - 2(3 - n) < 3(7n + 4) + 2$

(o) $\dfrac{3}{8}\left(2x - \dfrac{1}{3}\right) - \dfrac{2}{9}(3x + 33) \ge \dfrac{5x-3}{4} + \dfrac{1}{3}$

14.3   Regions in a plane

- When the relationship between two variables is expressed as an inequality, that relationship is represented graphically as a region on the Cartesian plane.
- When the inequality includes equal to ($\le$ or $\ge$), the boundary line on the graph must be included as a solid line on the graph.
- When the inequality does not include equal to ($<$ or $>$), the boundary line is shown as a broken line.

Exercise 14.3

1 On separate axes, show the region that represents the following inequalities by shading the unwanted region:

(a) $y < 4x + 1$ (b) $y \ge -2x + 5$ (c) $y > -x + 1$

2 Shade the unwanted region that represents each inequality on separate axes.

(a) $2y \le -4$ (b) $x - y > 7$ (c) $3x - y \ge 3$

(d) $2x < 3y - 6$ (e) $-2 < y \le 4$ (f) $\dfrac{x-y}{4} > \dfrac{3}{2}$

3 For each of the following diagrams, find the inequality that is represented by the unshaded region.

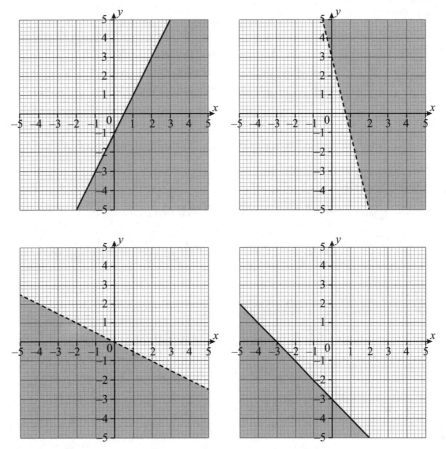

4 By shading the unwanted regions, show the region defined by the set of inequalities:

$2x + 3y < 6$, $x - y > 0$ and $y \geq -1$.

5 (a) By shading the unwanted regions, show the region that satisfies all the inequalities:

$2x + 4y \leq 6$, $x - 5y \leq -5$ and $x \geq -2$

(b) Write down the integer coordinates (x, y) which satisfy all the inequalities in this case.

14.4 Linear programming

- A mathematical way to express constraints in business and industry to obtain greatest profit, least cost, etc.
- Constraints take the form of linear inequalities.

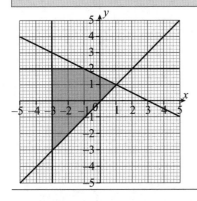

Exercise 14.4

1 In the diagram, the shaded region represents the set of inequalities $y \leq 2$, $x \geq -3$, $y \geq x$ and $x + 2y \leq 3$. Find the greatest and least possible values of $x + y$ subject to these inequalities.

2 (a) On a grid, shade to indicate the region satisfying all the inequalities $y \geq 0$, $0 \leq x \leq 3$, $y \leq x + 3$ and $y \leq -x + 7$.

(b) What is the greatest possible value of $2y + x$ if x and y satisfy all the inequalities in **(a)**?

3 At a school bake sale, chocolate fudge is sold for a profit of $3 and vanilla fudge for a profit of $2. Sally has ingredients to make at most 30 bags of chocolate fudge and 20 bags of vanilla fudge. She has enough time to make a maximum of 40 bags altogether. How many bags of each type should she make to maximise her profit and what is this maximum profit?

4 A factory makes different concentrates for cold drinks. The process requires the production of at least three litres of orange for each litre of lemon concentrate. For the summer, at least 1000 litres but no more than 1800 litres of orange concentrate needs to be produced in a month. The demand for lemon, on the other hand, is not more than 600 litres a month. Lemon concentrate sells for $1.90 per litre and orange concentrate sells for $1 per litre. How many litres of each should be produced in order to maximise income?

14.5 Completing the square

- Completing the square is a method used for solving quadratic equations that cannot be solved by factors.

- Expressions of the form $x^2 + ax$ can be written in the form, $\left(x + \dfrac{a}{2}\right)^2 - \left(\dfrac{a}{2}\right)^2$.

Exercise 14.5

1 Write the following expressions in the form $(x + a)^2 + b$.

(a) $x^2 + 6x + 4$ (b) $x^2 - 4x + 7$ (c) $x^2 + 14x + 44$

(d) $x^2 - 12x + 30$ (e) $x^2 + 10x + 17$ (f) $x^2 + 22x + 141$

(g) $x^2 + 24x + 121$ (h) $x^2 - 16x + 57$ (i) $x^2 + 18x + 93$

(j) $x^2 - 2x + 10$ (k) $x^2 - 8x - 5$ (l) $x^2 + 20x + 83$

2 Solve the following quadratic equations by the method of completing the square, giving your final answer to two decimal places if necessary.

(a) $x^2 - 5x - 6 = 0$ (b) $x^2 - x - 6 = 0$ (c) $x^2 - 4x + 3 = 0$ (d) $x^2 - 6x - 7 = 0$

(e) $x^2 - 16x + 3 = 0$ (f) $x^2 + 7x + 1 = 0$ (g) $x^2 + 9x - 1 = 0$ (h) $x^2 + 11x + 27 = 0$

(i) $x^2 - 2x - 100 = 0$

3 Solve the following equations by completing the square (answers to two decimal places if necessary).

(a) $2x^2 - 3x - 2 = 0$ (b) $x(x - 4) = -3$ (c) $3x^2 = 2(3x + 2)$

(d) $2x - 5 = \dfrac{3}{x}$ (e) $(x + 1)(x - 7) = 4$ (f) $x + 2x^2 = 8$

14.6 Quadratic formula

- The general form of the quadratic equation is $ax^2 + bx + c = 0$.
- The quadratic formula is $x = \dfrac{-b \pm \sqrt{b^2 - 4ac}}{2a}$.
- The quadratic formula is used primarily when the quadratic expression cannot be factorised.

> **Tip**
> The $\pm$ in the formula tells you to calculate two values.

> **Tip**
> Take care when the coefficient of x^2 is not equal to 1.

> **Tip**
> You must make sure that your equation takes the form of a quadratic expression equal to zero. If it does not then you will need to collect all terms on to one side so that a zero appears on the other side!

> Consecutive numbers are one unit apart.

Exercise 14.6

1 Each of the following quadratics will factorise. Solve each of them by factorisation and then use the quadratic formula to show that you get the same answers in both cases.

(a) $x^2 - 14x + 40 = 0$ (b) $x^2 + 14x - 120 = 0$ (c) $x^2 + 5x - 6 = 0$

(d) $x^2 - 8x + 15 = 0$ (e) $x^2 - 3x - 4 = 0$ (f) $x^2 - 4x + 4 = 0$

(g) $x^2 + 4x - 12 = 0$ (h) $x^2 + 10x + 25 = 0$ (i) $x^2 + 2x - 8 = 0$

(j) $x^2 - 4x - 12 = 0$ (k) $x^2 - 9x + 20 = 0$ (l) $x^2 + 3x - 40 = 0$

2 Solve each of the following equations by using the quadratic formula. Give your answers correct to two decimal places where necessary. These quadratic expressions do not factorise.

(a) $x^2 + 6x + 4 = 0$ (b) $x^2 + x - 4 = 0$ (c) $x^2 + 14x + 44 = 0$

(d) $x^2 - 6x - 8 = 0$ (e) $x^2 + 10x + 17 = 0$ (f) $x^2 + 7x + 1 = 0$

(g) $x^2 + 24x + 121 = 0$ (h) $x^2 + 11x + 27 = 0$ (i) $x^2 + 18x - 93 = 0$

(j) $x^2 - 2x - 10 = 0$ (k) $x^2 - 8x - 5 = 0$ (l) $x^2 - 2x - 100 = 0$

3 Solve each of the following equations. Give your answers correct to two decimal places where necessary.

(a) $x^2 - 4x - 8 = 0$ (b) $6x^2 + 11x - 35 = 0$ (c) $2x^2 - 3x + \dfrac{1}{2} = 0$

(d) $2x^2 - 5x = 25$ (e) $4x^2 - 13x + 9 = 0$ (f) $8x^2 - 4x = 18$

(g) $9x^2 - 1 = 6x$ (h) $x(x - 16) + 57 = 0$ (i) $9(x + 1) = x^2$

(j) $2x^2 + 5x = 3$ (k) $6x^2 + 13x + 6 = 0$ (l) $4x^2 - x - 3 = 0$

4 Two consecutive numbers have a product of 3306. Form a quadratic equation to find what the two numbers are.

5 The width of a postage stamp is two thirds its height. The postage stamp is to be enlarged to create a poster. If the area of the poster is to be 216 cm², what will the dimensions of the poster be?

14.7 Factorising quadratics where the coefficient of x^2 is not 1

- The coefficient of x^2 is not always 1. Extra care must be taken when expressing such a quadratic as a product of its factors.

Exercise 14.7

Tip

Always look for common factors as the first step when factorising expressions.

Note: $(2-x) = -(x-2)$.

1 Factorise each of the following expressions.

(a) $2x^2 - x - 3$ (b) $9x^2 + 6x + 1$ (c) $4x^2 - 12x + 9$ (d) $6x^2 - 7x - 5$

(e) $4x^2 + x - 3$ (f) $14x^2 - 51x + 7$ (g) $3x^2 + 11x - 20$ (h) $6x^2 + 11x - 7$

(i) $3x^2 - 10x - 25$ (j) $3x^2 + 7x - 66$ (k) $15x^2 - 16x - 15$ (l) $8x^2 + 25x + 3$

2 Factorise completely. You may need to remove a common factor before factorising the trinomials.

(a) $4x^2 + 12x + 9$ (b) $2x^2 - \dfrac{1}{2}$ (c) $50x^2 + 40x + 8$

(d) $6x^2 - 7xy - 5y^2$ (e) $4x^4 + x^2 - 3$ (f) $12x^2 - 2x - 2$

(g) $2(x+1) - 4x^2 - 4x$ (h) $(x+1)^2 + 3(x+1) + 2$ (i) $3(x+1)^2 - 10(x+1) - 25$

(j) $6x^2 + 14x - 132$ (k) $3(x^2-1) + x(x+1)$ (l) $8x^2 + 25xy + 3y^2$

14.8 Algebraic fractions

- You can use the techniques for working with number fractions and for simplifying indices.
- Numerator and denominator can be divided (cancelled) by the HCF.
- Factorise, if possible, first.

Exercise 14.8

Tip

Always look for common factors first.

1 Simplify the following fractions.

(a) $\dfrac{2x}{14}$ (b) $\dfrac{3x}{x}$ (c) $\dfrac{x}{7x}$ (d) $\dfrac{12x}{30}$

(e) $\dfrac{16z}{6}$ (f) $\dfrac{34x}{17xy}$ (g) $\dfrac{12x^2}{18xy}$ (h) $\dfrac{5a}{25a^2b}$

(i) $\dfrac{24ab^2}{36a^2b}$

2 Simplify the following fractions.

(a) $\dfrac{x^2+x-6}{x^2-2x}$ (b) $\dfrac{a^2-b^2}{a^2+2ab+b^2}$ (c) $\dfrac{2x^2-xy-y^2}{x^2-xy}$ (d) $\dfrac{3x^2+10x+3}{x^2-2x-15}$

(e) $\dfrac{a^2-5a-14}{a^2-7a}$ (f) $\dfrac{a^2-b^2}{a^2+ab-2b^2}$ (g) $\dfrac{2x^2+7x-15}{2x^2+x-6}$ (h) $\dfrac{x^4-2x^2-3}{x^2+1}$

(i) $\dfrac{35x^2+49x}{15x^2+21x}$

> **Tip**
> Dividing by a fraction is the same as multiplying by the reciprocal of the fraction.

3 Write each of the following as a single fraction in its lowest terms.

(a) $\dfrac{8x}{15} \times \dfrac{5x}{16}$

(b) $\dfrac{3y}{4} \times \dfrac{2y}{9}$

(c) $\dfrac{5}{a} \times \dfrac{7}{a}$

(d) $\dfrac{7x^2}{5y} \div \dfrac{14x}{25y^2}$

(e) $\dfrac{a}{b} \div \left(\dfrac{a}{b} \times \dfrac{c}{a}\right)$

(f) $\dfrac{4a^2}{3b^2} \times \dfrac{b^4 - b^2}{2a} \div \dfrac{2a}{3}$

(g) $\dfrac{4a^2}{7b} \times \dfrac{b^2}{8a} \div \dfrac{3ab}{1}$

(h) $\dfrac{x^2 - 6x + 8}{3x + 9} \times \dfrac{x + 3}{2 - x}$

(i) $\dfrac{4 - 9x^2}{6x^2 - x - 2}$

> **Tip**
> A negative sign in front of a fraction affects all the terms in the numerator.

4 Simplify the following.

(a) $\dfrac{3}{x} + \dfrac{2}{y}$

(b) $\dfrac{3}{2} - \dfrac{4 - p}{8p} + \dfrac{3}{4p}$

(c) $\dfrac{3}{2p} + \dfrac{7}{5p}$

(d) $\dfrac{5}{p + 1} + \dfrac{4}{2p + 2}$

(e) $\dfrac{3}{x + 2} + \dfrac{2}{x + 1}$

(f) $\dfrac{2m}{3} - \dfrac{3(m - 2)}{2}$

(g) $\dfrac{5}{x^2 - x - 6} + \dfrac{4}{x^2 + x - 2}$

(h) $\dfrac{2}{x^2 - 3x} - \dfrac{3}{x^2 + 4x}$

(i) $\dfrac{1}{2x^2 - x - 3} - \dfrac{2}{x^2 - 1}$

Mixed exercise

1 Solve for x and y if $3x + y = 1$ and $x - 2y = 12$.

2 Solve for x and y if $3y + 4x = 7$ and $2y + 3x - 4 = 0$.

> p.a. stands for 'per annum', which means 'per year'.

3 Mr Habib has \$15 000 to invest. His portfolio has two parts, one which yields 5% p.a. and the other 8% p.a. The total interest on the investment was \$1050 at the end of the first year. How much did he invest at each rate?

4 Simplify the following inequalities:

(a) $-3 < x + 2$

(b) $5 - 2x \geq 7$

5 Represent $-2 < x \leq 3$ graphically.

6 The whole numbers x and y satisfy the following inequalities:

$y > 1.5$, $y \leq 4$, $x \geq -2$, $y > x + 1$ and $y \geq -x + 1$.

Graphically find the greatest and least possible integer values of x and y for the expression:

$\dfrac{x}{2} + y$.

7 Factorise:

(a) $x^2 - 2xy$

(b) $a^4 - b^2$

(c) $x^2 + 6x - 55$

(d) $2y^2 + 13y - 7$

(e) $-4x^2 + 2x + 6$

(f) $(x + 1)^2 - 5(x + 1) - 14$

8 Solve the following equations:

(a) $2a^2 + 2a - 6 = 0$
(b) $3x^2 - x - 4 = 0$
(c) $x^2 + 2x - 15 = 0$
(d) $3x^2 - 5x + 2 = 0$
(e) $5x^2 - 3x = -3x^2 + 5$
(f) $3x^2 + 6x = 6x^2 + 3$

9 Use the quadratic formula to find the value(s) of x:

(a) $5x^2 + 8x - 4 = 0$
(b) $px^2 - qx + r = 0$

10 Simplify the following:

(a) $\dfrac{x^2 - y^2}{(x+y)^2}$

(b) $\dfrac{16 - 4x^2}{4x + 8}$

(c) $\dfrac{1}{2p^2} + \dfrac{1}{5p}$

(d) $\dfrac{7x^2}{5y} \times \dfrac{15y^2}{14x}$

(e) $\dfrac{x}{2y} \div \left(\dfrac{2x}{yz^2} \times \dfrac{z}{xy^3} \right)$

(f) $\dfrac{3a}{2} - \dfrac{5-a}{3a} + \dfrac{a}{5a}$

(g) $\dfrac{4}{x^2 + 2x - 8} \div \dfrac{4}{x^2 - x - 2} - \dfrac{2}{x^2 + 4x}$

(h) $\dfrac{3x}{6x^2 - 3x}$

(i) $\dfrac{1}{2x^2 + 11x + 5} - \dfrac{1}{2x^2 - x - 1}$

15 Scale drawings, bearings and trigonometry

15.1 Scale drawings

- The scale of a diagram, or a map, can be given in the form of a fraction or a ratio.
- A scale of 1 : 50 000 means that every line in the diagram has a length which is $\frac{1}{50000}$ of the length of the line that it represents in real life. For example 1 cm in the diagram represents 50 000 cm (or 0.5 km) in real life.

Exercise 15.1

◄ REWIND
Revise your metric conversions from chapter 13. ◄

1 (a) The basic pitch size of a rugby field is 100 m long and 70 m wide. A scale drawing of a field is made with a scale of 1 cm to 10 m. What is the length and width of the field in the drawing?

  (b) The pitch size, including the area inside the goal, is 144 m long and 70 m wide. What are these dimensions in the drawing of this pitch?

2 (a) The pitch size of a standard hockey field is 91.4 m long and 55 m wide. A scale drawing of a hockey field is made with a scale of 1 : 1000. What are the dimensions of the hockey field in the drawing?

  (b) A school that wants to hold a Seven-A-Side hockey tournament has three standard hockey fields at their Sports Centre. Would it be possible to have five matches taking place at the same time, if the size of the pitch used for Seven-A-Side hockey is 55 m × 43 m?

A5 is half A4 and has dimensions 14.8 cm × 21 cm.

3 (a) The size of a tennis court is 23.77 m × 10.97 m. What would be a good scale for a drawing of a tennis court if you can only use half of an A4 page? Express this scale as a fraction.

  (b) (i) Make an accurate scale drawing, using your scale. Include all the markings as shown in the diagram below.

   (ii) The net posts are placed 1 m outside the doubles side lines. Mark each net post with an × on your scale drawing.

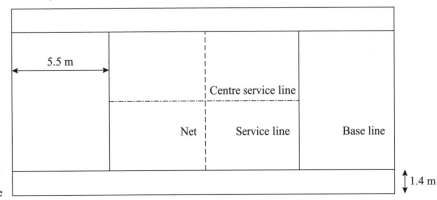

4 **(a)** The karate combat area measures 8 m × 8 m. Using a scale drawing and a scale of your choice, calculate the length of the diagonal.

(b) What would be a more accurate way to determine the length of the diagonal?

15.2 Bearings

- A bearing is a way of describing direction.
- Bearings are measured clockwise from the north direction.
- Bearings are always expressed using three figures.

Exercise 15.2

1 Give the three-figure bearing corresponding to:

(a) east   **(b)** south-west   **(c)** north-west.

2 Write down the three-figure bearings of X from Y.

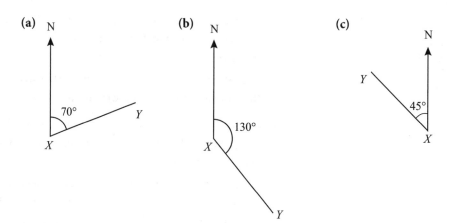

3 Village A is 7.5 km east and 8 km north of village B. Village C is 5 km from village B on a bearing of 300°. Using a scale drawing with a scale of 1 : 100 000 find:

(a) the bearing of village B from village A

(b) the bearing of village A from village C

(c) the direct distance between village B and village A

(d) the direct distance between village C and village A.

15.3 Understanding the tangent, cosine and sine ratios

- The hypotenuse is the longest side of a right-angled triangle.
- The opposite side is the side opposite a specified angle.
- The adjacent side is the side that forms a specified angle with the hypotenuse.
- The tangent ratio is $\dfrac{\text{the opposite side}}{\text{the adjacent side}}$ of a specified angle.

$$\tan\theta = \frac{\text{opp}(\theta)}{\text{adj}(\theta)}, \qquad \text{opp}(\theta) = \text{adj}(\theta) \times \tan\theta, \qquad \text{adj}(\theta) = \frac{\text{opp}(\theta)}{\tan\theta}$$

- The sine ratio is $\dfrac{\text{the opposite side}}{\text{the hypotenuse}}$ of a specified angle.

$$\sin\theta = \frac{\text{opp}(\theta)}{\text{hyp}}, \qquad \text{opp}(\theta) = \text{hyp} \times \sin\theta, \qquad \text{hyp} = \frac{\text{opp}(\theta)}{\sin\theta}$$

- The cosine ratio is $\dfrac{\text{the adjacent side}}{\text{the hypotenuse}}$ of a specified angle.

$$\cos\theta = \frac{\text{adj}(\theta)}{\text{hyp}}, \qquad \text{adj}(\theta) = \text{hyp} \times \cos\theta, \qquad \text{hyp} = \frac{\text{adj}(\theta)}{\cos\theta}$$

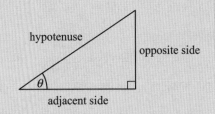

Exercise 15.3

1 Copy and complete the following table:

	(a)	(b)	(c)	(d)
	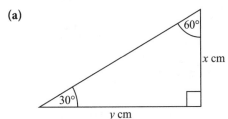			
hypotenuse				
opp(A)				
adj(A)				

2 Copy and complete the statement(s) alongside each triangle.

> Remember, when working with right-angled triangles you may still need to use Pythagoras.

(a)

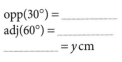

opp(30°) = ...
adj(60°) = ...
.... = y cm

(b)

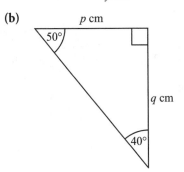

.... (40°) = q cm
.... (50°) = q cm
.... = p cm

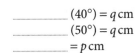

The memory aid, SOHCAHTOA, or the triangle diagrams

may help you remember the trigonometric relationships.

3 Calculate the value of the following tangent ratios, using your calculator. Give your answers to two decimal places where necessary.

(a) tan 33°   (b) tan 55°   (c) tan 79°

(d) tan 22.5°   (e) tan 0°

4 Copy and complete the statements for each of the following triangles, giving your answer as a fraction in its lowest terms where necessary:

(a)

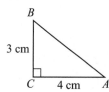

tan $A =$

(b)

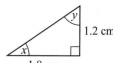

tan $x =$
tan $y =$

(c)

tan 55° =
$x =$
tan $B =$

(d)

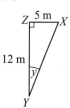

tan $y =$
$\angle X =$
tan $X =$

(e)

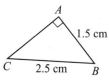

$AC =$
tan $B =$
tan $C =$

5 Calculate the unknown length (to two decimal places) in each case presented below.

(a)

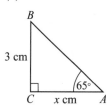

(b)

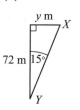

(c)

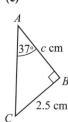

(d)

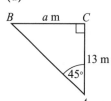

(e)

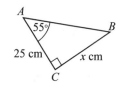

6 Find, correct to one decimal place, the acute angles that have the following tangent ratios:

(a) 0.5   (b) 0.866   (c) 1.25   (d) 12

(e) $\frac{1}{4}$ (f) $\frac{13}{15}$ (g) $5\frac{1}{2}$ (h) $\frac{61}{63}$

7 Find, correct to the nearest degree, the value of the lettered angles in the following diagrams.

(a)

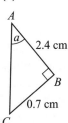

(b)

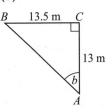

(c)

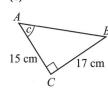

(d)

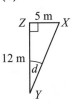

(e)

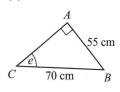

8 For each triangle find:

(i) hyp =   (ii) adj(θ) =   (iii) cos θ =

(a)   (b)   (c)   (d)   (e)

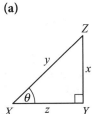 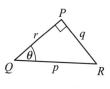 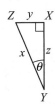

9 For each of the following triangles write down the value for:

(i) sine   (ii) cosine   (iii) tangent of the marked angle.

(a)   (b)   (c)   (d)   (e)

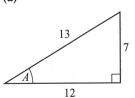 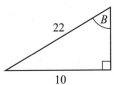 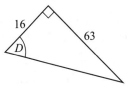

10 Use your calculator to find to the nearest degree:

    (a) an acute angle whose sine is 0.707

    (b) an acute angle whose cosine is 0.438

    (c) an acute angle whose cosine is 0.55

    (d) an acute angle whose sine is $\dfrac{\sqrt{3}}{2}$

    (e) an acute angle whose sine is $\dfrac{1}{2}$

    (f) an acute angle whose tangent is 0.5.

11 The diagram shows two ladders placed in an alley, both reaching up to window ledges on opposite sides: one is twice as long as the other and reaches height H, while the shorter one reaches a height h. The length of the longer ladder is 7.5 m. If the angles of inclination of the ladders are as shown, how much higher is the window ledge of the one window than that of the other?

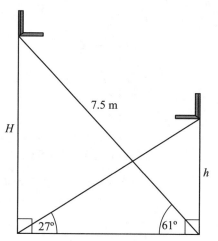

> **Tip**
> Remember, only round your working at the final step.

12 For each of the following triangles find the length of the unknown lettered side (correct to two decimal places) or the size of the lettered angle (correct to one decimal place).

(a)

(b)

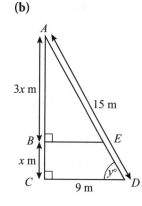

(c)

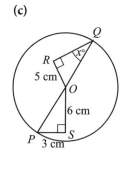

(d)

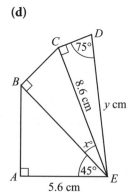

15.4 Solving problems using trigonometry

- If no diagram is given, draw one yourself.
- Mark the right angles in the diagram.
- Show all the given measurements.

Tip

Make sure you know that:

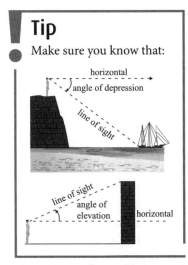

Exercise 15.4

1   At a certain time of the day Samuel's shadow is 0.75 m long. The angle of elevation from the end of his shadow to the top of his head is 66°. How tall is Samuel?

2   Sarah's line of sight is 1.5 m above the ground. She is looking at the top of a tree that is 23.5 m away.

   (a) If the tree is 15 m tall, what is the angle of elevation through which she is looking (correct to the nearest degree)?

   (b) A bird sits on top of the tree. Calculate (correct to the nearest degree) the angle of depression from the bird to Sarah's feet.

15.5 Angles between 0° and 180°

- If two angles sum (add up) to 180° they are said to be supplementary.
- An angle and its supplement have the same sine value ($\sin\theta = \sin(180° - \theta)$).
- The cosine of an angle and its supplement have the same value but different signs ($\cos\theta = -\cos(180° - \theta)$).
- The tangent of an angle and its supplement have the same value but different signs ($\tan\theta = -\tan(180° - \theta)$).

Exercise 15.5

Tip

$\sin\theta = \sin(180° - \theta)$
$\cos\theta = -\cos(180° - \theta)$

1   Express each of the following in terms of the supplementary angle between 0° and 180°.

   (a) $\cos 112°$ (b) $\sin 156°$ (c) $-\cos 75°$ (d) $\sin 125°$
   (e) $-\cos 45°$ (f) $\sin 145°$ (g) $\cos 120°$ (h) $\sin 98°$
   (i) $\cos 55°$ (j) $\cos 130°$

2   Given that θ is an angle of a triangle, find all possible values of θ between 0° and 180° (to the nearest degree) if:

   (a) $\sin\theta = 0.255$ (b) $\cos\theta = -0.566$ (c) $\sin\theta = 0.789$ (d) $\cos\theta = 0.345$
   (e) $\sin\theta = 0.343$ (f) $\cos\theta = 0.669$ (g) $\cos\theta = 0.782$ (h) $\cos\theta = -0.344$
   (i) $\sin\theta = 0.125$ (j) $\sin\theta = 0.995$

15.6 The sine and cosine rules

- The sine and cosine rules can be used in triangles that do not have a right angle.
- The sine rule: $\dfrac{\sin A}{a} = \dfrac{\sin B}{b} = \dfrac{\sin C}{c}$ or $\dfrac{a}{\sin A} = \dfrac{b}{\sin B} = \dfrac{c}{\sin C}$.
- The cosine rule: $a^2 = b^2 + c^2 - 2bc\cos A$ or $b^2 = a^2 + c^2 - 2ac\cos B$ or $c^2 = a^2 + b^2 - 2ab\cos C$.

Tip

Remember, the standard way of labelling a triangle is to label the vertices with upper case (capital) letters and the sides opposite with the same lower case letters.

Tip

The sine rule is used when dealing with pairs of opposite sides and angles.

Exercise 15.6

1 To one decimal place find the value of x in each of the following equations:

(a) $\dfrac{\sin x}{11} = \dfrac{\sin 45°}{12}$ (b) $\dfrac{x}{\sin 50°} = \dfrac{23}{\sin 72°}$

(c) $\dfrac{\sin x}{7.4} = \dfrac{\sin 38°}{5.2}$ (d) $\dfrac{x}{\sin 35°} = \dfrac{30}{\sin 71°}$

(e) $\dfrac{x}{\sin 55°} = \dfrac{8}{\sin 68°}$ (f) $\dfrac{\sin x}{4} = \dfrac{\sin 45°}{6}$

(g) $\dfrac{\sin x}{24} = \dfrac{\sin 35°}{36}$ (h) $\dfrac{x}{\sin 59°} = \dfrac{8.5}{\sin 62°}$

(i) $\dfrac{\sin x}{4} = \dfrac{\sin 105°}{16}$

2 Find the length of the marked side in each of the following triangles:

(a)

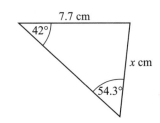

(b)

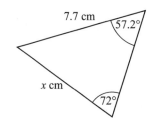

(c)

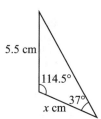

(d)

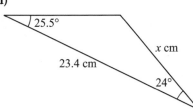

(e)

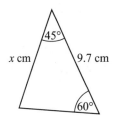

(f)

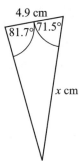

3 Find the size of the (acute) marked angle in the following triangles:

(a)

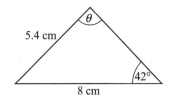

(b)

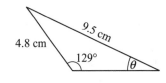

(c)

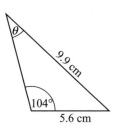

(d)

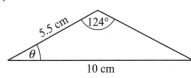

(e)

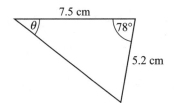

(f)

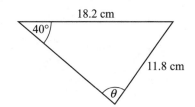

4 Given $b^2 = a^2 + c^2 - 2ac \cos B$, copy and complete the following equation:

$\cos B = \dots\dots\dots\dots\dots$

5 Find the size of the angle marked θ in each of the triangles below (correct to one decimal place).

(a)

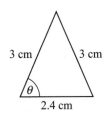

(b)

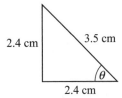

(c)

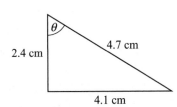

(d)

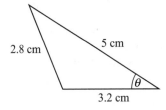

6 Find the third side of the following triangles (correct to one decimal place).

> **Tip**
> The cosine rule is used when all three sides are known or when you know two sides and the included angle.

(a)

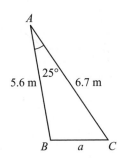

(b)

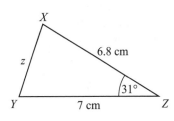

(c)

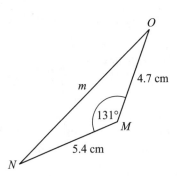

(d)

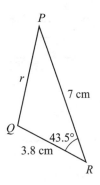

15.7 Area of a triangle

- You can find the area of a triangle even if you do not have a perpendicular height, as long as you have two sides and the included angle.
- Area of triangle ABC: area $= \frac{1}{2}ab \sin C$ or area $= \frac{1}{2}ac \sin B$ or area $= \frac{1}{2}bc \sin A$.

Exercise 15.7

Tip
To find the area of a triangle you need two sides and the angle between the two given sides.

If you are given two angles and a side, use the sine rule to find another side first.

1 Draw a rough sketch of each of these figures before calculating their area.

(Note: the convention of using a lower case letter to name the side opposite the vertex of the same letter has been used for some of these triangles.)

  (a) $\triangle ABC$ with $BC = 8$ cm, $AC = 5$ cm and $\angle C = 34°$.
  (b) $\triangle ABC$ with $a = 4.5$ cm, $b = 12$ cm and $\angle C = 110°$.
  (c) $\triangle XYZ$ with $XZ = 6$ cm, $XY = 7$ cm and $\angle X = 54°$.
  (d) $\triangle PQR$ with $q = 12$ cm, $\angle Q = 54°$ and $\angle R = 60°$.
  (e) $\triangle XYZ$ with $XY = 2$ cm, $\angle X = 63°$ and $\angle Y = 89°$.
  (f) $\triangle PQR$ with $p = 12$ cm, $q = 12$ cm and $\angle Q = 80°$.

2 Find the area of a triangle with sides 13 cm, 10 cm and 9 cm.

Tip
To find the area of other polygons, divide the shape into triangles, find their areas and add them together.

3 For each of the polygons below, find x and the area of the polygon:

  (a)   (b)   (c)

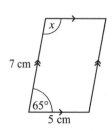 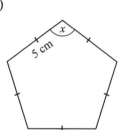 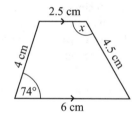

15.8 Trigonometry in three dimensions

- Pythagoras, trigonometric ratios, the sine rule, the cosine rule and the area rule can all be used to solve 3-D problems.
- You can find angles between lines and between planes.

Exercise 15.8

Tip
Drawing separate right-angled triangles found in the 3-D drawing can help.

1 The diagram shows a rectangular prism. Use Pythagoras and trigonometry to find the following distances (correct to three signifigant figures) and angles (correct to one decimal place).

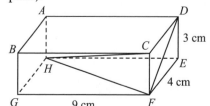

  (a) $D\hat{E}F$ (b) FD
  (c) $D\hat{F}E$ (d) GH
  (e) HF (f) $G\hat{H}F$
  (g) CH (h) $C\hat{H}F$

2 The diagram shows a square-based pyramid.

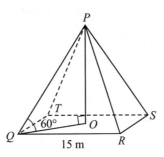

Use Pythagoras and trigonometry to find the following distances (correct to three significant figures).

(a) *QS* (b) *QO* (c) *PQ* (d) *PO*

3 The diagram shows a triangular prism.

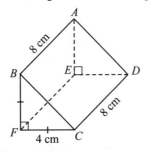

(a) Calculate the length of *BD* (correct to two decimal places).

(b) Calculate $B\hat{D}F$, the angle *BD* makes with the base *CDEF* (correct to one decimal place).

> **Tip**
>
> ! Always check that the solution you have found is reasonable.

Mixed exercise

1 Find the value of *x*:

(a) $\dfrac{\sin x}{5.2} = \dfrac{\sin 121°}{7.3}$

(b)

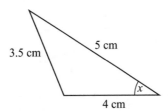

(c)

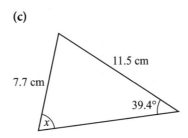

2 A triangle has sides of length 5.7 cm, 7.1 cm and 4.1 cm. Use the cosine rule to find the size of the smallest angle (correct to three significant figures).

3 In the figure, $CD = 530$ m. Find AB.

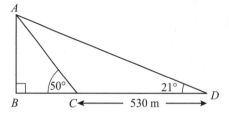

4 $BD = 50$ cm. Find AC.

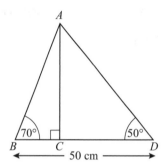

5 A man is standing at a lookout point 25 m above the sea. He spots a shark in the water at an angle of depression of 50°. A swimmer in the water is 5 m from the foot of the lookout point. How far is the shark from the swimmer?

6 The diagram (not drawn to scale) shows two aeroplanes, X and Y, flying over an airfield. The aeroplanes are flying directly behind each other and are 1500 metres above the ground. R, S and T are points on the ground and the angle of elevation of plane X from T is 58° and the angle of elevation of Y is 77°. Find the distance between the two aeroplanes (RS) showing all working and give your final answer correct to the nearest metre.

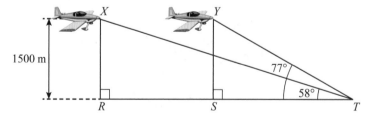

16 Scatter diagrams and correlation

16.1 Introduction to bivariate data

- When you collect two sets of data in pairs, it is called bivariate data. For example you could collect height and mass data for various students.
- Bivariate data can be plotted on a scatter diagram in order to look for correlation – a relationship between the data. For example, if you wanted to know whether taller students weighed more than smaller students, you could plot the two sets of data (height and mass) on a scatter diagram.
- Correlation is described as positive or negative, and strong or weak. When the points follow no real pattern, there is no correlation.
- A line of best fit can be drawn on a scatter diagram to describe the correlation. This line should follow the direction of the points on the graph and there should be more or less the same number of points on each side of the line. You can use a line of best fit to make predictions within the range of the data shown. It is not statistically accurate to predict beyond the values plotted.

Exercise 16.1

1 Match each graph below to a description of the correlation shown.

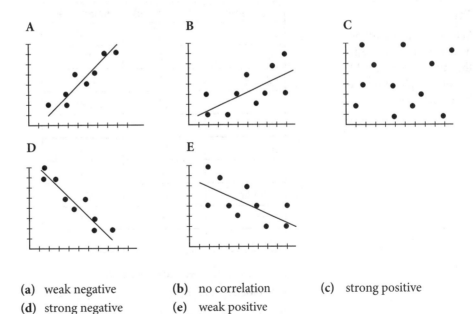

    (a) weak negative   **(b)** no correlation   **(c)** strong positive

    (d) strong negative   **(e)** weak positive

2 Sookie collected data from 15 students in her school athletics team. She wanted to see if there was a correlation between the height of the students and the distance they could jump in the long-jump event. She drew a scatter diagram to show the data.

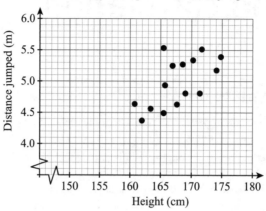

Student heights compared to distance jumped

(a) Copy the diagram and draw the line of best fit on to it.

(b) Use your line of best fit to estimate how far a student 165 cm tall could jump.

(c) For the age group of Sookie's school team, the girls' record for long jump is 6.07 m. How tall would you expect a girl to be who could equal the record jump?

(d) Describe the correlation shown on the graph.

(e) What does the correlation indicate about the relationship between height and how far you can jump in the long jump event?

3 The table below shows the ages of ten students and the distance they can swim in half an hour.

Student	Age (years)	Distance (m)
Amy	12	200
Beth	8	350
Cherie	7	400
Dani	13	450
Emma	9	550
Fran	10	350
Gita	6	0
Hannah	12	500
Inge	9	250
Jen	11	300

> **Tip**
> When time is one of the data pairs, it is normally the independent variable, so you will plot it on the horizontal axis.

(a) What is the dependent variable?

(b) Plot a scattergram.

(c) Describe the correlation.

(d) Draw a line of best fit.

(e) How old would you estimate Kate to be if she is able to swim 450 m in half an hour?

(f) How reliable is your answer to **(e)**?

(g) How far would you estimate Lynne (who is 15) can swim in half an hour?

Mixed exercise

Accidents at a road junction

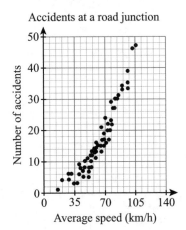

1 Study the scatter diagram and answer the questions.

   (a) What does this diagram show?

   (b) What is the independent variable?

   (c) Copy the diagram and draw a line of best. Use your best fit line to predict:

       (i) the number accidents at the junction when the average speed of vehicles is 100 km/h

       (ii) what the average speed of vehicles is when there are fewer than 10 accidents.

   (d) Describe the correlation.

   (e) What does your answer to **(d)** tell you about the relationship between speed and the number of accidents at a junction?

2 A brand new car (Model X) costs $15 000. Mr Smit wants to find out what price second-hand Model X cars are sold for. He drew this scatter graph to show the relationship between the price and the age of cars in a second-hand car dealership.

Comparison of car age with re-sale price

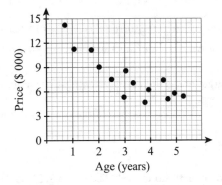

   (a) Describe the trend shown on this graph.

   (b) Between which two years does the price of the car fall in value by the largest amount?

   (c) Describe what happens to the price when the car is 3 to 5 years old.

   (d) How old would you expect a second-hand Model X car to be if it was advertised for sale at $7500?

   (e) What price range would you expect a 3-year-old Model X to fall into?

17 Managing money

17.1 Earning money

- People who are formally employed may be paid a salary, wage or earn commission.
    - A salary is a fixed amount for a year of work, usually paid in monthly instalments.
    - A wage is an agreed hourly rate for an agreed number of hours, normally paid weekly.
    - Workers who sell things for a living are often paid a commission. This is a percentage of the value of the goods sold.
- Additional amounts may be paid to employees in the form of overtime or bonuses.
- Employers may deduct amounts from employees' earnings such as insurance, union dues, medical aid and taxes.
- The amount a person earns before deductions is their gross earnings. The amount they actually are paid after deductions is their net earnings.

Exercise 17.1

Casual workers are normally paid an hourly rate for the hours they work.

 Tip
Remember, work out all percentage deductions on the gross income and then subtract them all from the gross.

Some workers are paid for each piece of work they complete. This is called piece work.

1 A woman works a 38-hour week. She earns $731.88. What is her hourly rate of pay?

2 What is the annual salary of a person who is paid $2130 per month?

3 An electrician's assistant earns $25.50 per hour for a 35-hour week. He is paid 1.5 times his hourly rate for each hour he works above 35 hours. How much would he earn in a week if he worked:

    (a) 36 hours   **(b)** 40 hours   **(c)** 30 hours   **(d)** $42\frac{1}{2}$ hours?

4 Sandile earns a gross salary of $1613.90 per month. His employer deducts 15% income tax, $144.20 insurance and 1.5% for union dues. What is Sandile's net salary?

5 A clothing factory worker in Indonesia is paid the equivalent of $1.67 per completed garment. How much would he earn if he completed 325 garments in a month?

6 Naadira receives an annual salary of $32 500. She pays 4% of her weekly gross earnings into her pension fund. An additional $93.50 is deducted each week from her salary. Calculate:

    (a) her weekly gross earnings
    (b) her weekly pension fund payment
    (c) her net income per week.

17.2 Borrowing and investing money

- When you borrow money you may pay interest on the amount borrowed.
- When you invest or save money you may earn interest on the amount invested.
- If the amount of interest paid (or charged) is the same for each year, then it is called simple interest.
- When the interest for one year is added to the investment (or debt) and the interest for the next year is calculated on the increased investment (or debt), it is called compound interest.
- The original amount borrowed or invested is called the principal.
- For simple interest, the interest per annum = interest rate × principal (original sum invested).
- The formula used to calculate simple interest is: $I = \dfrac{PRT}{100}$ where:
  - P = the principal
  - R = the interest rate
  - T = the time (in years).
- For compound interest, knowing how to use a multiplier can help you do the calculations faster.
  - For example, if the compound interest is 5%, then the multiplier is $\dfrac{105}{100} = 1.05$.
  - Multiply the principal by a power of the multiplier. The number of years of the investment tells you what the power is. So, if it you invest a sum for three years at 5%, you would multiply by $(1.05)^3$. This gives you the final amount.
- Hire purchase (HP) is a method of buying things on credit and paying them off over an agreed period of time. Normally you pay a deposit and equal monthly instalments.

Exercise 17.2

'per annum' (p.a.) means 'per year'

Tip

You can change the subject of the simple interest formula:

$$I = \frac{PRT}{100}$$

$$P = \frac{100I}{RT}$$

$$R = \frac{100I}{PT}$$

$$T = \frac{100I}{PR}$$

1 Calculate the simple interest on:

   (a) $250 invested for a year at the rate of 3% per annum
   (b) $400 invested for five years at the rate of 8% per annum
   (c) $700 invested for two years at the rate of 15% per annum
   (d) $800 invested for eight years at the rate of 7% per annum
   (e) $5000 invested for 15 months at the rate of 5.5% per annum.

2 $7500 is invested at 3.5% per annum simple interest. How long will it take for the amount to reach $8812.50?

3 The total simple interest on $1600 invested for five years is $224. What is the percentage rate per annum?

4 The cash price of a car was $20 000. The hire purchase price was a $6000 deposit and instalments of $700 per month for two years. How much more than the cash price was the hire purchase price?

5 Lebo can pay $7999 cash for a new car or he can buy it on HP by paying a $2000 deposit and 36 monthly payments of $230. How much extra will he pay by buying on HP?

Using the multiplying factor for compound interest gives the new amount. Subtract the principal to find the actual interest.

6 Calculate the compound interest on:

   (a) $250 invested for a year at the rate of 3% per annum

   (b) $400 invested for five years at the rate of 8% per annum

   (c) $700 invested for two years at the rate of 15% per annum

   (d) $800 borrowed for eight years at the rate of 7% per annum

   (e) $5000 borrowed for 15 months at the rate of 5.5% per annum.

7 How much will you have in the bank if you invest $500 for four years at 3% interest, compounded annually?

8 Mrs Genaro owns a small business. She borrows $18 500 dollars from the bank to finance some new equipment. She repays the loan in full after two years. If the bank charged her compound interest at the rate of 21% per annum, how much did she owe them after two years?

17.3 Buying and selling

- The amount a business pays for an item is called the cost price. The price they sell it to the public for is called the selling price. The amount the seller adds onto the cost price to make a selling price is called a mark up. For example, a shopkeeper may buy an item for $2 and mark it up by 50 cents to sell it for $2.50.
- The difference between the cost price and the selling price is called the profit (if it is higher than the cost price) or the loss (if it is lower than the cost price).
  - Profit = selling price − cost price.
  - Loss = cost price − selling price.
- The rate of profit (or loss) is the percentage profit (or loss). Rate of profit (or loss) $= \dfrac{\text{profit (or loss)}}{\text{cost price}} \times 100\%$.
- A discount is an intentional reduction in the price of an item. Discount = original selling price − new marked price.
- The rate of discount is a percentage. Rate of discount $= \dfrac{\text{discount}}{\text{original selling price}} \times 100\%$.

Exercise 17.3

1 Find the cost price in each of the following:

   (a) selling price $120, profit 20%

   (b) selling price $230, profit 15%

   (c) selling price $289, loss 15%

   (d) selling price $600, loss $33\frac{1}{3}\%$.

2 Find the cost price of an article sold at $360 with a profit of 20%.

3 If a shopkeeper sells an article for $440 and loses 12% on the sale, find his cost price.

4 A dentist offers a 5% discount to patients who pay their accounts in cash within a week. How much will someone with an account of $67.80 pay if they pay promptly in cash?

5 Calculate the new selling price of each item with the following discounts.

(a) $199 discount 10%

(b) $45.50 discount 12%

(c) $1020 discount $5\frac{1}{2}$%

Mixed exercise

1 Nerina earns $19.50 per hour. How many hours does she need to work to earn:

(a) $234

(b) $780

(c) $497.25?

2 A mechanic works a 38-hour week for a basic wage of $28 per hour. Overtime is paid at time and a half on weekdays and double time on weekends. Calculate his gross earnings for a week if he works his normal hours plus:

(a) three hours overtime on Thursday

(b) one extra hour per day for the whole week

(c) two hours overtime on Tuesday and $1\frac{1}{2}$ hours overtime on Saturday.

3 Jamira earns a monthly salary of $5234.

(a) What is her annual gross salary?

(b) She pays 12% tax and has a further $456.90 deducted from her monthly salary. Calculate her net monthly income.

4 A $10 000 investment earns interest at a rate of 3% p.a. This table compares the simple and compound interest.

Years	1	2	3	4	5	6	7	8
Simple interest	300	600						
Compound interest	300	609						

(a) Copy and complete the table.

(b) What is the difference between the simple interest and compound interest earned after five years?

(c) Draw a bar chart to compare the value of the investment after one, five and 10 years for both types of interest. Comment on what your graph shows about the difference between simple and compound interest.

5 Find the selling price of an article that was bought for $750 and sold at a profit of 15%.

6 Calculate the selling price of an item of merchandise bought for $3000 and sold at a profit of 12%.

7 A gallery owner displays paintings for artists. She puts a 150% mark up on the price asked by the artist to cover her expenses and make a profit. An artist supplies three paintings at the prices listed below. For each one, calculate the mark up in dollars, and the selling price the gallery owner would charge.

(a) Painting A, $890

(b) Painting B, $1300

(c) Painting C, $12 000

8 An art collector wants to buy paintings A and B (from question 7). He agrees to pay cash on condition that the gallery owner gives him a 12% discount on the selling price of the paintings.

(a) What price will he pay?

(b) What percentage profit does the gallery owner make on the sale?

9 A boy bought a bicycle for $500. After using it for two years, he sold it at a loss of 15%. Calculate the selling price.

10 It is found that an article is being sold at a loss of 12%. The cost of the article was $240. Calculate the selling price.

11 A woman makes dresses. Her total costs for ten dresses were $377. At what price should she sell the dresses to make 15% profit?

12 Sal wants to buy a used scooter. The cash price is $495. To buy on credit, she has to pay a 20% deposit and then 24 monthly instalments of $25 each. How much will she save by paying cash?

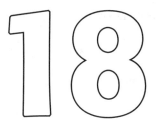

Curved graphs

18.1 Plotting quadratic graphs (the parabola)

- The highest power of a variable in a quadratic equation is two.
- The general formula for a quadratic graph is $y = ax^2 + bx + c$
- The axis of symmetry of the graph divides the parabola into two symmetrical halves.
- The turning point is the point at which the graph changes direction. This point is also called the vertex of the graph.
  - If the value of a in the general form of a quadratic equation is positive, the parabola will be a 'valley shape' and the y-value of the turning point a minimum value.
  - If the value of a in the general form of a quadratic equation is negative, the parabola will be a 'hill shape' and the y-value of the turning point a maximum value.

Exercise 18.1

Remember, the constant term (c in the general formula) is the y-intercept.

1 Copy and complete the following tables. Plot all the graphs onto the same set of axes. Use values of −12 to 12 on the y-axis.

(a)

x	−3	−2	−1	0	1	2	3
$y = -x^2 + 2$							

(b)

x	−3	−2	−1	0	1	2	3
$y = x^2 - 3$							

(c)

x	−3	−2	−1	0	1	2	3
$y = -x^2 - 2$							

(d)

x	−3	−2	−1	0	1	2	3
$y = -x^2 - 3$							

(e)

x	−3	−2	−1	0	1	2	3
$y = x^2 + \dfrac{1}{2}$							

2 Match each of the five parabolas shown here to one of the equations given.

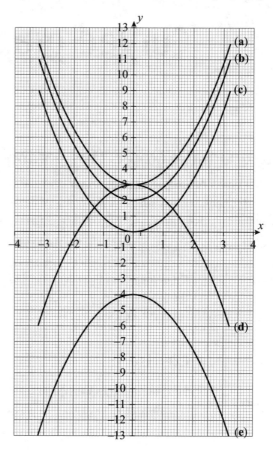

$$y = -4 - x^2 \qquad y = -x^2 + 3 \qquad y = 3 + x^2 \qquad y = x^2 + 2 \qquad y = x^2$$

3 Copy and complete the table of values for each of the equations given below. Plot the points on separate pairs of axes and join them, with a smooth curve, to draw the graph of the equation.

(a)

x	−2	−1	0	1	2	3	4	5
$y = x^2 - 3x + 2$								

(b)

x	−3	−2	−1	0	1	2	3
$y = x^2 - 2x - 1$							

(c)

x	−2	−1	0	1	2	3	4	5	6
$y = -x^2 + 4x + 1$									

4 A toy rocket is thrown up into the air. The graph below shows its path.

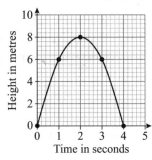

(a) What is the greatest height the rocket reaches?

(b) How long did it take for the rocket to reach this height?

(c) How high did the rocket reach in the first second?

(d) For how long was the rocket in the air?

(e) Estimate for how long the rocket was higher than 3 m above ground.

18.2 Plotting reciprocal graphs (the hyperbola)

- The general formula for a hyperbola graph is $y = \dfrac{a}{x}$ or $xy = a$.
- $x \neq 0$ and $y \neq 0$.
- The x-axis and the y-axis are asymptotes. This means the graph approaches the x-axis and the y-axis but never intersects with them.
- The graph is symmetrical about the $y = x$ and $y = -x$ line.

> **Tip**
> Reciprocal equations have a constant product. This means in $xy = a$, x and y are variables but a is a constant.

Exercise 18.2

1 Draw graphs for the following reciprocal graphs. Plot at least three points in each of the two quadrants and join them up with a smooth curve.

    (a) $xy = 5$ (b) $y = \dfrac{16}{x}$ (c) $xy = 9$

    (d) $y = -\dfrac{8}{x}$ (e) $y = -\dfrac{4}{x}$

2 The length and width of a certain rectangle can only be a whole number of metres. The area of the rectangle is 24 m².

    (a) Draw a table that shows all the possible combinations of measurements for the length and width of the rectangle.

    (b) Plot your values from (a) as points on a graph.

    (c) Join the points with a smooth curve. What does this graph represent?

    (d) Assuming, now, that the length and width of the rectangle can take any positive values that give an area of 24 m², use your graph to find the width if the length is 7 m.

18.3 Using graphs to solve quadratic equations

- If a quadratic equation has real roots the graph of the equation will intersect with the x-axis. This is where $y = 0$.
- To solve quadratic equations graphically, read off the x-coordinates of the points for a given y-value.

Exercise 18.3

1 Use this graph of the relationship $y = x^2 - x - 6$ to solve the following equations.

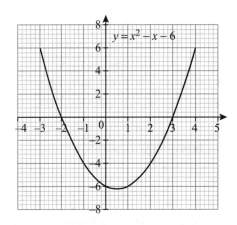

> **Tip**
>
> For part **(c)** you might find it helpful to rearrange the equation so the left-hand side matches the equation of the graph, i.e. subtract 6 from both sides.

   (a) $x^2 - x - 6 = 0$ **(b)** $x^2 - x - 6 = -4$ **(c)** $x^2 - x = 12$

2 **(a)** Draw the graph of $y = -x^2 - x + 2$ for values of x from -3 to 2.

   (b) Use your graph to find the approximate solutions to the equations:
     (i) $-x^2 - x + 2 = 0$
     (ii) $-x^2 - x + 2 = 1$
     (iii) $-x^2 - x + 2 = -2$

3 **(a)** Use an interval of $-4 \le x \le 5$ on the x-axis to draw the graph $y = x^2 - x - 6$.

   (b) Use the graph to solve the following equations:
     (i) $-6 = x^2 - x - 6$
     (ii) $x^2 - x - 6 = 0$
     (iii) $x^2 - x = 12$

18.4 Using graphs to solve simultaneous linear and non-linear equations

- The solution is the point where the graphs intersect.

Exercise 18.4

1 Draw these pairs of graphs and find the points where they intersect.

   (a) $y = \dfrac{4}{x}$ and $y = 2x + 2$

   (b) $y = x^2 + 2x - 3$ and $y = -x + 1$

   (c) $y = -x^2 + 4$ and $y = \dfrac{3}{x}$

2 Use a graphical method to solve the following equations simultaneously.

    (a) $y = 2x^2 + 3x - 2$ and $y = x + 2$

    (b) $y = x^2 + 2x$ and $y = -x + 4$

    (c) $y = -2x^2 + 2x + 4$ and $y = -2x - 4$

    (d) $y = -0.5x^2 + x + 1.5$ and $y = \frac{1}{2}x$

18.5 Other non-linear graphs

- A cubic equation has three as the highest power of its variable.
  - If x is positive, then x^3 is positive and $-x^3$ is negative.
  - If x is negative, then x^3 is negative and $-x^3$ is positive.
- Cubic equations produce graphs called cubic curves.
- The general form of a cubic equation is $y = ax^3 + bx^2 + cx + d$.
- Exponential growth is found in many real life situations.
- The general equation for an exponential function is $y = x^a$.

Exercise 18.5

Tip

Before drawing your graphs check the range of y-values in your table of values.

1 Construct a table of values from $-5 \leq x \leq 5$ and plot the points to draw graphs of the following equations.

  (a) $y = x^3 - 4x^2$ **(b)** $y = x^3 + 5$ **(c)** $y = -2x^3 + 5x^2 + 5$

  (d) $y = -x^3 + 4x^2 - 5$ **(e)** $y = x^3 + 2x - 10$ **(f)** $y = 2x^3 + 4x^2 - 7$

  (g) $y = -x^3 - 3x^2 + 6$ **(h)** $y = -3x^3 + 5x$

Tip

Rearrange the equation so that the LHS of the equation is equivalent to the given equation to help you solve the new equation.

2 (a) Copy and complete the table of values for the equation $y = x^3 - 5x^2 + 10$.

x	-2.5	-2	-1.5	-1	-0.5	0	0.5	1	1.5	2	2.5	3	4	5	6
y															

  (b) On a set of axes, draw the graph of the equation $y = x^3 - 5x^2 + 10$ for $-2.5 \leq x \leq 6$.

  (c) Use the graph to solve the equations:

    (i) $x^3 - 5x^2 + 10 = 0$ **(ii)** $x^3 - 5x^2 + 10 = 10$

    (iii) $x^3 - 5x^2 + 10 = x - 5$

Tip

When you have to plot graphs of equations with a combination of linear, quadratic, cubic, reciprocal or constant terms you need to draw up a table of values with at least eight values of x to get a good indication of the shape of the graph.

3 Construct a table of values for $-3 \leq x \leq 3$ for each of the following equations and draw the graphs.

  (a) $y = x - \frac{1}{x}$ **(b)** $y = x^3 + \frac{1}{x}$ **(c)** $y = x^2 + 2 - \frac{4}{x}$

  (d) $y = 2x + \frac{3}{x}$ **(e)** $y = x^3 - \frac{2}{x}$ **(f)** $y = x^2 - x + \frac{1}{x}$

4 On to the same set of axes draw the graphs of:

  (a) $y = 2^x$ and $y = 2^{-x}$ for $-4 \leq x \leq 4$

  (b) $y = 10^x$ and $y = 2x - 1$ for $0 \leq x \leq 1$.

5 A single-celled algae has been discovered that splits into three separate cells every hour.

(a) Represent the first five hours of growth on a graph.

(b) (i) On to the same set of axes used for (a) sketch the graph of $y = 12x + 1$, which represents the growth of another single-celled organism with a fixed rate of growth.

(ii) What is the growth rate of the second organism?

(c) Use your graph to answer the following.

(i) After how many hours are there equal numbers of each organism?

(ii) How many cells of each organism is this?

18.6 Finding the gradient of a curve

- A curve does not have a constant gradient.
- The gradient of a curve at a point is equal to the gradient of the tangent to the curve at that point.
- Gradient $= \dfrac{y \text{ change}}{x \text{ change}} = \dfrac{\text{vertical change}}{\text{horizontal change}}$.

Exercise 18.6

1 Draw the graph of $y = x^2 - 2x - 8$. Find the gradient of the graph:

(a) at the point where the curve intersects with the y-axis

(b) at each of the points where the curve intersects with the x-axis.

2 (a) Draw the graph of $y = x^3 - 1$ for $-4 \leqslant x \leqslant 4$.

(b) Find the gradient of the curve at the point A (2, 7).

3 The graph shows how the rate of growth of a bean plant is affected by sunlight. Find the rate of growth with and without light on the thirteenth day.

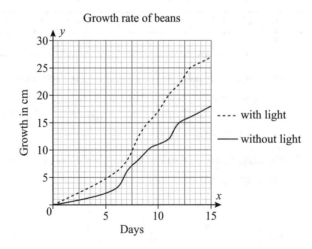

Mixed exercise

1

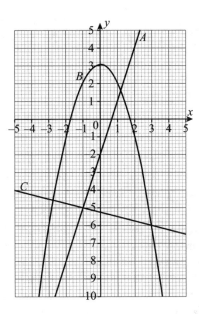

(a) Write an equation for each of the graphs above, *A*, *B* and *C*.

(b)   (i)   Solve equations *A* and *C* simultaneously.

     (ii)   How would you check your solution graphically?

(c) What is the maximum value of *B*?

2 (a) Draw the graphs of the following equations on the same grid: $y = x^2$ and $y = x^3$.

  (b) Use your graph to solve the two equations simultaneously.

  (c) By drawing a suitable straight line, or lines, on to the same grid, solve the equations:

    (i) $x^2 = 4$

    (ii) $x^3 + 8 = 0$

  (d) Find the rate of change for each graph at the points where $x = 2$.

3 The dotted line on the grid below is the axis of symmetry for the given hyperbola.

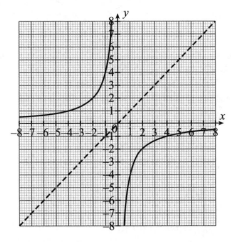

(a) Give the equation for the hyperbola.

(b) Give the equation for the given line of symmetry.

(c) Copy the diagram and draw in the other line of symmetry, giving the equation for this line.

Symmetry and loci

19.1 Symmetry in two dimensions

- Two-dimensional (flat) shapes have line symmetry if you are able to draw a line through the shape so that one side of the line is the mirror image (reflection) of the other side. There may be more than one possible line of symmetry in a shape.
- If you rotate (turn) a shape around a fixed point and it fits on to itself during the rotation, then it has rotational symmetry. The number of times the shape fits on to its original position during a rotation is called the order of rotational symmetry.

If a shape can only fit back into itself after a full 360° rotation, it has no rotational symmetry.

Exercise 19.1

1 For each of the following shapes:

    (a) copy the shape and draw in any lines of symmetry

    (b) determine the order of rotational symmetry.

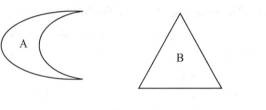

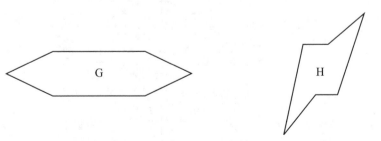

2 **(a)** How many lines of symmetry does a rhombus have? Draw a diagram to show your solution.

    (b) What is the order of rotational symmetry of a rhombus?

3 Draw a quadrilateral that has no lines of symmetry and no rotational symmetry.

19.2 Symmetry in three dimensions

- Three-dimensional shapes (solids) can also be symmetrical.
- A plane of symmetry is a surface (imaginary) that divides the shape into two parts that are mirror images of each other.
- If you rotate a solid around an axis and it looks the same at different positions on its rotation, then it has rotational symmetry. The axis is called the axis of symmetry.

Exercise 19.2

> **Tip**
>
> Think of a *plane of symmetry* as a slice or cut through a solid to divide it into two halves that are mirror images of each other.

1 For each of the following solids, state the number of planes of symmetry.

(a) 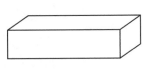 (b) 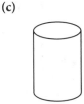 (c) 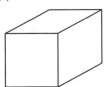 (d)

(e) 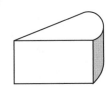 (f) 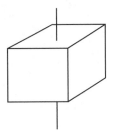 (g) 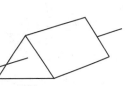 (h)

> **Tip**
>
> Think of an *axis of symmetry* as a rod or axle through a solid. When the solid turns on this axis and reaches its original position during a turn, it has rotational symmetry.

2 What is the order of rotational symmetry about the given axis in each of these solids?

(a) (b) (c)

(d)  (e) 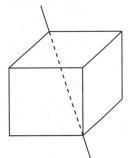 (f)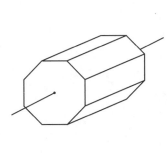

19.3 Symmetry properties of circles

- A circle has line symmetry about any diameter and it has rotational symmetry around its centre.
- The following theorems can be used to solve problems related to circles:
  - the perpendicular bisector of a chord passes through the centre
  - equal chords are equidistant from the centre and chords equidistant from the centre are equal in length
  - two tangents drawn to a circle from the same point outside the circle are equal in length.

> **Tip**
>
> You need to learn the circle theorems. State the theorem you are using when solving a problem in an exam.

Exercise 19.3

1 Find the size of the angles marked x and y.

(a)

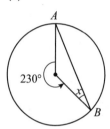

(b)

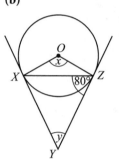

2 In the diagram, MN and PQ are equal chords. S is the midpoint of MN and R is the midpoint of PQ. $MN = 12.5$ cm. Find the length of SO correct to two significant figures.

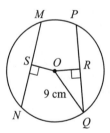

3 In diagram **(a)**, MN and PQ are equal chords and $MN = 12$ cm. S and T are the midpoints of MN and PQ respectively. $SO = 5$ cm.
In diagram **(b)**, chord $AB = 40$ mm.
Find the length of the diameter of each circle, and hence calculate its circumference, correct to two decimal places.

(a)

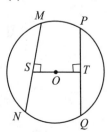

(b)

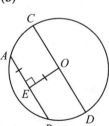

19.4 Angle relationships in circles

- When a triangle is drawn in a semi-circle, so that one side is the diameter and the vertex opposite the diameter touches the circumference, the angle of the vertex opposite the diameter is a right angle (90°).
- Where a tangent touches a circle, the radius drawn to the same point meets the tangent at 90°.
- The angle formed from the ends of a chord and the centre of a circle is twice the angle formed by the ends of the chord and a point at the circumference (in the same segment).
- Angles in the same segment are equal.
- The opposite angles of a cyclic quadrilateral add up to 180°.
- Each exterior angle of a cyclic quadrilateral is equal to the interior angle opposite to it.

> ## ! Tip
> If you learn the circle theorems well you should be able to solve most circle problems.

Exercise 19.4

The angle relationships for triangles, quadrilaterals and parallel lines (chapter 3), as well as Pythagoras' theorem (chapter 11), may be needed to solve circle problems.

1 In the diagram, O is the centre of the circle, $\angle NPO = 15°$ and $\angle MOP = 70°$.

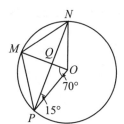

Find the size of the following angles, giving reasons.

(a) $\angle PNO$ (b) $\angle PON$ (c) $\angle MPN$ (d) $\angle PMN$

2 O is the centre of the circle.

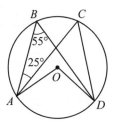

Calculate:

(a) $\angle ACD$ (b) $\angle AOD$ (c) $\angle BDC$

3 Calculate the angles of the cyclic quadrilateral.

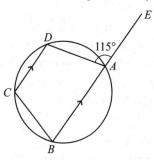

4 *AB* is the diameter of the circle. Calculate the size of angle *ABD*.

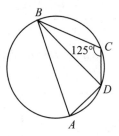

5 *SPT* is a tangent to a circle with centre *O*. *SR* is a straight line which goes through the centre of the circle and $\angle PSO = 29°$. Find the size of $\angle TPR$.

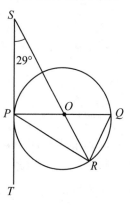

6 Given that *O* is the centre of the circle below and $\angle BAC = 72°$, calculate the size of $\angle BOC$.

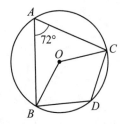

7 In the diagram, $AB \parallel DC$, $\angle ADC = 64°$ and $\angle DCA = 22°$.

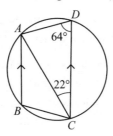

Calculate the size of:

(a) $\angle BAC$ (b) $\angle ABC$ (c) $\angle ACB$.

8 SNT is a tangent to a circle with centre O. $\angle QMO = 18°$ and $\angle MPN = 56°$.

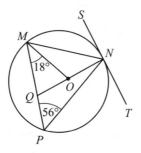

Find the size of:

(a) $\angle MNS$ (b) $\angle MOQ$ (c) $\angle PNT$.

19.5 Locus

- A locus is a set of points (that may or may not be connected) that satisfy a given rule. A locus can be a straight line, a curve or a combination of straight and curved lines.
- The locus of points equidistant from a given point is a circle.
- The locus of points equidistant from a fixed line is two lines parallel to the given line.
- The locus of points equidistant from a given line segment is a 'running track' shape around the line segment.
- The locus of points equidistant from the arms of an angle is the bisector of the angle.
- To find the locus of points that are the same distance from two or more given points you have to use a combination of the loci above to find the intersections of the loci.

REWIND

Make sure you know to bisect an angle as this is often required in loci problems (see chapter 3). ◄

Exercise 19.5

1 Copy the diagrams and draw the locus of the points that are 3 cm from the point or lines in each case.

(a) • A   (b) A •———————• B   (c) A

B ————— C

2 Construct a circle with centre *O* and a radius of 4 cm.

    (a) Draw the locus of points that are 1 cm from the circumference of the circle.

    (b) Shade the locus of points that are less than 1 cm from circumference of the circle.

3 In this scale diagram, the shaded area represents a fishpond. The fishpond is surrounded by a concrete walkway 2 m wide. Copy the diagram and draw the locus of points that are 2 m from the edges of the fishpond. Shade the area covered by the concrete walkway.

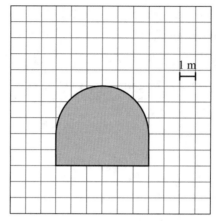

4 Nick lives 3 km from the road and 1.5 km from the school. The closest distance of the school from the road is 4 km. Using a scale of 1 cm to 1 km, construct the loci to show two possible positions for Nick's home.

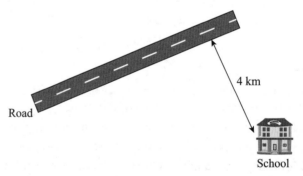

5 Anna lives at *A* and Betty lives at *B*. They want to meet at a point equidistant from both homes. By construction, show the locus of possible meeting points.

                  ● *A*

                          ● *B*

6 Follow the instructions carefully to find the location of a water main on a copy of the diagram below.

Cell tower
A

Radio mast
C

30 m

15 m

B Flagpole   Scale 1 cm = 5 m

(a) Find the locus of points that are equidistant from the cell tower and the flagpole, then the single locus that is equidistant from *AB* and *BC*. Label this point *D* and draw a line to join it to the base of the flagpole.

(b) The water main is ten metres from point *D* and on the line segment joining point *D* to the base of the flagpole. Mark this as point *X* on your diagram.

Mixed exercise

1 Here are five shapes.

(a)   (b)   (c)   (d)   (e)

For each one:

(i) indicate the axes of symmetry (if any)
(ii) state the order of rotational symmetry.

2 Study the diagram.

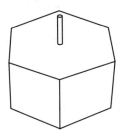

(a) What type of solid is this?
(b) What is the correct mathematical name for the rod through the solid?
(c) What is the order of rotational symmetry of this solid?
(d) How many planes of symmetry does this solid have?

3 In each of the following *O* is the centre of the circle. Find the value of the marked angles. Give reasons for your statements.

(a)   **(b)**   **(c)**   **(d)**

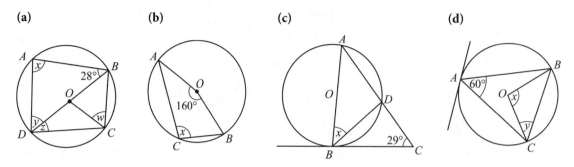

4 Find the length of *x* and *y* in each of these diagrams. *O* is the centre of the circle in each case.

(a)   **(b)**

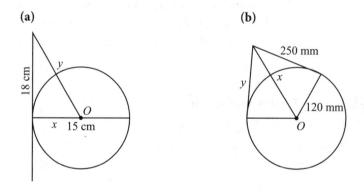

5 Jessica tells a friend that her house is 3 km from the petrol station on Route 66 and 2 km from Route 66 itself. Use a scale of 1 cm to 1 km to show all possible locations for Jessica's house.

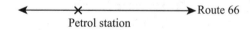

6 Construct line segment *AB* 6 cm long. Show the locus of points that are equidistant from both *A* and *B* and also 5 cm from *A*.

20 Histograms and frequency distribution diagrams

20.1 Histograms

- A histogram is a specialised graph. It is used to show grouped numerical data using a continuous scale on the horizontal axis. (This means there are no gaps in between the data categories – where one ends, the other begins.)
- Because the scale is continuous, each column is drawn above a particular class interval.
- When the class intervals are equal, the bars are all the same width and it is common practice to label the vertical scale as frequency.
- When the class intervals are not equal, the vertical axis shows the frequency density.

  Frequency density $= \dfrac{\text{frequency}}{\text{class interval}}$. The area of each 'bar' represents the frequency.

- A gap will only appear between bars if an interval has a frequency/frequency density of zero.

Exercise 20.1

1 The table shows the marks obtained by a number of students for English and Mathematics in a mock exam.

Remember there can be no gaps between the bars: use the upper and lower bounds of each class interval to prevent gaps.

Marks class interval	English frequency	Mathematics frequency
1–10	0	0
11–20	3	2
21–30	7	5
31–40	4	6
41–50	29	34
51–60	51	48
61–70	40	45
71–80	12	6
81–90	3	2
91–100	1	2

◀ REWIND
You met the mode in chapter 12. ◀

(a) Draw two separate histograms to show the distribution of marks for English and Mathematics.
(b) What is the modal class for English?
(c) What is the modal class for Mathematics?
(d) Write a few sentences comparing the students' performance in English and Mathematics.

2 Study this graph and answer the questions about it.

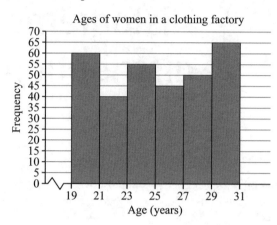

Ages of women in a clothing factory

(a) How do you know this is a histogram and not a bar graph?

(b) How many women aged 23–25 work in the clothing factory?

(c) How many women work in the factory altogether?

(d) What is the modal class of this data?

(e) Explain why there is a broken line on the horizontal axis.

3 Sally did a survey to find the ages of people using an internet café. These are her results:

Age (a)	$15 \leq a < 20$	$20 \leq a < 25$	$25 \leq a < 35$	$35 \leq a < 50$	$50 \leq a < 55$
No. of people	14	12	12	12	8

Draw an accurate histogram to show these data. Use a scale of 1 cm to five years on the horizontal axis and an area scale of one square centimetre to represent one person.

> **Tip**
>
> It helps to remember that the frequency density tells you what the column height should be. If one column is twice as wide as another, it will only be half as high for the same frequency.

4 This histogram shows the number of houses in different price ranges that are advertised in a property magazine.

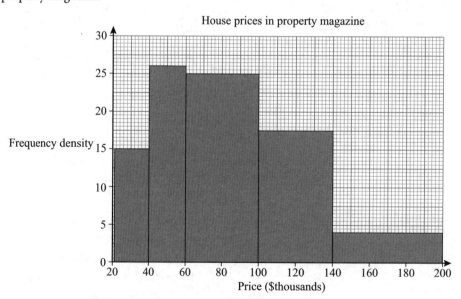

House prices in property magazine

(a) How many houses were in the $20 000–$40 000 price range?

(b) How many houses were in the $140 000–$200 000 price range?

(c) How many houses are represented by one square centimetre on this graph?

20.2 Cumulative frequency

- Cumulative frequency is a 'running total' of the class frequencies up to each upper class boundary.
- When cumulative frequencies are plotted they give a cumulative frequency curve or graph.
- You can use the curve to estimate the median value of the data.
- You can divide the data into four equal groups called quartiles. The interquartile range (IQR) is the difference between the upper and lower quartiles $(Q_3 - Q_1)$.
- Data can also be divided into 100 equal groups called percentiles. The 50th percentile is equivalent to the median.

Exercise 20.2

1   The table shows the percentage scored by a number of students in an examination.

Percentage	Number of students
$0 \leq m < 10$	0
$10 \leq m < 20$	3
$20 \leq m < 30$	7
$30 \leq m < 40$	4
$40 \leq m < 50$	29
$50 \leq m < 60$	51
$60 \leq m < 70$	40
$70 \leq m < 80$	12
$80 \leq m < 90$	3
$90 \leq m < 100$	1

(a) Draw a cumulative frequency curve to show this data. Use a scale of 1 cm per ten percent on the horizontal axis and a scale of 1 cm per ten students on the vertical axis.

(b) Use your curve to estimate the median, Q_1 and Q_3.

(c) Estimate the IQR.

(d) The pass rate for this test is 40%. What percentage of the students passed the test?

(e) Indicate the 60th and 80th percentiles on your graph. What do these percentiles indicate?

> **Tip**
> You will normally be given a scale to use when you have to draw a cumulative frequency curve in an examination.

> **Tip**
> To find the position of the quartiles from a cumulative frequency curve, use the formulae $\frac{n}{4}$, $\frac{n}{2}$ and $\frac{3n}{4}$. Note that this is different to the formulae used for discrete data.

2   This cumulative frequency curve shows the height in centimetres of 200 professional basketball players.

(a) Estimate the median height of players in this sample.

(b) Estimate Q_1 and Q_3.

(c) Estimate the IQR.

(d) What percentage of basketball players are over 1.82 m tall?

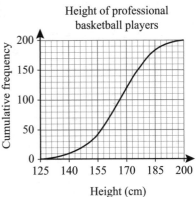

Height of professional basketball players

Mixed exercise

1 This partially completed histogram shows the heights of trees in a section of tropical forest.

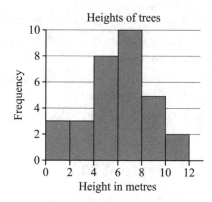

Heights of trees

(a) A scientist measured five more trees and their heights were: 2.09 m, 3.34 m, 6.45 m, 9.26 m and 3.88 m. Redraw the graph to include this data.

(b) How many trees in this sector of forest are ≥ 6 m tall?

(c) What is the modal class of tree heights?

2 A nurse measured the masses of a sample of students in a high school and drew the following table.

Mass (kg)	Frequency
$54 \leq m < 56$	4
$56 \leq m < 58$	7
$58 \leq m < 60$	13
$60 \leq m < 62$	19
$62 \leq m < 64$	11

(a) Draw a histogram to show the distribution of masses.

(b) What is the modal mass?

(c) What percentage of students weighed less than 56 kg?

(d) What is the maximum possible range of the masses?

3 The table shows the average minutes of airtime that teenagers bought from a pre-paid kiosk in one week.

Minutes	$20 \leq m < 30$	$30 \leq m < 40$	$40 \leq m < 60$	$60 \leq m < 80$	$80 \leq m < 100$	$100 \leq m < 150$
No. of teenagers	10	15	40	50	60	50

Draw an accurate histogram to display this data. Use a scale of 1 cm to represent ten minutes on the horizontal axis and an area scale of 1 cm² per five persons.

4 Thirty seedlings were planted for a biology experiment. The heights of the plants were measured after three weeks and recorded as below.

Heights (h cm)	$0 \leq h < 3$	$3 \leq h < 6$	$6 \leq h < 9$	$9 \leq h < 12$
Frequency	3	8	15	4

(a) Find an estimate for the mean height.

(b) Draw a cumulative frequency curve and use it to find the median height.

(c) Estimate Q_1 and Q_3 and the IQR.

21 Ratio, rate and proportion

21.1 Working with ratio

- A ratio is a comparison of two or more quantities measured in the same units. In general, a ratio is written in the form $a:b$.
- Ratios should always be given in their simplest form. To express a ratio in simplest form, divide or multiply by the same factor.
- Quantities can be shared in a given ratio. To do this you need to work out the number of equal parts in the ratio and then work out the value of each share. For example, a ratio of $3:2$ means that there are 5 equal parts. One share is $\frac{3}{5}$ of the total and the other is $\frac{2}{5}$ of the total.

Remember, simplest form is also called 'lowest terms'.

Exercise 21.1

1 Express the following as ratios in their simplest form.

(a) $2\frac{3}{4}:3\frac{2}{3}$

(b) $1\frac{1}{2}$ hours : 15 minutes

(c) 175 cm to 2 m

(d) 600 g to three kilograms

(e) 12.5 g to 50 g

Tip

You can cross multiply to make an equation and solve for x.

2 Find the value of x in each of the following.

(a) $2:3 = 6:x$

(b) $2:5 = x:10$

(c) $2:x = 3:24$

(d) $x:12 = 2:8$

(e) $10:15 = x:6$

(f) $\frac{2}{7} = \frac{x}{4}$

(g) $\frac{5}{x} = \frac{16}{6}$

(h) $\frac{x}{4} = \frac{10}{15}$

(i) $\frac{x}{21} = \frac{1}{3}$

(j) $\frac{5}{x} = \frac{3}{8}$

3 A length of rope 160 cm long must be cut into two parts so that the lengths are in the ratio $3:5$. What are the lengths of the parts?

4 To make salad dressing, you mix oil and vinegar in the ratio $2:3$. Calculate how much oil and how much vinegar you will need to make the following amounts of salad dressing:

(a) 50 ml

(b) 600 ml

(c) 750 ml.

5 The sizes of three angles of a triangle are in the ratio $A:B:C = 2:1:3$. What is the size of each angle?

6 A metal disc consists of three parts silver and two parts copper (by mass). If the disc has a mass of 1350 mg, how much silver does it contain?

21.2 Ratio and scale

- Scale is a ratio. It can be expressed as
  length on the drawing : real length.
- All ratio scales must be expressed in the form of $1:n$ or $n:1$.
- To change a ratio so that one part = 1, you need to divide both parts by the number that you want to be expressed as 1. For example with $2:7$, if you want the 2 to be expressed as 1, you divide both parts by 2. The result is $1:3.5$.

! Tip

With reductions (such as maps) the scale will be in the form $1:n$, where $n > 1$. With enlargements the scale will be in the form $n:1$, where $n > 1$. n may not be a whole number.

Exercise 21.2 A

1 Write these ratios in the form of $1:n$.

(a) $4:9$ (b) $400\,\text{m}:1.3\,\text{km}$ (c) 50 minutes$:1\frac{1}{2}$ hours

2 Write these ratios in the form of $n:1$.

(a) $12:8$ (b) $2\,\text{m}:40\,\text{cm}$ (c) $2.5\,\text{g}$ to $500\,\text{mg}$

Exercise 21.2 B

1 The distance between two points on a map with a scale of $1:2\,000\,000$ is 120 mm. What is the distance between the two points in reality? Give your answer in kilometres.

2 A plan is drawn using a scale of $1:500$. If the length of a wall on the plan is 6 cm, how long is the wall in reality?

3 Miguel makes a scale drawing to solve a trigonometry problem. 1 cm on his drawing represents 2 m in real life. He wants to show a 10 m long ladder placed 7 m from the foot of a wall.

(a) What length will the ladder be in the diagram?
(b) How far will it be from the foot of the wall in the diagram?

4 A map has a scale of $1:700\,000$.

(a) What does a scale of $1:700\,000$ mean?
(b) Copy and complete this table using the map scale.

Map distance (mm)	10		50	80		
Actual distance (km)		50			1200	1500

5 Mary has a rectangular picture 35 mm wide and 37 mm high. She enlarges it on the photocopier so that the enlargement is 14 cm wide.

(a) What is the scale factor of the enlargement?
(b) What is the height of her enlarged picture?
(c) In the original picture, a fence was 30 mm long. How long will this fence be on the enlarged picture?

21.3 Rates

- A rate compares two quantities measured in different units. For example speed is a rate that compares kilometres travelled per hour.
- Rates can be simplified just like ratios. They can also be expressed in the form of $1:n$.
- You solve rate problems in the same way that you solved ratio and proportion problems. Use the unitary or ratio methods.

Tip

The word 'per' is often used in a rates. Per can mean 'for every', 'in each', 'out of every', or 'out of' depending on the context.

Remember, speed is a very important rate.

$$speed = \frac{distance}{time}$$

$$distance = speed \times time$$

$$time = \frac{distance}{speed}$$

Exercise 21.3

1 At a market, milk costs $1.95 per litre. How much milk can you buy for $50?

2 Sam travels a distance of 437 km and uses 38 litres of petrol. Express his petrol consumption as a rate in km/l.

3 Calculate the average speed of the following vehicles.

    (a) A car that travels 196 km in 2.5 hours.
    (b) A plane that travels 650 km in one hour 15 minutes.
    (c) A train that travels 180 km in 45 minutes.

4 How long would it take to travel these distances?

    (a) 400 km at 80 km/h   (b) 900 km at 95 km/h
    (c) 1800 km at 45 km/h   (d) 500 m at 7 km/h

5 How far would you travel in $2\frac{1}{2}$ hours at these speeds?

    (a) 60 km/h   (b) 120 km/h
    (c) 25 metres per minute   (d) two metres per second

21.4 Kinematic graphs

- Distance–time graphs show the connection between the distance an object has travelled and the time taken to travel that distance. They are also called travel graphs.
- Time is normally shown along the horizontal axis because it is the independent variable. Distance is shown on the vertical axis because it is the dependent variable.
- You can determine speed on a distance–time graph by looking at the slope (steepness) of the line. The steeper the line, the greater the speed; a straight line indicates constant speed; upward and downward slopes represent movement in opposite directions; and a horizontal line represents no movement:
  - Average speed $= \dfrac{\text{distance travelled}}{\text{time taken}} = \dfrac{\text{change in } y\text{-coordinate}}{\text{change in } x\text{-coordinate}}$
- Speed–time graphs show speed on the vertical axis and time on the horizontal axis.
- For a speed–time graph, gradient = acceleration. Positive gradient (acceleration) is an increase in speed. Negative gradient (deceleration) is a decrease in speed.
- Distance = speed × time. You can find the distance covered in a certain time by calculating the area below each section of the graph. Apply the area formulae for quadrilaterals and triangles to do this.

Exercise 21.4

1 The graph below shows the distance covered by a vehicle in a six-hour period.

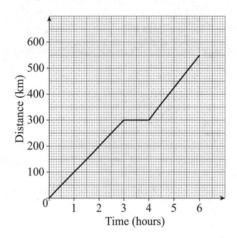

(a) Use the graph to find the distance covered after:

    (i) one hour   **(ii)** two hours   **(iii)** three hours.

(b) Calculate the average speed of the vehicle during the first three hours.

(c) Describe what the graph shows between hour three and four.

(d) What distance did the vehicle cover during the last two hours of the journey?

(e) What was its average speed during the last two hours of the journey?

2 Dabilo and Pam live 200 km apart from each other. They decide to meet up at a shopping centre in-between their homes on a Saturday. Pam travels by bus and Dabilo catches a train. The graph shows both journeys.

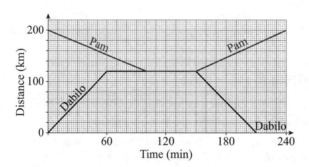

(a) How much time did Dabilo spend on the train?

(b) How much time did Pam spend on the bus?

(c) At what speed did the train travel for the first hour?

(d) How far was the shopping centre from:

    (i) Dabilo's home?   **(ii)** Pam's home?

(e) What was the average speed of the bus from Pam's home to the shopping centre?

(f) How long did Dabilo have to wait before Pam arrived?

(g) How long did the two girls spend together?

(h) How much faster was Pam's journey on the way home?

(i) If they left home at 8:00 a.m., what time did each girl return home after the day's outing?

3 This speed–time graph shows the speed of a car in km/h against the time in minutes.

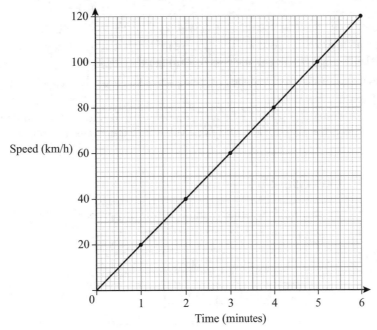

(a) What is the speed of the car after:

(i) two minutes

(ii) six minutes?

(b) When is the car travelling at 70 km/h?

(c) Calculate the acceleration of the car in km/h².

(d) What distance did the car cover in the first six minutes?

4 This speed–time graph shows the speed of a train in m/s against the time in seconds.

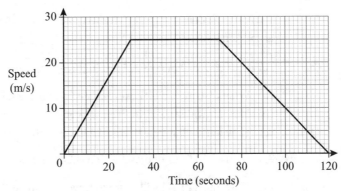

> **Tip**
>
> Acceleration = change in speed ÷ time taken. As the units of speed in this example are metres per second, then the units of acceleration are metres per second per second. This is written as m s^{-2} or m/s².

(a) When was the train accelerating and what was the acceleration?

(b) When did the train start decelerating and what was the deceleration?

(c) When the train was travelling at constant speed, what was the speed in km/h?

(d) What distance did the train travel in two minutes?

21.5 Proportion

- Proportion is a constant ratio between the corresponding elements of two sets.
- When quantities are in direct proportion they increase or decrease at the same rate. The graph of a directly proportionate relationship is a straight line passing through the origin.
- When quantities are inversely proportional, one increases as the other decreases. The graph of an inversely proportional relationship is a curve.
- The unitary method is useful for solving ratio and proportion problems. This method involves finding the value of one unit (of work, time, etc.) and using that value to find the value of a number of units.

> **! Tip**
>
> If x and y are directly proportional, then $\frac{x}{y}$ is the same for various values of x and y.

Exercise 21.5

1 Determine whether A and B are directly proportional in each case.

(a)

A	2	4	6
B	300	600	900

(b)

A	2	5	8
B	2	10	15

(c)

A	1	2	3	4
B	0.1	0.2	0.3	0.4

2 A textbook costs $25.

   (a) What is the price of seven books?

   (b) What is the price of ten books?

3 Find the cost of five identically priced items if seven items cost $17.50.

4 If a 3.5 m tall pole casts a 10.5 m shadow, find the length of the shadow cast by a 20 m tall pole at the same time.

5 A car travels a distance of 225 km in three hours at a constant speed.

   (a) What distance will it cover in one hour at the same speed?

   (b) How far will it travel in five hours at the same speed?

   (c) How long will it take to travel 250 km at the same speed?

6 A truck uses 20 litres of diesel to travel 240 kilometres.

   (a) How much diesel will it use to travel 180 km at the same rate?

   (b) How far could the truck travel on 45 litres of diesel at the same rate?

7 It takes one employee ten days to complete a project. If another employee joins him, it only takes five days. Five employees can complete the job in two days.

   (a) Describe this relationship.

   (b) How long would it take to complete the project with:

      (i) four employees

      (ii) 20 employees?

8 After a tsunami, ten people have enough fresh water to last them for six days at a set rate per person.

   (a) How long would the water last, if there were only five people drinking it at the same rate?
   (b) Another two people join the group. How long will the water last if it is used at the same rate?

9 Nick took four hours to complete a journey at 110 km/h. Marie did the same journey at 80 km/h. How long did it take her?

10 A plane travelling at an average speed of 1000 km/h takes 12 hours to complete a journey. How fast would it need to travel to cover the same distance in ten hours?

21.6 Direct and inverse proportion in algebraic terms

- When two quantities are directly proportional then $P = kQ$, where k is a constant.
- When two quantities are inversely proportional then $PQ = k$, where k is a constant.

Exercise 21.6

> **Tip**
>
> The symbol $\propto$ means proportional to.

1 Given that a varies directly with b and that $a = 56$ when $b = 8$,

   (a) find the value of the constant of proportionality (k)
   (b) find the value of a when $b = 12$.

2 The table shows values of m and T. Show that T is directly proportional to m.

m	7.5	11.5	18
T	16.35	25.07	39.24

3 F is directly proportional to m and $F = 16$ when $m = 2$.

   (a) Find the value of F when $m = 5$.
   (b) Find the value of m when $F = 36$.

4 In the following relationship, $xy = k$. Find the missing values.

x	3	6	b	9
y	4	a	1.5	c

5 $y \propto \dfrac{1}{x}$ and $y = 5$ when $x = 4$.

   (a) Find the value of y when $x = 10$.
   (b) Find the value of x when $y = 40$.

6 y is directly proportional to x^2, and $y = 50$ when $x = 5$.

   (a) Write the equation for this relationship.
   (b) Find y if $x = 25$.
   (c) Find x if $y = 162$.

7 y is inversely proportional to $\sqrt{x}$ and $y = 20$ when $x = 16$.

   (a) Write the equation for this relationship.

   (b) Find y if $x = 100$

   (c) Find x if $y = \frac{1}{3}$.

8 a varies inversely with b and $a = 10$ when $b = 16$.

   (a) Find the value of b when $a = 4$

   (b) Find the value of a when $b = 9$

9 The relationship between x and y is given as $y = \dfrac{10}{x}$.

   (a) Find the value of y when $x = 4$.

   (b) Calculate x when $y = 5$.

10 A length of wire 18 m long is cut into a number (y) of equal lengths (x m).

   (a) Show that y is inversely proportional to x.

   (b) Write an equation to describe the relationship between x and y.

   (c) Find the value of y when $x = 0.5$ m.

21.7 Increasing and decreasing amounts by a given ratio

- You can increase or decrease amounts in a given ratio.

- $\dfrac{\text{new amount}}{\text{old amount}} = \dfrac{x}{y}$, new amount $= \dfrac{x \times \text{old amount}}{y}$. For an increase, $x > y$. For a decrease $x < y$.

Exercise 21.7

1 The price of an article costing \$240 is increased in the ratio 5 : 4. What is the new price?

2 An apartment purchased for \$80 000 has decreased in value in the ratio 9 : 10. What is it worth now?

3 A car purchased for \$85 000 has decreased in value in the ratio 3 : 5.

   (a) What is the new value of the car?

   (b) How much money would the owner lose if she sold the car for the decreased value?

4 Increase 10 250 in the ratio 7 : 5.

Mixed exercise

1 A triangle of perimeter 360 mm has side lengths in the ratio 3 : 5 : 4.

   (a) Find the lengths of the sides.

   (b) Is the triangle right-angled? Give a reason for your answer.

2 On a floor plan of a school, 2 cm represents 1 m in the real school. What is the scale of the plan?

3 A car travels at an average speed of 85 km/h.

(a) What distance will the car travel in:

(i) 1 hour   (ii) $4\frac{1}{2}$ hours   (iii) 15 minutes?

(b) How long will it take the car to travel:

(i) 30 km   (ii) 400 km   (iii) 100 km?

4 This travel graph shows the journey of a petrol tanker doing deliveries.

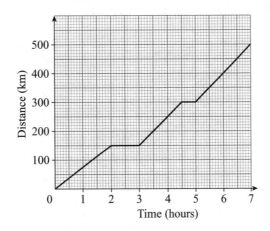

(a) What distance did the tanker travel in the first two hours?

(b) When did the tanker stop to make its first delivery? For how long was it stopped?

(c) Calculate the average speed of the tanker between the first and second stop on the route.

(d) What was the average speed of the tanker during the last two hours of the journey?

(e) How far did the tanker travel on this journey?

5 This speed–time graph shows the speed in m/s for a car journey.

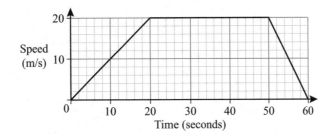

(a) For how long was the car accelerating?

(b) Calculate the rate at which it decelerated from 50 to 60 seconds.

(c) What distance did the car cover during the first 20 seconds?

(d) How many metres did the car take to stop once it started decelerating?

6 Nine students complete a task in three minutes. How long would it take six students to complete the same task if they worked at the same rate?

7 A cube with sides of 2 cm has a mass of 12 grams. Find the mass of another cube made of the same material if it has sides of 5 cm.

8 The pressure (P) of a given amount of gas is inversely proportional to the volume (V) of the gas.

   (a) Express the relationship between P and V in a generalised equation.

   (b) It is found that $P = 60$ when $V = 40$. Find the value of P when $V = 30$.

9 Salma has a photograph 104 mm long and 96 mm wide. This is too big for her album. She reduces it on the computer so that it is 59.43 mm long.

   (a) In what ratio did Salma reduce the photograph?

   (b) Calculate the new width of the photo correct to two decimal places.

22 More equations, formulae and functions

22.1 Setting up equations to solve problems

- You can set up your own equations and use them to solve problems that have a number as an answer.
- The first step in setting up an equation is to work out what needs to be calculated. Represent this amount using a variable (usually x). You then construct an equation using the information you are given and solve it to find the answer.

> **Tip**
> When you have to give a formula, you should express it in simplest terms by collecting like terms.

Exercise 22.1 A

1 A rectangle is 4 cm longer than it is wide. If the rectangle is x cm long, write down:

    (a) the width (in terms of x)

    (b) a formula for calculating the perimeter (P) of the rectangle.

    (c) a formula for finding the area (A) of the rectangle in simplest terms.

2 Three numbers are represented by x, $3x$ and $x + 2$.

    (a) Write a formula for finding the sum (S) of the three numbers.

    (b) Write a formula for finding the mean (M) of the three numbers.

3 The smallest of three consecutive numbers is x.

    (a) Express the other two numbers in terms of x.

    (b) Write a formula for finding the sum (S) of the numbers.

4 Sammy is two years older than Max. Tayo is three years younger than Max. If Max is x years old, write down:

    (a) Sammy's age in terms of x

    (b) Tayo's age in term of x

    (c) a formula for finding the combined ages of the three boys.

> **Tip**
> There is usually one word or short statement in the problem that means 'equal to'. Examples are: total, gives, the answer is, the result is, product of is, and sum of is.

Exercise 22.1 B

1 There are 12 more girls than boys in a class of 40 students. How many boys are there?

2 A rectangle has an area of 36 cm² and the breadth is 4 cm. Find the length of the rectangle.

3 There are ten times as many silver cars than red cars in a parking area. If there 88 silver and red cars altogether, find the number of cars of each colour.

4 Nadira is 25 years younger than her father. Nadira's mother is two years younger than her father. Together Nadira, her mother and father have a combined age of 78. Work out their ages.

5   The perimeter of a parallelogram is 104 cm. If the length is three times the breadth, calculate the dimensions of the parallelogram.

6   Three items, X, Y and Z are such that the price of Y is 90c more than the price of X and the price of Z is 60c cheaper than the price of X. Two of item X plus three of item Y plus six of item Z cost \$9. What is the price of each item?

7   Rushdi's father is presently five times his age. In three years' time, he will be four times Rushdi's age. How old is Rushdi now?

8   A concert ticket costs \$25. Pensioners and students pay \$15. For one performance, 32 more discount tickets than regular priced tickets were sold at the door. If \$4360 was collected, how many regular priced tickets were sold?

22.2 Using and transforming formulae

- To change the subject of a formula:
  - expand to get rid of any brackets
  - use inverse operations to isolate the variable you require.
- When a formula contains squared terms or square roots, remember that a squared number has both a negative and a positive root.
- The variable that is to be made the subject may occur more than once in the formula. If this is the case, gather the like terms and factorise before you express the formula in terms of the subject variable.

REWIND

You have met this topic in chapter 6. This exercise uses the same principles to transform slightly more complicated formulae. ◄

Exercise 22.2

1   The variable that needs to be the subject is in brackets. Change the subject of each formula to that variable.

   (a) $U + T = V + W$ (V)
   (b) $3(V + W) = U - T^2$ (V)
   (c) $A = \dfrac{C}{B}$ (B)
   (d) $A = \dfrac{B}{C}$ (B)
   (e) $2P = Q^2$ (Q)
   (f) $P = 2Q^2$ (Q)
   (g) $P = Q^2R$ (Q)
   (h) $Q = \sqrt{2P}$ (P)
   (i) $Q = \sqrt{PR}$ (P)
   (j) $Q = \sqrt{(P - R)}$ (P)
   (k) $PQ = R^2$ (Q)

2   Ohm's law is a formula that links voltage (V), current (I) and resistance (R). Given that $V = RI$:

   (a) change the subject of the formula to I
   (b) find the current (in amps) for a voltage of 50 volts and a resistance of 2.5 ohms.

3 The area of a circle can be found using the formula $A = \pi r^2$.

    (a) Change the subject of the formula to r.

    (b) Find the length of the radius of a circle with an area of $100\,\text{mm}^2$. Give your answer correct to three signifigant figures.

4 The formula for finding degrees Celsius from degrees Fahrenheit is $C = \frac{5}{9}(F - 32)$.

    (a) Make F the subject of the formula.

    (b) Find the temperature in degrees Fahrenheit when it is $27\,°\text{C}$.

    (c) The temperature in Kelvin can be found using the formula, $K = C + 273$, where K is the temperature in Kelvin and C is the temperature in degrees Celsius. Use this information together with the previous formula, as necessary, to find the Kelvin equivalent of $122\,°\text{F}$.

22.3 Functions and function notation

- A function is a rule (or set of instructions) for changing an input value into an output value.
- The symbol f(x) is used to denote a function of x. This is called function notation. For example: f(x) = $5x - 2$.
- To find the value of a function, such as f(3), you substitute the given number for x and calculate the value of the expression.
- A composite function is a combination of two or more functions. The order in which the functions are written is important: gf means first apply f and then apply g.
- The notation for the inverse of a function of f is f^{-1}. This is read as f-inverse. You can think of the inverse of a function as its reverse. Applying the inverse means working backwards and undoing (doing the inverse) of each operation.

! Tip

Finding the inverse of a function in practice means making x the subject of the formula instead of y.

Exercise 22.3

1 f(x) = $2x + 5$, calculate:

    (a) f(3)   **(b)** f(-3)   **(c)** f(0)   **(d)** f(m).

2 Given f: $x \to 3x^2 + 5$,

    (a) Write down the expression for f(x).

    (b) Calculate:

        (i) f(2)   **(ii)** f(4)   **(iii)** f(6)

    (c) Show whether f(2) + f(4) = f(6).

    (d) Find:

        (i) f(a)   **(ii)** f(b)   **(iii)** f($a + b$)

    (e) Find a if f(a) = 32

3 Given h: $x \to \sqrt{5 - x}$,

    (a) Write down the expression for h(x).

    (b) Find

        (i) h(1)   **(ii)** h(-4)

4 If f(x) = $4x$ and g(x) = $x - 5$, find:

    (a) fg   **(b)** gf

5 If g(x) = $2x$ and h(x) = $2x + 3$, find gh(3).

6 Write down the inverse of each of the following functions using the correct notation.

(a) $f(x) = x + 4$ (b) $f(x) = x - 9$ (c) $f(x) = 5x$ (d) $f(x) = \dfrac{x}{-2}$

7 Given $f(x) = x - 3$ and $g(x) = \dfrac{x}{2}$, find:

(a) $fg(x)$ (b) $gf(x)$ (c) $(fg)^{-1}(x)$

(d) $(gf)^{-1}(x)$ (e) $f^{-1}g^{-1}(x)$ (f) $g^{-1}f^{-1}(x)$

Mixed exercise

1 A certain number increased by six is equal to twice the same number decreased by four. What is the number?

2 The sum of three consecutive numbers is 126. Find the numbers.

3 Zorina is a quarter of the age of her mother, who is 32 years' old. In how many years time will she be a third of her mother's age?

4 Cedric has $16 more than Nathi. Together they have $150. How much does each person have?

5 Sindi, Jonas and Mo put money together to contribute $130 to charity. Jonas puts in half the amount that Sindi puts in and Mo puts in $10 less than twice the amount that Sinid puts in. Work out how much each person put in.

6 Altogether 72 adults and children take part in a fun hike. Adults pay $7.50 and children pay $5.00. If $430 was collected, how many children took part?

7 Make b the subject of each formula:

(a) $a = \dfrac{5(b+7)}{9} + \dfrac{(b-3)}{3}$

(b) $a^2 = 2(b - 3) + 5(2 + 3b)$

8 Given $f(x) = \dfrac{2x - 3}{5}$, find $f^{-1}(x)$.

9 $f(x) = 3x + 4$ and $g(x) = \dfrac{x-2}{5}$, find:

(a) $f^{-1}(x)$ (b) $f^{-1}(13)$ (c) the value of a if $f(a) = 22$

(d) $ff(x)$ (e) $g^{-1}f(1)$.

23 Transformations and matrices

23.1 Simple plane transformations

- A transformation is a change in the position or size of a point or a shape.
- There are four basic transformations: reflection, rotation, translation and enlargement.
  - The original shape is called the object (O) and the transformed shape is called the image (O′).
- A reflection flips the shape over.
  - Under reflection, every point on a shape is reflected in a mirror line to produce a mirror-image of the object. Points on the object and corresponding points on the image are the same distance from the mirror line, when you measure the distance perpendicular to the mirror line.
  - To describe a reflection you need to give the equation of the mirror line.
- A rotation turns the shape around a point.
  - The point about which a shape is rotated is called the centre of rotation. The shape may be rotated clockwise or anticlockwise.
  - To describe a rotation you need to give the centre of rotation and the angle and direction of turn.
- A translation is a slide movement.
  - Under translation, every point on the object moves the same distance in the same direction to form the image. Translation involves moving the shape sideways and/or up and down. The translation can therefore be described using a column vector $\begin{pmatrix} x \\ y \end{pmatrix}$ where x is the movement to the side (along the x-axis) and y is the movement up or down. The sign of the x or y value gives you the direction of the translation. Positive means to the right or up and negative means to the left or down.
- An enlargement involves changing the size of an object to produce an image that is similar in shape to the object.
  - The enlargement factor $= \dfrac{\text{length of a side on the image}}{\text{length of the corresponding side on the object}}$. When an object is enlarged from a fixed point, it has a centre of enlargement. The centre of enlargement determines the position of the image. Lines drawn through corresponding points on the object and the image will meet at the centre of enlargement.
- The transformations above can be combined.

Tip

Reflection and rotation change the position and orientation of the object while translation only changes the position. Enlargement changes the size of the object to produce the image but its orientation is not changed.

Exercise 23.1 A

You will need squared paper for this exercise.

1 Draw and label any rectangle $ABCD$.

   (a) Rotate the rectangle clockwise 90° about point D. Label the image $A'B'C'D'$.
   (b) Reflect $A'B'C'D'$ about $B'D'$.

2 Make a copy of the diagram below and carry out the following transformations.

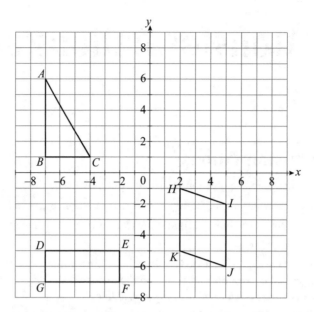

(a) Translate △ABC three units to the right and four units up. Label the image correctly.

(b) Reflect rectangle DEFG about the line $y = -3$. Label the image correctly.

(c) (i) Rotate parallelogram HIJK 90° anticlockwise about point $(2, -1)$.

   (ii) Translate the image $H'I'J'K'$ one unit left and five units up.

3 Make a copy of the diagram below and carry out the following transformations.

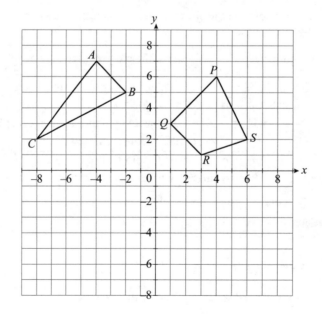

(a) △ABC is translated using the column vector $\begin{pmatrix} 10 \\ -9 \end{pmatrix}$ to form the image $A'B'C'$. Draw and label the image.

(b) Quadrilateral PQRS is reflected in the y-axis and then translated using the column vector $\begin{pmatrix} 0 \\ -6 \end{pmatrix}$. Draw the resultant image $P'Q'R'S'$.

4 For each of the reflections shown in the diagram, give the equation of the mirror line.

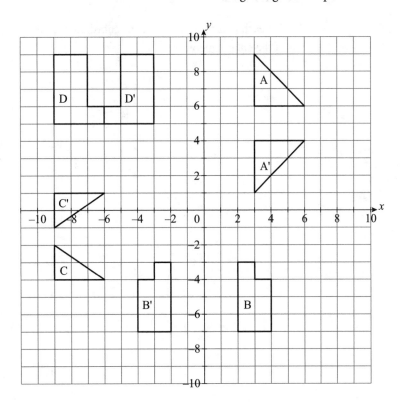

5 Copy the diagram for question 4 and draw the reflection of each shape (A–D) in the *x*-axis.

6 In each of the following, fully describe at least two different transformations that map the object onto its image.

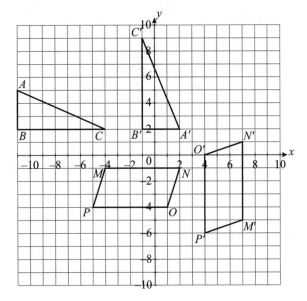

Exercise 23.1 B

REWIND

You dealt with enlargement and scale factors in chapter 21. ◄

You can find the centre of enlargement by drawing lines through the corresponding vertices on the two shapes. The lines will meet at the centre of enlargement.

When the image is smaller than the object, the scale factor of the 'enlargement' will be a fraction.

1   For each pair of shapes, give the coordinates of the centre of enlargement and the scale factor of the enlargement.

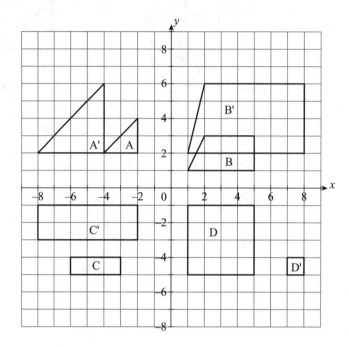

2   Copy each shape onto squared grid paper. Using point X as a centre of enlargement and a scale factor of two, draw the image of each shape under the given enlargement.

(a)
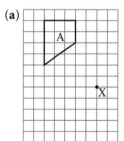

(b)
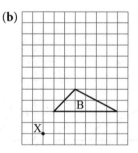

(c)
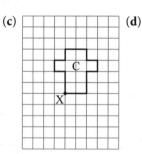

(d)
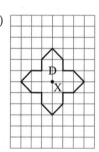

Exercise 23.1 C

1 Triangle *ABC* is to be reflected in the *y*-axis and its image Δ*A'B'C'* is then to be reflected in the *x*-axis to form Δ*A"B"C"*.

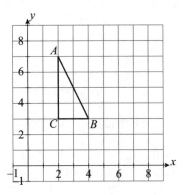

(a) Draw a set of axes, extending them into the negative direction. Copy Δ*ABC* onto your grid and draw the transformations described.

(b) Describe the single transformation that maps Δ*ABC* directly onto Δ*A"B"C"*.

2 Shape A is to be enlarged by a scale factor of two, using the origin as the centre of enlargement, to get shape B. Shape B is then translated, using the column vector $\begin{pmatrix} -8 \\ 1 \end{pmatrix}$, to get shape C.

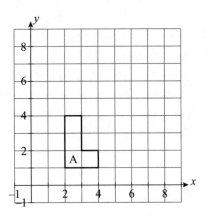

(a) Draw a set of axes, extending the *x*-axis into the negative direction. Copy shape A onto your grid and draw the two transformations described.

(b) What single transformation would have the same results as these two transformations?

3 A trapezium *ABCD* with its vertices at coordinates *A* (2, 4), *B* (3, 4), *C* (3, 1) and *D* (1, 1) is to be reflected in the line *x* = 4. The image is to be reflected in the line *y* = 5.

(a) Draw the shape and show its position after each reflection. Label the final image F′.

(b) Describe the single transformation you could use to transform *ABCD* to F′.

23.2 Vectors

- A vector is a quantity that has both magnitude (size) and direction.
- Vectors can be represented by line segments. The length of the line represents the magnitude of the vector and the arrow on the line represents the direction of the vector. A vector represented by line segment AB starts at A and extends in the direction of B.
- The notation $\mathbf{a}$, $\mathbf{b}$, $\mathbf{c}$ or $\mathbf{AB}$, $\overrightarrow{AB}$ is used for vectors.
- Vectors can also be written as column vectors in the form $\begin{pmatrix} x \\ y \end{pmatrix}$.

  A column vector represents a translation (how the point at one end of the vector moves to get to the other end of the line).

  The column vector $\begin{pmatrix} 1 \\ 2 \end{pmatrix}$ represents a translation one unit in the x-direction and two units in the y-direction.
- Vectors are equal if they have the same magnitude and the same direction.
- The negative of a vector is the vector with the same magnitude but the opposite direction. So, the negative of $\mathbf{a}$ is $-\mathbf{a}$ and the negative of $\overrightarrow{AB}$ is $\overrightarrow{AB}$.
- Vectors cannot be multiplied by each other, but they can be multiplied by a scalar (a number).

  Multiplying any vector $\begin{pmatrix} x \\ y \end{pmatrix}$ by a scalar k, gives $\begin{pmatrix} kx \\ ky \end{pmatrix}$.
- Vectors can be added and subtracted using the 'nose-to-tail' method or triangle rule, so:

  $\begin{pmatrix} x_1 \\ y_1 \end{pmatrix} + \begin{pmatrix} x_2 \\ y_2 \end{pmatrix} = \begin{pmatrix} x_1 + x_2 \\ y_1 + y_2 \end{pmatrix}$.

  To subtract vectors, you need to remember that subtracting a vector is the same as adding its negative.

  So $\overrightarrow{AB} - \overrightarrow{CA} = \overrightarrow{AB} + \overrightarrow{AC}$
- You can use Pythagoras' theorem to find the magnitude (length) of a vector. If the vector is $\begin{pmatrix} x \\ y \end{pmatrix}$ then its magnitude is $\sqrt{x^2 + y^2}$. The notation $|\mathbf{a}|$ or $|\overrightarrow{AB}|$ is used to represent the magnitude of the vector.
- A vector that starts from the origin (O) is called a position vector. If $\overrightarrow{OA}$ is a position vector, then the coordinates of O must be $(0, 0)$ and the coordinates of point A have to be the same as the components of the column vector $\overrightarrow{OA}$.
- You can use position vectors to find the magnitude of any related vector because you know the coordinates of the points. You can then use Pythagoras to work out the lengths of the sides of a related right-angled triangle.

Exercise 23.2 A

Remember, a scalar is a quantity without direction, basically just a number or measurement.

Remember, equal vectors have the same magnitude and direction; negative vectors have the same magnitude and opposite directions.

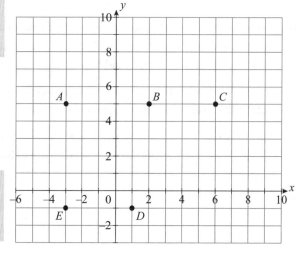

1 Using the points on the grid, express each of the following as a column vector:

(a) $\overrightarrow{AB}$ (b) $\overrightarrow{BC}$

(c) $\overrightarrow{AE}$ (d) $\overrightarrow{BD}$

(e) $\overrightarrow{DB}$ (f) $\overrightarrow{EC}$

(g) $\overrightarrow{CD}$ (h) $\overrightarrow{BE}$

(i) What is the relationship between $\overrightarrow{BE}$ and $\overrightarrow{CD}$?

(j) What is $\overrightarrow{AB} + \overrightarrow{BC}$?

(k) What is $\overrightarrow{AE} - \overrightarrow{AB}$?

(l) Is $\overrightarrow{BC} = \overrightarrow{ED}$?

Remember, A is the object and A' is the image.

2 Represent the following vectors on squared paper.

(a) $\overrightarrow{AB} = \begin{pmatrix} 2 \\ 3 \end{pmatrix}$ (b) $\overrightarrow{CD} = \begin{pmatrix} -1 \\ 4 \end{pmatrix}$ (c) $\overrightarrow{EF} = \begin{pmatrix} 4 \\ 5 \end{pmatrix}$ (d) $\overrightarrow{GH} = \begin{pmatrix} 3 \\ -4 \end{pmatrix}$

3 Find the column vector that describes the translation from the object to its image in each of the following examples.

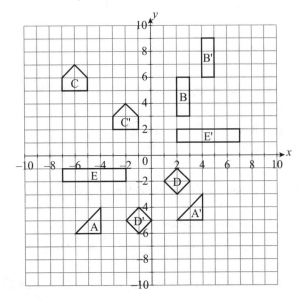

Exercise 23.2 B

1 Given that $\mathbf{a} = \begin{pmatrix} 1 \\ 3 \end{pmatrix}$, $\mathbf{b} = \begin{pmatrix} -2 \\ 4 \end{pmatrix}$ and $\mathbf{c} = \begin{pmatrix} 0 \\ -3 \end{pmatrix}$, find:

(a) $4\mathbf{b}$ (b) $2\mathbf{a}$ (c) $-4\mathbf{c}$ (d) $\mathbf{a} + \mathbf{b}$ (e) $\mathbf{b} + \mathbf{c}$
(f) $\mathbf{a} + \mathbf{b} + \mathbf{c}$ (g) $2\mathbf{a} + 3\mathbf{b}$ (h) $4\mathbf{b} - 2\mathbf{c}$ (i) $-4\mathbf{a} - 2\mathbf{b}$ (j) $2\mathbf{a} - 4\mathbf{b} + 2\mathbf{c}$

2 The diagram shows the pattern on a floor tile. The tiles are squares divided into four congruent triangles by the intersecting diagonals of each square.

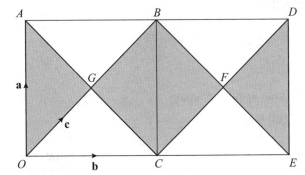

The vectors $\overrightarrow{OA} = \mathbf{a}$, $\overrightarrow{OC} = \mathbf{b}$ and $\overrightarrow{OG} = \mathbf{c}$ are shown. Use this information to write each of the following in terms of $\mathbf{a}$, $\mathbf{b}$ and $\mathbf{c}$.

(a) $\overrightarrow{DE}$ (b) $\overrightarrow{AD}$ (c) $\overrightarrow{AG}$ (d) $\overrightarrow{OB}$
(e) $\overrightarrow{OE}$ (f) $\overrightarrow{CD}$ (g) $\overrightarrow{BF} + \overrightarrow{FD}$ (h) $\overrightarrow{DE} + \overrightarrow{EF}$
(i) $4\overrightarrow{BF} - 3\overrightarrow{EF}$ (j) $\frac{1}{2}\overrightarrow{OC} + 3\overrightarrow{GB}$

Tip

If you cannot remember the rule for finding the magnitude of a vector, then draw the vector on a grid as the hypotenuse of a right-angled triangle. You will quickly see how to work out its length using Pythagoras' theorem.

3 Draw any position vector $\overrightarrow{OA}$ = a on a set of axes and then indicate:

  (a) –a   (b) 4a   (c) $\frac{1}{2}$a   (d) –2a   (e) $-\frac{1}{2}$a

4 The following vectors are drawn on a 1 cm squared grid. Calculate the magnitude of each vector in centimetres. Give your answers correct to two decimal places:

  (a) $\overrightarrow{MD} = \begin{pmatrix} 4 \\ 5 \end{pmatrix}$ (b) $\overrightarrow{PQ} = \begin{pmatrix} -2 \\ 7 \end{pmatrix}$

  (c) $\overrightarrow{XY} = \begin{pmatrix} 9 \\ -12 \end{pmatrix}$ (d) $\overrightarrow{ST} = \begin{pmatrix} -13 \\ -12 \end{pmatrix}$

5 Point O is the origin. Point X is (1, 5), point Y is (3, –4) and point Z is (–7, –4). Find the value of:

  (a) $|\overrightarrow{OX}|$ (b) $|\overrightarrow{OY}|$
  (c) $|\overrightarrow{OZ}|$ (d) $|\overrightarrow{XY}|$

6 Given the position vectors $\overrightarrow{OA} = \begin{pmatrix} -6 \\ 2 \end{pmatrix}$, $\overrightarrow{OB} = \begin{pmatrix} -2 \\ -4 \end{pmatrix}$ and $\overrightarrow{OC} = \begin{pmatrix} 5 \\ 1 \end{pmatrix}$:

  (a) give the coordinates of points A, B and C

  (b) express vectors $\overrightarrow{AB}$, $\overrightarrow{BC}$ and $\overrightarrow{CA}$ as column vectors.

7 In $\triangle XYZ$, $\overrightarrow{XY}$ = x and $\overrightarrow{YZ}$ = y. M is the midpoint of $\overrightarrow{XY}$. Express $\overrightarrow{XZ}$, $\overrightarrow{ZX}$ and $\overrightarrow{MZ}$ in terms of x and y.

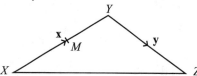

Tip

When two vectors are equal they have the same magnitude and direction, hence the lines associated with them are equal and parallel.

Vectors with the same direction are parallel, even if they do not have the same magnitude.

8 a $= \begin{pmatrix} 1 \\ 2 \end{pmatrix}$, b $= \begin{pmatrix} 3 \\ 0 \end{pmatrix}$ and c $= \begin{pmatrix} -2 \\ 5 \end{pmatrix}$.

  (a) Write a column vector for **x**, **y** and **z**, if:

    (i) x = a + b + c
    (ii) y = a – 2b – c
    (iii) z = 3a + b – 2c

  (b) Calculate and give your answers to three significant figures:

    (i) |x| (ii) |y| (iii) |2z|

Tip

Draw a diagram to represent this situation and then apply the vector calculations.

9 In this triangle, X and Y are the midpoints of AB and AC respectively. D is the midpoint of XY, $\overrightarrow{AX}$ = **a** and $\overrightarrow{AY}$ = **b**.

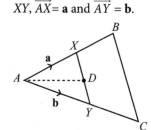

(a) Express these vectors in terms of **a** and **b**, giving your answers in their simplest form.

    (i) $\overrightarrow{XY}$ (ii) $\overrightarrow{AD}$ (iii) $\overrightarrow{BC}$

(b) Show that $XY \parallel BC$ and is half its length.

10 Carlos jogged for 40 minutes at a steady pace of 9 km/h in a north-easterly direction. He then walked westwards until he was due north of his starting point, where he stopped for lunch. If Carlos jogged home travelling due south at the same pace as he set off, how many minutes did the last leg of his journey take him? (Give your answer to one decimal place.)

23.3 Further transformations

- A shear is a transformation that keeps one line of a shape fixed (invariant) and moves all other points on the shape parallel to the invariant line.
  - The distance that the points move is proportional to the distance of the points from the invariant line, the constant of proportionality is called the shear factor.
  - To describe a shear you need to give the shear factor and state which line is invariant.
- A one-way stretch is a transformation that enlarges the shape in one-direction, perpendicular to an invariant line.
  - The distance that the points move from the invariant line is proportional to their original distance from the invariant line, the constant of proportionality is called the scale factor.
  - To describe a one-way stretch you need to give the scale factor and state which line is invariant.
- A two-way stretch is a combination of two one-way stretches at 90° to each other.
  - The only invariant point on the object is the point where the two perpendicular invariant lines cross (think of this as the origin of the stretch – one stretch is then in y direction and the other is in x direction).
  - A two-way stretch affects both the x and y-coordinates of each point by the respective scale factors.

Exercise 23.3

1 Draw the image of each shape after the given transformation.

    (a) Shear factor = 1.5, $x = 0$ is invariant.   (b) Shear factor = 1, $y = 0$ is invariant.

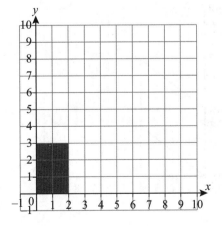 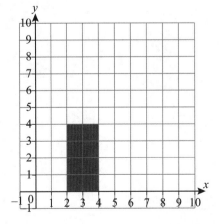

Tip

- You can think of a one-way stretch as a shear perpendicular to the invariant line.
- A scale factor $k < 1$ reduces the size of the shape in a stretch and the image will be closer to (rather than further from) the invariant line.

(c) Shear factor = 3, *y*-axis is invariant. **(d)** Stretch, scale factor = 2, *y*-axis is invariant.

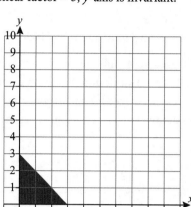
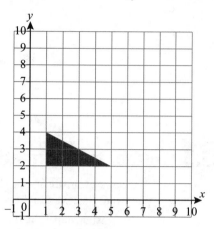

2 Describe the single transformation that maps each object onto its image.

(a)

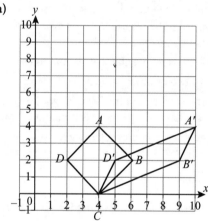

(b)

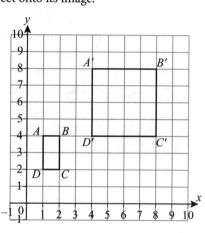

(c)

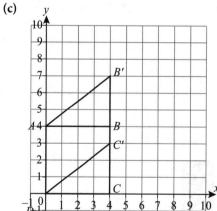

(d)

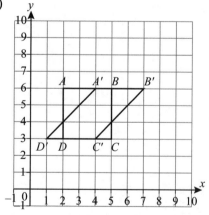

23.4 Matrices and matrix transformation

- A matrix is an array of numbers. The numbers in the matrix are called the elements of the matrix.
- The order of matrix is the number of rows multiplied by the number of columns. So a matrix with three rows and four columns has an order of 3×4.
- Matrices of the same order can be added and subtracted. To do this, add or subtract the corresponding elements of the two matrices to find the solution (which will be a matrix of the same order as the originals).
- Matrices can be multiplied by scalars (numbers). Multiply each element of the matrix by the scalar. Your answer will be a matrix of the same order as the original.
- You can multiply two matrices ($A \times B$) only if the number of columns in **A** is equal to the number of rows in **B**. The elements of a row in **A** are multiplied by the corresponding elements of a column in **B** and the products added – the result goes into a position equivalent to the row number of **A** and the column number of **B**. This is repeated for all combinations of rows from **A** with columns from **B**.
- The square 2×2 matrix $I = \begin{pmatrix} 1 & 0 \\ 0 & 1 \end{pmatrix}$ is called the *identity* matrix. When you multiply a 2×2 matrix **A** by I or I by a 2×2 matrix **A** then $AI = A$ and $IA = A$.
- The square 2×2 matrix $O = \begin{pmatrix} 0 & 0 \\ 0 & 0 \end{pmatrix}$ is called the *zero* matrix for 2×2 matrices. Multiplication by the zero matrix is equal to the zero matrix (each element is multiplied by 0, giving 0 all round).
- For any 2×2 matrix $A = \begin{pmatrix} a & b \\ c & d \end{pmatrix}$ the calculation $(ad - bc)$ is called the *determinant* of the matrix. The symbol $|A|$ denotes the determinant of **A**.
- You cannot divide matrices, but you can find the inverse of a non-singular matrix. Just as a number × its inverse = 1, a matrix × its inverse = **I** (the *identity* matrix). The inverse of matrix **A** is denoted by A^{-1}, so $A \times A^{-1} = I$ (where the inverse exists).
- For $A = \begin{pmatrix} a & b \\ c & d \end{pmatrix}$, $A^{-1} = \frac{1}{(ad - bc)} \begin{pmatrix} d & -b \\ -c & a \end{pmatrix}$. The multiplier $\frac{1}{(ad - bc)}$ is the reciprocal of the determinant of the matrix and the elements of the matrix in the multiplication are found by swapping elements a and d and changing the sign of elements b and c of the original matrix **A**.
- When $ad = bc$, then $\frac{1}{(ad - bc)} = \frac{1}{0}$. Because $\frac{1}{0}$ is undefined (you cannot divide by 0), the matrix has no inverse and it is called a singular matrix.

Exercise 23.4

1 Given $A = \begin{pmatrix} -1 & 2 & 3 \\ 4 & 3 & -3 \end{pmatrix}$ and $B = \begin{pmatrix} 1 & 4 & 2 \\ 3 & -1 & 0 \end{pmatrix}$, find:

   (a) $A + B$ (b) $A - B$ (c) $B - A$.

2 $D = \begin{pmatrix} 1 & 4 \\ 5 & 8 \end{pmatrix}$.

   (a) Find the determinant of **D**.
   (b) Find D^{-1}

3 Given $\mathbf{A} = \begin{pmatrix} 3 & 0 \\ 1 & -2 \end{pmatrix}$ and $\mathbf{B} = \begin{pmatrix} 1 & 3 \\ -4 & 2 \end{pmatrix}$.

(a) Show by calculation that $\mathbf{AB} \neq \mathbf{BA}$

(b) Find:

    (i) $|\mathbf{A}|$ (ii) $|\mathbf{AB}|$

4 Given $\mathbf{A} = \begin{pmatrix} 1 & -3 & 0 \\ 4 & 2 & -1 \end{pmatrix}$ and $\mathbf{B} = \begin{pmatrix} 6 & 3 & -3 \\ 7 & -2 & 5 \end{pmatrix}$, find:

(a) $\mathbf{A} + \mathbf{B}$ (b) $3\mathbf{A}$ (c) $-2\mathbf{B}$

5 Given that $\mathbf{C} = \begin{pmatrix} 2 & x \\ 1 & 4 \end{pmatrix}$ and $|\mathbf{C}| = 5$.

(a) Find the value of x.

(b) Find $\mathbf{C}^{-1}$.

23.5 Matrices and transformations

- Column vectors can be used to represent translations on a grid and 2×2 matrices can represent reflection, rotation, enlargement, stretch and shear transformations.

- To find the image of any point you multiply the matrix by the position vector of the point. (Remember the position vector of a point $\begin{pmatrix} x \\ y \end{pmatrix}$ gives you the coordinates (x, y) of the point.)

- To find what 2×2 matrix represents a given transformation:
  - select the points $(1, 0)$ and $(0, 1)$
  - find the images of these points under the given transformation
  - write down the position vectors of these images
  - the position vector of the image of the first point becomes the first column and the position vector of the image of the second point is the second column of the required matrix.

- For combined transformations represented by two matrices (transformation by $\mathbf{A}$ and then by $\mathbf{B}$), the matrix product $\mathbf{BA}$ describes the combined transformation. Note that the order of multiplication is very important in matrices because $\mathbf{AB} \neq \mathbf{BA}$.

Exercise 23.5

> **Tip**
>
> You don't need to know the matrices that represent different transformations from memory but you must be able to work them out and use them to describe transformations.

1 For both pairs of shapes:

    (i) describe fully the transformation that maps shape A onto shape B

    (ii) find the 2×2 matrix that represents each transformation.

(a)

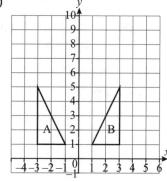

(b)

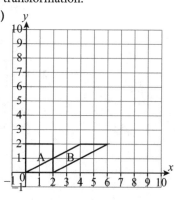

2 A square with vertices at $P\,(0, 0)$, $Q\,(0, 2)$, $R\,(2, 2)$ and $S\,(2, 0)$ is transformed by the matrix $\begin{pmatrix} 1 & 0 \\ 0 & 4 \end{pmatrix}$.

    (a) Find the coordinates of vertex R' under this transformation.

    (b) Describe the transformation in words.

3 The transformation T is defined by the matrix $\mathbf{A}$ where $\mathbf{A} = \begin{pmatrix} 3 & 0 \\ 0 & 3 \end{pmatrix}$

    (a) Describe the transformation T in words.

    (b) A second transformation, T2, is represented by the matrix $\mathbf{B}$ where $\mathbf{B} = \begin{pmatrix} -1 & 0 \\ 0 & 1 \end{pmatrix}$. Find the matrix that represents the combined transformation $\mathbf{BA}$.

4 Find the matrix that represents the combined transformation reflection in the x-axis followed by an enlargement of scale factor 3 about the origin.

Mixed exercise

1

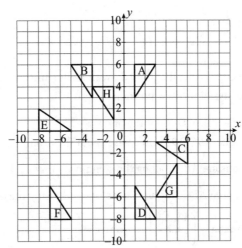

    (a) Describe a single transformation that maps triangle A onto:

        (i) triangle B   **(ii)** triangle C   **(iii)** triangle D.

    (b) Describe the pair of transformations that you could use to map triangle A onto:

        (i) triangle E   **(ii)** triangle F   **(iii)** triangle G   **(iv)** triangle H.

2 Sally translated parallelogram *DEFG* along the column vector $\begin{pmatrix} -4 \\ 5 \end{pmatrix}$ and then rotated it 90° clockwise about the origin to get the image $D'E'F'G'$ shown on the grid.

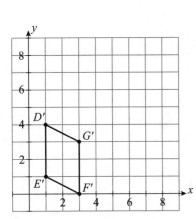

    (a) Draw a diagram and reverse the transformations Sally performed on the shape to show the original position of *DEFG*.

    (b) Enlarge *DEFG* by a scale factor of 2 using the origin as the centre of enlargement. Label your enlargement $D''E''F''G''$.

3 Square *ABCD* is shown on the grid.

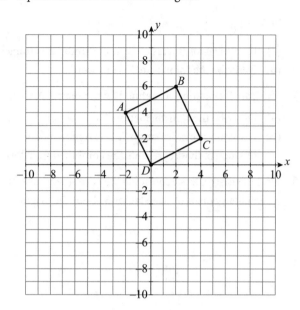

Onto a copy of the diagram, draw the following transformations and, in each case, give the coordinates of the new position of vertex *B*.

(a) Reflect *ABCD* about the line $x = -2$.

(b) Rotate *ABCD* 90° clockwise about the origin.

(c) Translate *ABCD* along the column vector $\begin{pmatrix} -3 \\ 2 \end{pmatrix}$.

(d) Enlarge *ABCD* by a scale factor of 1.5 using the origin as the centre of enlargement.

4 Given that $\mathbf{a} = \begin{pmatrix} 3 \\ 6 \end{pmatrix}$, $\mathbf{b} = \begin{pmatrix} 2 \\ -4 \end{pmatrix}$ and $\mathbf{c} = \begin{pmatrix} -2 \\ -4 \end{pmatrix}$,

(a) find:

    (i) $2\mathbf{a}$ (ii) $\mathbf{b} + \mathbf{c}$ (iii) $\mathbf{a} - \mathbf{b}$ (iv) $2\mathbf{a} + 3\mathbf{b}$

(b) Draw four separate vector diagrams on squared paper to represent:

    (i) $\mathbf{a}, 2\mathbf{a}$ (ii) $\mathbf{b}, \mathbf{c}, \mathbf{b} + \mathbf{c}$ (iii) $\mathbf{a}, \mathbf{b}, \mathbf{a} - \mathbf{b}$ (iv) $\mathbf{a}, \mathbf{b}, 2\mathbf{a} + 3\mathbf{b}$

5 *ABCDEF* is a regular hexagon with centre *O*. $\overrightarrow{FA} = \mathbf{x}$ and $\overrightarrow{AB} = \mathbf{y}$.

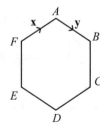

(a) Express the following vectors in terms of **x** and **y**.

    (i) $\overrightarrow{ED}$ (ii) $\overrightarrow{DE}$ (iii) $\overrightarrow{FB}$

    (iv) $\overrightarrow{EF}$ (v) $\overrightarrow{FD}$

(b) If the coordinates of point *E* are (0, 0) and the coordinates of point *B* are (4, 2). Calculate $|\overrightarrow{EB}|$ correct to three significant figures.

6 Describe the following transformations.

(a)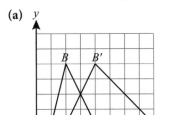

(b)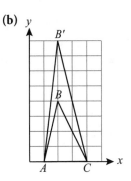

(c)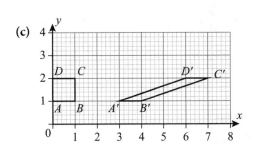

(d)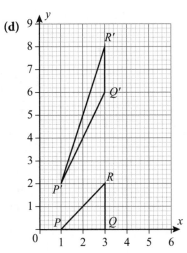

7 Draw the image of *ABCD* under a stretch of scale factor $\frac{1}{2}$ with the *x*-axis invariant.

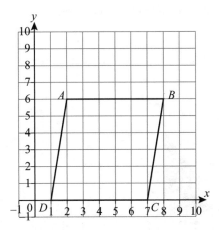

8 Draw the image of *ABCD* under a shear of factor 3 with $y = 0$ invariant.

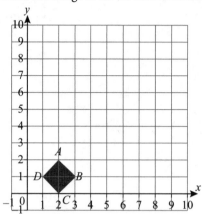

9 $P = \begin{pmatrix} 1 & 2 \\ 2 & 1 \end{pmatrix}$ and $Q = \begin{pmatrix} 1 & 3 \\ 2 & 2 \end{pmatrix}$. Calculate:

(a) **P + Q**

(b) **P − Q**

(c) **PQ**

(d) **QP**

(e) **|P|**

(f) **P−I**

10 Given $\begin{pmatrix} 2 & 5 & a \\ 3 & 4 & 6 \\ -2 & 4 & -1 \end{pmatrix} \begin{pmatrix} a \\ b \\ 3 \end{pmatrix} = \begin{pmatrix} 45 \\ 47 \\ c \end{pmatrix}$, find the values of *a*, *b* and *c*.

11 Copy the diagram onto a set of axes.

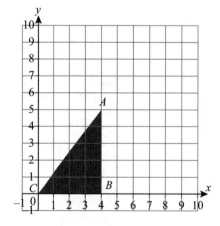

(a) Draw the image of *ABC* after reflection in the *x*-axis.

(b) Write down the 2 × 2 matrix **A** that represents this transformation.

(c) Enlarge the image *A′B′C′* by a scale factor of 2 with centre of enlargement at (0, 0)

(d) Write down the 2 × 2 matrix **B** that represents this transformation.

(e) Find the matrix of the combined transformation **A** followed by **B**.

24 Probability using tree diagrams

24.1 Using tree diagrams to show outcomes

- A probability tree shows all the possible outcomes for simple combined events.
- Each line segment or branch represents one outcome. The end of each branch segment is labelled with the outcome and the probability of each outcome is written on the branch.

! Tip

Remember, for independent events
$P(A \text{ and then } B) = P(A) \times P(B)$ and for mutually exclusive events
$P(A \text{ or } B) = P(A) + P(B)$.

Exercise 24.1

1 Anita has four cards. They are yellow, red, green and blue. She draws a card at random and then tosses a coin. Draw a tree diagram to show all possible outcomes.

2 The spinner shown has numbers on an inner circle and letters on an outer ring. When spun, it gives a result consisting of a number and a letter. Draw a tree diagram to show all possible outcomes when you spin it.

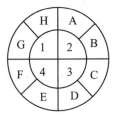

3 A tin contains eight green counters and four yellow counters. One counter is drawn and not replaced, and then another is drawn from the bag.

 (a) Draw a tree diagram to show the possible outcomes for drawing two counters.

 (b) Label the branches to show the probability of each event.

24.2 Calculating probability from tree diagrams

- To determine the probability of a combination of outcomes, multiply along each of the consecutive branches. If several combinations satisfy the same outcome conditions, then add the probabilities of the different paths.
- The sum of all the probabilities on a set of branches must equal one.

Exercise 24.2

1 When a coloured ball is drawn from a bag, a coin is tossed once or twice, depending on the colour of the ball drawn. There are three blue balls, two yellow balls and a black ball in the bag. The tree diagram shows the possible outcomes.

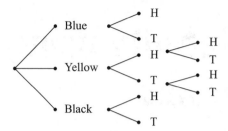

(a) Copy and label the diagram to show the probability of each event. Assume the draw of the balls is random and the coin is fair.

(b) Calculate the probability of a blue ball and a head.

(c) Calculate the probability of a yellow ball and two heads.

(d) Calculate the probability that you will not get heads at all.

2 The tree diagram below shows the possible outcomes when two coins are tossed.

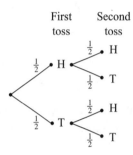

(a) Copy and the tree diagram to show the possible outcomes when a third coin is tossed.

(b) Calculate the probability of tossing three heads.

(c) Calculate the probability of getting at least two tails.

(d) Calculate the probability of getting fewer heads than tails.

(e) Calculate the probability of getting an equal number of heads and tails.

Mixed exercise

1 Dineo is playing a game where she rolls a normal six-sided die and tosses a coin. If the score on the die is even, she tosses the coin once. If the score on the die is odd, she tosses the coin twice.

(a) Draw a tree diagram to show all possible outcomes.

(b) Assuming the die and the coin are fair and all outcomes are equally likely, label the branches with the correct probabilities.

(c) What is the probability of obtaining two tails?

(d) What is the probability of obtaining a five, a head and a tail (in any order)?

2 A bag contains two 5c and five 10c coins. You are asked to draw a coin from the bag at random without replacing any until you get a 10c coin.

(a) Draw a probability tree to show the possible outcomes.

(b) Label the branches to show the probability of each event.

(c) Calculate the probability of getting a 10c on your first draw.

(d) What is the probability of drawing the two 5c coins before you draw a 10c coin?

(e) If you draw two 5c coins on your first two draws, what is the probability of getting a 10c coin on your third draw? Why?

> **Tip**
> This is an example of conditional probability. The first coin is removed and not replaced, leaving fewer possible outcomes for the second coin in each case.

Answers

Chapter 1

Exercise 1.1

1

Number	Natural	Integer	Prime	Fraction
−0.2				✓
−57		✓		
3.142				✓
0				
$0.\dot{3}$				✓
1	✓	✓		
51	✓	✓		
10 270	✓	✓		
$-\frac{1}{4}$				✓
$\frac{2}{7}$				✓
$\sqrt{9}$	✓	✓	✓	
11	✓	✓	✓	
$\sqrt[3]{512}$	✓	✓		

2 **(a)** 121, 144, 169, 196, ...

(b) $\frac{1}{4}, \frac{1}{6}, \frac{2}{7}, \frac{2}{9}$, etc.

(c) 83, 89, 97, 101, ...

(d) 2, 3, 5, 7

Exercise 1.2 A

1 **(a)** 18 **(b)** 36 **(c)** 90
(d) 24 **(e)** 36 **(f)** 24
(g) 72 **(h)** 96

2 **(a)** 6 **(b)** 18 **(c)** 9
(d) 3 **(e)** 10 **(f)** 1
(g) 12 **(h)** 50

Exercise 1.2 B

1 18 m

2 120 shoppers

3 20 students

4 after 420 seconds; 21 laps (Francesca), 5 laps (Ayuba) and 4 laps (Claire)

5 **(a)** 1024 cm² **(b)** 200 tiles

Exercise 1.3

1 **(a)** 2, 3, 5, 7
(b) 53, 59
(c) 97, 101, 103

2 **(a)** $2 \times 2 \times 3 \times 3$
(b) 5×13
(c) $2 \times 2 \times 2 \times 2 \times 2 \times 2$
(d) $2 \times 2 \times 3 \times 7$
(e) $2 \times 2 \times 2 \times 2 \times 5$
(f) $2 \times 2 \times 2 \times 5 \times 5 \times 5$
(g) $2 \times 5 \times 127$
(h) 13×151

3 **(a)** LCM = 378, HCF = 1
(b) LCM = 255, HCF = 5
(c) LCM = 864, HCF = 3
(d) LCM = 848, HCF = 1
(e) LCM = 24 264, HCF = 2
(f) LCM = 2574, HCF = 6
(g) LCM = 35 200, HCF = 2
(h) LCM = 17 325, HCF = 5

Exercise 1.4

1 square: 121, 144, 169, 196, 225, 256, 289
cube: 125, 216

2 **(a)** 7 **(b)** 5 **(c)** 14
(d) 10 **(e)** 3 **(f)** 25
(g) $\frac{3}{4}$ **(h)** 5 **(i)** 2
(j) 5 **(k)** $1\frac{3}{4}$ **(l)** 12
(m) −5 **(n)** $\frac{5}{6}$ **(o)** 6

3 **(a)** 23 cm **(b)** 529 cm²

Exercise 1.5

1 −3 °C

2 **(a)** −2 °C **(b)** −9 °C **(c)** −12 °C

3 **(a)** 4 **(b)** 7 **(c)** −1
(d) −2 **(e)** −3

Exercise 1.6

1 **(a)** 26 **(b)** 66
(c) 23.2 **(d)** 15.66
(e) 3.39 **(f)** 2.44
(g) 3.83 **(h)** 2.15
(i) 1.76 **(j)** 2.79
(k) 7.82 **(l)** 0.21
(m) 8.04 **(n)** 1.09
(o) 8.78 **(p)** 304.82
(q) 94.78 **(r)** 0.63

(s) 4.03 **(t)** 6.87
(u) 6.61 **(v)** 3.90
(w) −19.10 **(x)** 20.19

Exercise 1.7

1

	(i)	(ii)	(iii)
(a)	5.65	5.7	6
(b)	9.88	9.9	10
(c)	12.87	12.9	13
(d)	0.01	0.0	0
(e)	10.10	10.1	10
(f)	45.44	45.4	45
(g)	14.00	14.0	14
(h)	26.00	26.0	26

2 **(a)** 53 200 **(b)** 713 000
(c) 17.4 **(d)** 0.00728

3 **(a)** 36 **(b)** 5.2
(c) 12 000 **(d)** 0.0088
(e) 430 000 **(f)** 120
(g) 0.0046 **(h)** 10

Mixed exercise

1 natural: 24, 17

rational: $-\frac{3}{4}, 0.65, 3\frac{1}{2}, 0.66$

integer: 24, −12, 0, 17

prime: 17

2 **(a)** two are prime: 2 and 3
(b) $2 \times 2 \times 3 \times 3$
(c) 2 and 36 **(d)** 36

3 **(a)** $2 \times 2 \times 7 \times 7$
(b) $3 \times 3 \times 5 \times 41$
(c) $2 \times 2 \times 3 \times 3 \times 5 \times 7 \times 7$

4 14th and 28th March

5 **(a)** true **(b)** true
(c) false **(d)** false

6 **(a)** 5 **(b)** 5
(c) 64 **(d)** 145

7 **(a)** 16.07 **(b)** 9.79 **(c)** 13.51
(d) 11.01 **(e)** 0.12 **(f)** −7.74

8 **(a)** 1240 **(b)** 0.765
(c) 0.0238 **(d)** 31.5

9 **(a)** It is not strictly possible – to have a tile of 790 cm², the builders must be using rounded values.

(b) 28.1 cm
(c) 110 tiles

Chapter 2

Exercise 2.1

1 (a) $3(x+2)$ (b) $6(x-1)$
  (c) $2(11+x)$ (d) $18x$
  (e) $3x^2+4$ (f) x^2+8
  (g) $\frac{1}{5}-x$ (h) $x+\frac{1}{3}$
  (i) $4+3x$ (j) $12-5x$

2 (a) $p+5$ (b) $p-4$ (c) $4p$

3 (a) $\$\frac{x}{3}$

  (b) $\$\frac{x}{9}, \$\frac{2x}{9}$, and $\$\frac{2x}{3}$

Exercise 2.2

1 (a) $54\,\text{cm}^2$ (b) $1.875\,\text{m}^2$
  (c) $110.25\,\text{cm}^2$ (d) $8\,\text{cm}^2$

2 -104

3 17

4 17.75

5 (a) 6 (b) 91

Exercise 2.3

1 (a) $3x^2-2x+3$
  (b) $4x^2y-2xy$
  (c) $5ab-4ac$
  (d) $4x^2+5x-y-5$
  (e) $-30mn$ (f) $6x^2y$
  (g) $6xy^3$ (h) $-4x^3y$
  (i) $4b$ (j) $\frac{1}{4y}$
  (k) $3b$ (l) $\frac{9m}{4}$
  (m) $\frac{20y}{3x}$ (n) $\frac{3x^2}{y}$
  (o) $\frac{2y^2}{x^2}$ (p) $\frac{y^2}{2}$
  (q) $\frac{15a^2}{4}$ (r) $\frac{-14y}{5}$
  (s) $\frac{x}{6y}$ (t) $\frac{27x^2}{10}$

Exercise 2.4

1 (a) $2x^2-4x$ (b) $xy-3x$
  (c) $-2x-2$ (d) $-3x+2$
  (e) $-2x^2+6x$ (f) $3x+1$
  (g) x^3-2x^2-x (h) x^2+x+2

2 (a) $x^2+\frac{x}{2}$ (b) x^2+xy

  (c) $-8x^3+4x^2+2x$ (d) $\frac{x}{2}+\frac{3y}{2}$
  (e) $-2x^2+8x$ (f) $3x^2-6x$
  (g) $-5x^2-6x$

Exercise 2.5 A

1 (a) $\frac{x^6}{y^2}$ (b) $3x^4y$
  (c) $\frac{2x^2}{3y}$ (d) xy^{10}
  (e) $\frac{5x^9}{2y^3}$ (f) x^7y^3
  (g) $\frac{50x^3}{27y}$ (h) $\frac{49}{25x^3y}$
  (i) x^7y (j) $\frac{8x^{10}y^3}{3}$
  (k) $\frac{x^{16}}{y^{16}}$ (l) $\frac{3125x^4y^2}{16}$

2 (a) $\frac{x^8}{y^2}$ (b) $\frac{x^5}{y^4}$
  (c) $\frac{8}{x^5y^7}$ (d) $\frac{1}{x^9}$
  (e) $\frac{y^{16}}{x^{22}}$ (f) $\frac{y^{22}}{2x^4}$

3 (a) $x^{\frac{1}{2}}$ (b) $x^{\frac{8}{15}}$
  (c) $x^{\frac{1}{6}}$ (d) $x^{\frac{1}{9}}$
  (e) $8x^3$ (f) $2x^3y^{\frac{1}{3}}$
  (g) $x^{\frac{1}{2}}y^4$ (h) x^3y^{-1} or $\frac{x^3}{y}$
  (i) x^3 (j) $x^{-2}y^{-4}$ or $\frac{1}{x^2y^4}$
  (k) y^{-2} or $\frac{1}{y^2}$

4 (a) $x^{\frac{2}{3}}$ (b) x^2
  (c) $y^{\frac{7}{3}}$ (d) x^2
  (e) $x^{\frac{3}{4}}y^2$ (f) $x^{-\frac{1}{4}}y^{-\frac{29}{16}}$ or $\frac{1}{x^{\frac{1}{4}}y^{\frac{29}{16}}}$

Exercise 2.5 B

1 (a) -1296 (b) -1 (c) $\frac{8}{3}$
  (d) 2 (e) $\frac{1}{4}$ (f) $\frac{1}{625}$
  (g) 32 (h) 4 (i) $\frac{3}{2}$
  (j) $\frac{3}{2}$

2 (a) 17 (b) 65
  (c) 15 (d) -163

3 (a) $\frac{1}{4}$ (b) 4 (c) -4
  (d) $\frac{3}{4}$ (e) 2 (f) 2
  (g) 2 (h) $\frac{3}{2}$

Mixed exercise

1 (a) $x+12$ (b) $x-4$
  (c) $5x$ (d) $\frac{x}{3}$
  (e) $4x$ (f) $\frac{x}{4}$
  (g) $12-x$ (h) x^3-x

2 (a) -6 (b) 24 (c) $\frac{-14}{9}$

3 (a) -2 (b) $\frac{2}{3}$ (c) 5
  (d) 7 (e) -2

4 (a) $9a+b$
  (b) x^2+3x-2
  (c) $-4a^4b+6a^2b^3$
  (d) $-7x+4$
  (e) $\frac{4x}{y}$
  (f) $5x-\frac{5y}{2}$

5 (a) $11x-3$
  (b) $6x^2+15x-8$
  (c) $-2x^2+5x+12$
  (d) $-x^3+3x^2-x+5$

6 (a) $\frac{5x^5}{6}$ (b) 15
  (c) $\frac{1}{x^4}$ (d) $16x^4y^8$
  (e) $\frac{64x^9}{y^{15}}$ (f) x^9y^8
  (g) $\frac{27x^4}{4y^3}$ (h) $\frac{xy^6}{2}$

7 (a) $5xy^{\frac{1}{3}}$ (b) $x^{\frac{1}{2}}$
  (c) $x^{-9}y$ or $\frac{y}{x^9}$
  (d) $2x^{-\frac{1}{3}}y^{\frac{5}{3}}$ or $\frac{2y^{\frac{5}{3}}}{x^{\frac{1}{3}}}$

Chapter 3

Exercise 3.1 A

1 (a) (i) $150°$ (ii) $180°$ (iii) $135°$
  (b) $45°$

(c) (i) 810°   **(ii)** 72°
(d) quarter to one or 12:45

2 No. If the acute angle is ≤ 45° it will produce an acute or right angle.

3 Yes. The smallest obtuse angle is 91° and the largest is 179°. Half of those will range from 45.5° to 89.5°, all of which are acute.

4 (a) 45°
(b) $(90 - x)°$
(c) $x°$

5 (a) 135°   **(b)** 90°
(c) $(180 - x)°$ **(d)** $x°$
(e) $(90 + x)°$ **(f)** $(90 - x)°$

Exercise 3.1 B

1 $\angle QON = 48°$, so $a = 48°$ (vertically opposite)

2 (a) $\angle EOD = 41°$ (∠s on line), so $x = 41°$ (vertically opposite)
(b) $x = 20°$ (∠s round point)

Exercise 3.1 C

1 (a) $x = 85°$ (co-int ∠s); $y = 72°$ (alt ∠s)
(b) $x = 99°$ (co-int ∠s); $y = 123°$ ($\angle ABF = 123°$, co-int ∠s then vertically opposite)
(c) $x = 72°$ ($\angle BFE = 72°$, then alt ∠s); $y = 43°$ (∠s in triangle BCJ)
(d) $x = 45°$ (∠s round a point); $y = 90°$ (co-int ∠s)

2 (a) $x = 112°$
(b) $x = 45°$ ($\angle STQ$ corr ∠s then vertically opposite)
(c) $x = 90°$ ($\angle ECD$ and $\angle ACD$ co-int ∠s then ∠s round a point)
(d) $x = 18°$ ($\angle DFE$ co-int with $\angle CDF$ then $\angle BFE$ co-int with $\angle ABF$)
(e) $x = 85°$

Exercise 3.2

1 (a) 103° (∠s in triangle)
(b) 51° (ext ∠ equals sum int opps)
(c) 68° (ext ∠ equals sum int opps)
(d) 53° (base ∠s isosceles)
(e) 60° (equilateral triangle)

(f) $x = 58°$ (base ∠s isosceles and ∠s in triangle); $y = 26°$ (ext ∠s equals sum int opps)
(g) $x = 33°$ (base ∠s isosceles then ext ∠s equals sum int opps)
(h) $x = 45°$ (co-int ∠s then ∠s in triangle)
(i) $x = 45°$ (base ∠s isosceles); $y = 75°$ (base ∠s isosceles)

2 (a) $x = 36°$; so $A = 36°$ and $B = 72°$
(b) $x = 40°$; so $A = 80°$; $B = 40°$ and $\angle ACD = 120°$
(c) $x = 60°$
(d) $x = 72°$

3 $\angle B = 34°$; $\angle C = 68°$

Exercise 3.3

1 (a) square, rhombus
(b) rectangle, square
(c) square, rectangle
(d) square, rectangle, rhombus, parallelogram
(e) square, rectangle
(f) square, rectangle, parallelogram, rhombus
(g) square, rhombus, kite
(h) rhombus, square, kite
(i) rhombus, square, kite

2

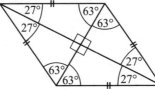

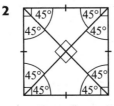

3 (a) $x = 69°$
(b) $x = 64°$
(c) $x = 52°$
(d) $x = 115°$
(e) $x = 30°$; $2x = 60°$; $3x = 90°$
(f) $a = 44°$; $b = 68°$; $c = 44°$; $d = e = 68°$

4 (a) $\angle Q + \angle R = 210°$
(b) $\angle R = 140°$
(c) $\angle Q = 70°$

5 (a) $\angle MNP = 42°$
(b) $\angle MNO = 104°$
(c) $\angle PON = 56°$

Exercise 3.4

1 (a) (i) 1080°   **(ii)** 135°
(b) (i) 1440°   **(ii)** 144°
(c) (i) 2340°   **(ii)** 156°

2 $\dfrac{900}{7} = 128.57°$

3 20 sides

4 (a) 165.6°   **(b)** $\dfrac{360}{14.4} = 25$ sides

5 (a) $x = 156°$
(b) $x = 85°$
(c) $x = 113°$; $y = 104°$

Exercise 3.5

1

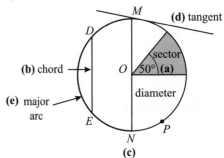

Exercise 3.6

1, 2 student's own diagrams

3 2.1 cm

4 (a) scalene   **(b)** yes

5 6.6 cm

Mixed exercise

1 (a) $x = 113°$
(b) $x = 41°$
(c) $x = 66°$
(d) $x = 74°$; $y = 106°$; $z = 37°$
(e) $x = 46°$; $y = 104°$
(f) $x = 110°$; $y = 124°$
(g) $x = 40°$; $y = 70°$; $z = 70°$
(h) $x = 35°$; $y = 55°$

2 (a) $x = 60 + 60 + 120 = 240°$
(b) $x = 90 + 90 + 135 = 315°$
(c) $x = 80°$

3 **(a)** **(i)** radius   **(ii)** chord
     (iii) diameter
  (b) *AO, DO, OC, OB*
  (c) 24.8 cm
  (d) student's own diagram

4 student's own diagram

5 student's own diagram

Chapter 4

Exercise 4.1

1 **(a)** gender, eye colour, hair colour
  (b) height, shoe size, mass, number of brothers/sisters
  (c) shoe size, number of brothers/sisters
  (d) height, mass
  (e) possible answers include: gender, eye colour, hair colour – collected by observation; height, mass – collected by measuring; shoe size, number of siblings – collected by survey, questionnaire

Exercise 4.2

1

Phone calls	Tally	Frequency
1	/	1
2	//	2
3	//	2
4	LH1	5
5	LH1 ////	9
6	LH1 //	7
7	LH1 /	6
8	///	3
9	///	3
10	//	2

2 **(a)**

No. of mosquitoes	0	1	2	3	4	5	6
Frequency	7	6	9	7	8	7	6

  (b) It is impossible to say; frequency is very similar for all numbers of mosquitoes.

3 **(a)**

Score	Frequency
0–29	1
30–39	1
40–49	7
50–59	19
60–69	12
70–79	6
80–100	4

  (b) 10   **(c)** 2   **(d)** 26
  (e) There are very few marks at the low and high end of the scale.

4 **(a)**

Eye colour	Brown	Blue	Green
Male	4	0	1
Female	2	1	2

  (b)

Hair colour	Brown	Black	Blonde
Male	2	2	1
Female	1	4	0

No. of brothers/sisters	0	1	2	3	4
Male	0	1	1	2	1
Female	2	1	1	1	0

  (c) student's own sentences

Exercise 4.3

1 **(a)** pictogram
  (b) number of students in each year group in a school
  (c) 30 students
  (d) half a stick figure
  (e) 225
  (f) Year 11; 285
  (g) rounded; unlikely the year groups will all be multiples of 15

2 student's own pictogram

3 **(a)** number of boys and girls in Class 10A
  (b) 18   **(c)** 30
  (d) the favourite sports of students in Class 10A, separated by gender
  (e) athletics
  (f) athletics
  (g) 9

4 **(a)** student's own chart
  (b) student's own chart

5 **(a)** cars   **(b)** 17%   **(c)** 20
  (d) handcarts and bicycles

6 **(a)** student's own chart
  (b) 6   **(c)** 50   **(d)** C

7 **(a)** 26 °C
  (b) May–Nov
  (c) northern hemisphere
  (d) No
  (e) 35 mm
  (f) April
  (g) none

Mixed exercise

1 **(a)** survey or questionnaire
  (b) discrete; you cannot have half a child
  (c) quantitative; it can be counted
  (d)

No. of children in family	0	1	2	3	4	5	6
Frequency	7	10	11	12	5	2	1

  (e) student's own chart
  (f) student's own chart

2 student's own pictogram

3 **(a)** compound bar chart
  (b) It shows how many people, out of every 100, have a mobile phone and how many have a land line phone.
  (c) No. The figures are percentages.
  (d) Canada, USA and Denmark
  (e) Germany, UK, Sweden and Italy
  (f) Denmark
  (g) own opinion with reason

4 **(a)** Student's own chart
  (b) Student's own chart
  (c) Student's own chart

5 **(a)**

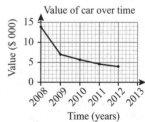

  (b) 49.6%
  (c) $3900

Chapter 5

Exercise 5.1

1 (a) $x = 65$ (b) $x = 168$ (c) $x = 55$
(d) $x = 117$ (e) $x = 48$ (f) $x = 104$

Exercise 5.2

1 (a) $\frac{25}{8}$ (b) $\frac{17}{11}$ (c) $\frac{59}{5}$

(d) $\frac{15}{4}$ (e) $\frac{59}{4}$ (f) $\frac{25}{9}$

2 (a) $\frac{108}{5}$ (b) $\frac{63}{13}$ (c) 14

(d) $\frac{28}{5}$ (e) 3 (f) $\frac{6}{19}$

(g) 120 (h) $\frac{3}{14}$ (i) 72

(j) 3 (k) $\frac{233}{50}$ (l) $\frac{7}{4}$

3 (a) $\frac{13}{24}$ (b) $\frac{19}{60}$ (c) $\frac{19}{21}$

(d) $\frac{35}{6}$ (e) $\frac{183}{56}$ (f) $\frac{161}{20}$

(g) $\frac{18}{65}$ (h) $\frac{41}{40}$ (i) $\frac{29}{21}$

(j) $\frac{-5}{6}$ (k) $\frac{-10}{3}$ (l) $\frac{-26}{9}$

4 (a) 24 (b) $\frac{96}{7}$ (c) $\frac{7}{96}$

(d) $\frac{10}{27}$ (e) $\frac{10}{9}$ (f) $\frac{9}{14}$

(g) 2 (h) $\frac{3}{5}$ (i) 4

5 (a) $\frac{38}{9}$ (b) $\frac{4}{5}$ (c) $\frac{39}{7}$

(d) $\frac{19}{4}$ (e) $\frac{5}{12}$ (f) $\frac{215}{72}$

(g) 0 (h) $\frac{11}{170}$ (i) $\frac{187}{9}$

6 (a) $525 (b) $375

7 (a) 300
(b) 6 hours 56 min

Exercise 5.3 A

1 (a) 16.7% (b) 62.5% (c) 29.8%
(d) 30% (e) 4% (f) 47%
(g) 112% (h) 207%

2 (a) $\frac{1}{8}$ (b) $\frac{1}{2}$ (c) $\frac{49}{50}$

(d) $\frac{3}{5}$ (e) $\frac{11}{50}$

3 (a) 83% (b) 60% (c) 7%
(d) 37.5% (e) 125% (f) 250%

4 (a) 60 kg (b) $24
(c) 150 litres (d) 55 ml
(e) $64 (f) £19.50
(g) 18 km (h) 0.2 grams
(i) $2.08 (j) 475 cubic metres

5 (a) +20% (b) −10%
(c) +53.3% (d) +3.3%
(e) −28.3% (f) +33.3%
(g) +2566.7%

6 (a) $54.72 (b) $945
(c) $32.28 (d) $40 236
(e) $98.55 (f) $99.68

7 (a) $58.48 (b) $520
(c) $83.16 (d) $19 882
(e) $76.93 (f) $45.24

Exercise 5.3 B

1 28 595 tickets

2 1800 shares

3 $129 375

4 21.95%

5 $15 696

6 $6228

7 2.5 grams

8 $\frac{7}{25}$ = 28% increase, so $7 more is better

Exercise 5.3 C

1 $50

2 (a) 1200 (b) 960

3 $150

4 (a) $12 (b) 27 750 (c) $114 885

Exercise 5.4 A

1 (a) 4.5×10^4 (b) 8×10^5
(c) 8×10 (d) 2.345×10^6
(e) 4.19×10^6 (f) 3.2×10^{10}
(g) 6.5×10^{-3} (h) 9×10^{-3}
(i) 4.5×10^{-4} (j) 8×10^{-7}
(k) 6.75×10^{-3} (l) 4.5×10^{-10}

2 (a) 2500 (b) 39 000
(c) 426 500 (d) 0.00001045
(e) 0.00000915 (f) 0.000000001

(g) 0.000028 (h) 94 000 000
(i) 0.00245

Exercise 5.4 B

1 (a) 6.56×10^{-17}
(b) 1.28×10^{-14}
(c) 1.44×10^{13}
(d) 1.58×10^{-20}
(e) 5.04×10^{18}
(f) 1.98×10^{12}
(g) 1.52×10^{17}
(h) 2.29×10^8
(i) 4.50×10^{-3}

2 (a) 12×10^{30}
(b) 4.5×10^{11}
(c) 3.375×10^{36}
(d) 1.32×10^{-11}
(e) 2×10^{26}
(f) 2.67×10^5
(g) 1.2×10^2
(h) 2×10^{-3}
(i) 2.09×10^{-8}

3 (a) the Sun (b) 6.051×10^6

4 (a) 500 seconds = 5×10^2 seconds
(b) 19 166.67 seconds = 1.92×10^4 seconds

Exercise 5.5

1 (a) $4 \times 5 = 20$
(b) $70 \times 5 = 350$
(c) $1000 \times 7 = 7000$
(d) $42 \div 6 = 7$

2 (a) 20 (b) 3
(c) 12 (d) 243

Mixed exercise

1 (a) 40 (b) 6
(c) 22 (d) 72

2 (a) $\frac{4}{5}$ (b) $\frac{2}{3}$ (c) $\frac{2}{3}$

3 (a) $\frac{1}{6}$ (b) 63 (c) $\frac{5}{3}$

(d) $\frac{3}{44}$ (e) $\frac{31}{48}$ (f) $\frac{71}{6}$

(g) $\frac{361}{16}$ (h) $\frac{334}{45}$ (i) $\frac{68}{15}$

(j) $\frac{14}{9}$

4 (a) $760 (b) $40 000

5 $10\,000

6 (a) 720   (b) 11 779

7 67.9%

8 (a) $5.9 \times 10^9\,\text{km}$
   (b) $5.753 \times 10^9\,\text{km}$

9 (a) $9.4637 \times 10^{12}\,\text{km}$
   (b) 1.6×10^{-5} light years
   (c) $3.975 \times 10^{13}\,\text{km}$

Chapter 6

Exercise 6.1

1 (a) $-2x - 2y$ (b) $-5a + 5b$
   (c) $6x - 3y$ (d) $8x - 4xy$
   (e) $-2x^2 - 6xy$ (f) $-9x + 9$
   (g) $12 - 6a$ (h) $3 - 4x - y$
   (i) 3 (j) $-3x - 7$
   (k) $2x^2 - 2xy$ (l) $-3x^2 + 6xy$

2 (a) $14x - 2y - 9x$
   (b) $-5xy + 10x$
   (c) $6x - 6y - 2xy$
   (d) $-2x - 6y - xy$
   (e) $12xy - 14 - y + 3x$
   (f) $4x^2 - 2x^2y - 3y$
   (g) $-2x^2 + 2x + 5$
   (h) $6x^2 + 4y - 8xy$
   (i) $-5x - 3$

Exercise 6.2

1 (a) $x = 3$ (b) $x = 4$
   (c) $x = \dfrac{9}{2} = 4\dfrac{1}{2}$ (d) $x = 4$
   (e) $x = \dfrac{36}{10} = \dfrac{18}{5} = 3\dfrac{3}{5}$ (f) $x = 5$
   (g) $x = 2$ (h) $x = -5$
   (i) $x = 4$ (j) $x = -\dfrac{3}{2} = -1\dfrac{1}{2}$
   (k) $x = \dfrac{11}{2} = 5\dfrac{1}{2}$ (l) $x = 3$

2 (a) $x = 10$ (b) $x = -2$
   (c) $x = -\dfrac{8}{3} = -2\dfrac{2}{3}$ (d) $x = \dfrac{4}{3} = 1\dfrac{1}{3}$
   (e) $x = 8$ (f) $x = \dfrac{1}{4}$
   (g) $x = -4$ (h) $x = -9$
   (i) $x = -10$ (j) $x = -13$
   (k) $x = -34$ (l) $x = \dfrac{20}{13} = 1\dfrac{7}{13}$

3 (a) $x = 18$ (b) $x = 27$
   (c) $x = 24$ (d) $x = -44$

(e) $x = 17$ (f) $x = \dfrac{23}{6} = 3\dfrac{5}{6}$

(g) $x = -1$ (h) $x = \dfrac{9}{2} = 4\dfrac{1}{2}$

(i) $x = -\dfrac{1}{3}$ (j) $x = 9$

(k) $x = \dfrac{16}{13} = 1\dfrac{3}{13}$ (l) $x = 10$

(m) $x = 42$ (n) $x = \dfrac{-11}{2}$

Exercise 6.3

1 (a) 3 (b) 8 (c) 5
   (d) a (e) $3y$ (f) $5ab$
   (g) $4xy$ (h) pq (i) $7ab$
   (j) xy^2z (k) ab^3 (l) $3xy$

2 (a) $12(x + 4)$ (b) $2(1 + 4y)$
   (c) $4(a - 4)$ (d) $x(3 - y)$
   (e) $a(b + 5)$ (f) $3(x - 5y)$
   (g) $8xz(3y - 1)$ (h) $3b(3a - 4c)$
   (i) $2y(3x - 2z)$ (j) $2x(7 - 13y)$

3 (a) $x(x + 8)$ (b) $a(12 - a)$
   (c) $x(9x + 4)$ (d) $2x(11 - 8x)$
   (e) $2b(3ab + 4)$ (f) $18xy(1 - 2x)$
   (g) $3x(2 - 3x)$ (h) $2xy^2(7x - 3)$
   (i) $3abc^2(3c - ab)$ (j) $x(4x - 7y)$
   (k) $b^2(3a - 4c)$ (l) $7ab(2a - 3b)$

4 (a) $(3 + y)(x + 4)$
   (b) $(y - 3)(x + 5)$
   (c) $(a + 2b)(3 - 2a)$
   (d) $(2a - b)(4a - 3)$
   (e) $(2 - y)(x + 1)$
   (f) $(x - 3)(x + 4)$
   (g) $(2 + y)(9 - x)$
   (h) $(2b - c)(4a + 1)$
   (i) $(x - 6)(3x - 5)$
   (j) $(x - y)(x - 2)$
   (k) $(2x + 3)(3x + y)$
   (l) $(x - y)(4 - 3x)$

Exercise 6.4 A

1 $m = \dfrac{D}{k}$

2 $c = y - mx$

3 $b = \dfrac{P + c}{a}$

4 $b = \dfrac{a - c}{x}$

5 (a) $a = c - b$ (b) $a = 2c + 3b$
   (c) $a = \dfrac{c + d}{b}$ (d) $a = \dfrac{d - c}{b}$
   (e) $a = bc - d$ (or $a = -d + bc$)

(f) $a = d + bc$ (g) $a = \dfrac{cd - b}{2}$

(h) $a = \dfrac{de - c}{b}$ (i) $a = \dfrac{e + d}{bc}$

(j) $a = \dfrac{ef - d}{bc}$ (k) $a = \dfrac{c(f - de)}{b}$

(l) $a = \dfrac{d(e - c)}{b}$ (m) $a = \dfrac{d}{c} + b$

(n) $a = \dfrac{d}{c} - 2b$

Exercise 6.4 B

1 (a) $b = \dfrac{P}{2} - l$ (b) $b = 35.5\,\text{cm}$

2 (a) $r = \dfrac{C}{2\pi}$ (b) $9\,\text{cm}$ (c) $46\,\text{cm}$

3 use $b = \dfrac{2A}{h} - a$; $b = 3.8\,\text{cm}$

4 (a) (i) $70\,\text{kg}$ (ii) $12\,\text{kg}$
   (b) $11\,656\,\text{kg}$
   (c) $\dfrac{T - 70P}{12} = B$
   (d) $960\,\text{kg}$

5 (a) $t = \sqrt{\dfrac{m}{5}}$ (b) 6 seconds

Mixed exercise

1 (a) $x = -3$ (b) $x = -6$
   (c) $x = 9$ (d) $x = -6$
   (e) $x = 2$ (f) $x = -13$
   (g) $x = 1.5$ (h) $x = 5$

2 (a) $x = \dfrac{m + r}{np}$ (b) $x = \dfrac{mq - p}{n}$

3 (a) $3x + 2$ (b) $-12x^2 + 8x$
   (c) $-8x + 4y - 6$ (d) $-16y + 2y^2$
   (e) $11x + 5$ (f) $5x^2 + 7x - 4$
   (g) $-2x^2 + 11x$ (h) $10x^2 + 24x$

4 (a) $4(x - 2)$ (b) $3(4x - y)$
   (c) $-2(x + 2)$ (d) $3x(y - 8)$
   (e) $7xy(2xy + 1)$ (f) $(x - y)(2 + x)$
   (g) $(4 + 3x)(x - 3)$
   (h) $4x(x + y)(x - 2)$

5 (a) $4(x - 7) = 4x - 28$
   (b) $2x(x + 9) = 2x^2 + 18x$
   (c) $4x(4x + 3y) = 16x^2 + 12xy$
   (d) $19x(x + 2y) = 19x^2 + 38xy$

6 (a) $x = 15°$
   (b) $x = 26°$
   (c) $x = 30°$

Chapter 7

Exercise 7.1 A

1 (a) 120 mm   (b) 45 cm
   (c) 128 mm   (d) 98 mm
   (e) 36.2 cm   (f) 233 mm

2 (a) 15.7 m   (b) 44.0 cm
   (c) 54.0 mm   (d) 21.6 m
   (e) 18.8 m   (f) 151 mm
   (g) 24.4 cm

3 90 m

4 $164 \times 45.50 = \$7462$

5 9 cm each

6 about 88 cm

7 (a) 197.82 cm   (b) 219.8 cm

Exercise 7.1 B

1 (a) 332.5 cm²   (b) 1.53 m²
   (c) 399 cm²   (d) 150 cm²
   (e) 59.5 cm²   (f) 71.5 cm²
   (g) 2296 mm²   (h) 243 cm²
   (i) 7261.92 cm²

2 (a) 7850 mm²   (b) 153.86 mm²
   (c) 7693 mm²   (d) 17.44 cm²
   (e) 167.47 cm²

3 (a) 288 cm²   (b) 82 cm²
   (c) 373.5 cm²   (d) 581.5 cm²
   (e) 366 cm²   (f) 39 cm²
   (g) 272.93 cm²   (h) 4000 cm²
   (i) 5639.63 cm²

4 (a) 30 cm²   (b) 90 cm²
   (c) 33.6 cm²   (d) 61.2 cm²
   (e) 720 cm²   (f) 2562.5 cm²

5 11.1 m²

6 70 mm = 7 cm

Exercise 7.1 C

1 (a) 43.96 mm   (b) 47.1 cm
   (c) 8.37 mm

2 6668.31 km

3 (a) 75.36 cm²   (b) 732.67 cm²
   (c) 92.34 mm²

4 61.33 cm²

Exercise 7.2

1 (a) cube
   (b) cuboid
   (c) square-based pyramid
   (d) octahedron

2 (a) cuboid
   (b) triangular prism
   (c) cylinder

3 The following are examples; there are other possible nets.

(a)

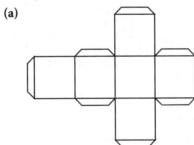

(b)

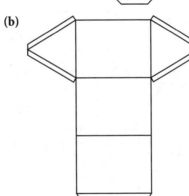

(c)

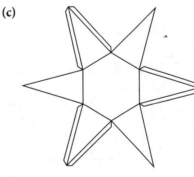

(d)

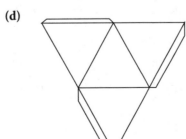

Exercise 7.3 A

1 (a) 2.56 mm²   (b) 523.2 m²
   (c) 13.5 cm²   (d) 401.92 mm²

2 (a) 384 cm²   (b) 8 cm

3 (a) 340 cm²   (b) 153 000 cm²
   (c) 4 tins

4 (a) 90 000 mm³   (b) 60 cm³
   (c) 20 410 mm³   (d) 1120 cm³
   (e) 960 cm³   (f) 5.76 m³
   (g) 1800 cm³   (h) 1.95 m³

5 332.5 cm³

6 (a) 224 m³   (b) 44 people

7 211.95 m³

8 various answers – for example:

Volume (mm³)	64 000	64 000	64 000	64 000
Length (mm)	80	50	100	50
Breadth (mm)	40	64	80	80
Height (mm)	20	20	8	16

Exercise 7.3 B

1 (a) 5.28 cm³   (b) 33 493.33 m³
   (c) 25.2 cm³   (d) 169.56 cm³
   (e) 65 111.04 mm³

2 (a) (i) 1.08×10^{12} km³
     (ii) 5.10×10^{8} km²
   (b) 1.48×10^{8} km²

Mixed exercise

1 (a) 346.19 cm²   (b) 65.94 cm

2 4.55 cm

3 (a) 2000 mm²   (b) 33 000 mm²
   (c) 40 cm²   (d) 80 cm²
   (e) 106 cm²   (f) 35 cm²
   (g) 175.84 cm²

4 15 m

5 (a) cuboid is smaller
   (b) 14 240 mm³
   (c) student's own diagram
   (d) cylinder 7536 mm², cuboid 9000 mm²

6 42

7 volume cone = 23.55 cm³
   volume pyramid = 30 cm³
   difference = 6.45 cm³

8 volume 3 balls = 1144.53 cm³
volume tube = 1860.39 cm³
space = 715.86 cm³

Chapter 8

Exercise 8.1

1 (a) red $=\frac{3}{10}$, white $=\frac{9}{25}$, green $=\frac{17}{50}$

(b) 30%   (c) 1   (d) $\frac{1}{3}$

2 (a) 0.61, 0.22, 0.11, 0.05, 0.01
(b) (i) highly likely
(ii) unlikely
(iii) highly unlikely

Exercise 8.2

1 (a) 1, 2, 3, 4, 5, 6, 7, 8, 9 or 10

(b) (i) $\frac{1}{10}=0.1$ (ii) 1 (iii) $\frac{3}{10}$

(iv) $\frac{3}{10}$ (v) $\frac{2}{5}$ (vi) $\frac{1}{2}$

(vii) $\frac{3}{10}$ (viii) $\frac{9}{10}$ (ix) 0

2 (a) $\frac{2}{5}$
(b) no sugar; probability $=\frac{3}{5}$

3 (a) $\frac{1}{4}$ (b) $\frac{1}{2}$

(c) $\frac{1}{2}$

4 (a) $\frac{1}{3}$ or 0.33   (b) $\frac{1}{2}$ or 0.5

(c) $\frac{1}{6}$ or 0.16

5 (a) $\frac{7}{20}$ (b) $\frac{1}{2}$ (c) $\frac{2}{5}$

(d) $\frac{3}{10}$ (e) $\frac{1}{5}$

6 $\frac{13}{40}$

Exercise 8.3

1 0.73

2 $\frac{5}{8}$

3 (a) 0.16   (b) 0.84   (c) 0.6
(d) strawberry 63, lime 66, lemon 54, blackberry 69, apple 48

4 (a) 0.6   (b) 0.97   (c) 11
(d) 114

Exercise 8.4

1

	H	T
H	HH	HT
T	HT	TT

(a) $\frac{3}{4}$ (b) $\frac{1}{4}$

2 (a)

		Yellow		
		1	**2**	**3**
Green	**1**	1, 1	1, 2	1, 3
	2	2, 1	2, 2	2, 3
	3	3, 1	3, 2	3, 3

(b) 9   (c) $\frac{1}{3}$ (d) $\frac{1}{3}$

3 (a)

	Snack		
Drink	cola, biscuit	cola, cake	cola, muffin
	fruit juice, biscuit	fruit juice, cake	fruit juice, muffin
	water, biscuit	water, cake	water, muffin

(b) $\frac{1}{9}$ (c) $\frac{2}{3}$

Exercise 8.5

1 (a)

	A	U	A
C	CA	CU	CA
L	LA	LU	LA
C	CA	CU	CA
T	TA	TU	TA
T	TA	TU	TA

(b) $\frac{4}{15}$ (c) $\frac{1}{5}$ (d) $\frac{14}{15}$

2 (a) $\frac{1}{15}$ (b) $\frac{2}{15}$ (c) $\frac{1}{45}$

(d) $\frac{1}{30}$ (e) $\frac{7}{15}$ (f) $\frac{2}{5}$

(g) $\frac{3}{10}$

3 (a) $\frac{5}{17}$ (b) $\frac{28}{153}$ (c) $\frac{40}{153}$

(d) $\frac{40}{153}$

(e) The four situations represent all the possible outcomes, so they must add up to one.

Mixed exercise

1 (a) 10 000   (b) heads 0.4083; tails 0.5917
(c) $\frac{1}{2}$
(d) could be – probability of the tails outcome is higher than the heads outcome for a great many tosses

2 (a) $\frac{1}{2}$ (b) $\frac{2}{5}$ (c) $\frac{1}{10}$

(d) 0   (e) $\frac{9}{10}$ (f) $\frac{9}{10}$

(g) $\frac{1}{2}$

3 (a) $\frac{1}{36}$ (b) 7, $\frac{1}{6}$

(c) $\frac{1}{2}$ (d) $\frac{1}{6}$

4 (a)

	$1	$1	$1	50c	50c	$5	20c	20c
$5	6	6	6	5.5	5.5	10	5.2	5.2
$5	6	6	6	5.5	5.5	10	5.2	5.2
$5	6	6	6	5.5	5.5	10	5.2	5.2
$5	6	6	6	5.5	5.5	10	5.2	5.2
$2	3	3	3	2.5	2.5	7	2.2	2.2
50c	1.5	1.5	1.5	1	1	5.5	0.7	0.7
50c	1.5	1.5	1.5	1	1	5.5	0.7	0.7

(b) $\frac{3}{14}$ (c) $\frac{1}{4}$ (d) $\frac{35}{56}$

5 $\frac{1}{8}$

6 $\frac{1}{3}$

Chapter 9

Exercise 9.1

1 (a) 17, 19, 21 (add 2)
(b) 121, 132, 143 (add 11)
(c) 8, 4, 2 (divide by 2)
(d) 40, 48, 56 (add 8)
(e) −10, −12, −14 (subtract 2)
(f) 2, 4, 8 (multiply by 2)

(g) 11, 16, 22 (add one more each time than added to previous term)

(h) 21, 26, 31 (add 5)

2 (a) 7, 9, 11, 13

(b) 37, 32, 27, 22

(c) $1, \frac{1}{2}, \frac{1}{4}, \frac{1}{8}$

(d) 5, 11, 23, 47

(e) 100, 47, 20.5, 7.25

3 (a) 5, 7, 9 $T_{35} = 73$

(b) 1, 4, 9 $T_{35} = 1225$

(c) 5, 11, 17 $T_{35} = 209$

(d) 0, 7, 26 $T_{35} = 42874$

(e) 0, 2, 6 $T_{35} = 1190$

(f) 1, −1, −3 $T_{35} = -67$

4 (a) $8n - 6$ **(b)** 1594   **(c)** 30th

(d) $T_{18} = 138$ and $T_{19} = 146$, so 139 is not a term

5 (a) $2n + 5$ $T_{50} = 105$

(b) $3 - 8n$ $T_{50} = -397$

(c) $6n - 4$ $T_{50} = 296$

(d) n^2 $T_{50} = 2500$

(e) $1.2n + 1.1$ $T_{50} = 61.1$

6 (a)

n	1	2	3	4	5	6
T_n	6	11	6	21	26	31

(b) $T_n = 5n + 1$

(c) 496   **(d)** 55th

Exercise 9.2

1 (a) $\sqrt[3]{16}, \sqrt{12}, 0.090090009\ldots$

(b) $\sqrt{45}, \sqrt[3]{90}, \pi, \sqrt{8}$

2 (a) $\frac{4}{9}$ **(b)** $\frac{74}{99}$ **(c)** $\frac{79}{90}$

(d) $\frac{103}{900}$ **(e)** $\frac{943}{999}$ **(f)** $\frac{928}{4995}$

Exercise 9.3 A

1 (a) false   **(b)** true   **(c)** false

(d) true   **(e)** false   **(f)** true

(g) false   **(h)** true

2 (a) The set of even number from two to twelve.

(b) 6

(c) {2}

(d) {2, 4, 6, 8}

(e) {2}

(f) {10, 12}

3 (a) {}

(b) {1, 3, 5, 6, 7, 9, 11, 12, 13, 15, 18}

(c) {1, 3, 5, 7, 9, 11, 13, 15}

(d) {1, 2, 4, 5, 6, 7, 8, 10, 11, 12, 13, 14, 16, 17, 18, 19, 20}

(e) {2, 4, 6, 8, 10, 12}

(f) {1, 2, 3, 4, 5, 6, 7, 8, 9, 10, 11, 12, 13, 15, 18}

4 (a) {−2, −1, 0, 1, 2}

(b) {1, 2, 3, 4, 5}

5 (a) {x: x is even, $x \le 10$}

(b) {x: x is square numbers, $x \le 25$}

Exercise 9.3 B

1

2 (a) 9

(b) 20

(c) {c, h, i, s, y}

(d) {c, e, h, i, m, p, r, s, t, y}

(e) {a, b, d, f, g, j, k, l, n, o, q, u, v, w, x, z}

(f) {c, h, i, s, y}

3 (a)

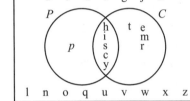

(b) 21   **(c)** 0.57

Mixed exercise

1 (a) $5n - 4$ $T_{120} = 596$

(b) $26 - 6n$ $T_{120} = -694$

(c) $3n - 1$ $T_{120} = 359$

2 (a) −4, −2, 0, 2, 4, 8

(b) 174

(c) T_{46}

3 $0.213231234\ldots, \sqrt{2}, 4\pi$

4 (a) $\frac{23}{99}$ **(b)** $\frac{286}{999}$

5 (a)

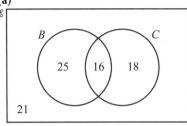

(b) 21   **(c)** 16

(d) (i) $\frac{17}{40}$ **(ii)** $\frac{41}{80}$ **(iii)** $\frac{1}{5}$

(iv) $\frac{59}{80}$ **(v)** $\frac{21}{80}$

Chapter 10

Exercise 10.1

1 (a)

x	−1	0	1	2	3
y	4	5	6	7	8

(b)

x	−1	0	1	2	3
y	1	−1	−3	−5	−7

(c)

x	−1	0	1	2	3
y	9	7	5	3	1

(d)

x	−1	0	1	2	3
y	−1	−2	−3	−4	−5

(e)

x	4	4	4	4	4
y	−1	0	1	2	3

(in fact, any five values of y are correct)

(f)

x	−1	0	1	2	3
y	−2	−2	−2	−2	−2

(g)

x	−1	0	1	2	3
y	1.5	−0.5	−2.5	−4.5	−6.5

(h)

x	−1	0	1	2	3
y	−1.2	−0.8	−0.4	0	0.4

(i)

x	−1	0	1	2	3
y	−1	−0.5	0	0.5	1

(j)

x	−1	0	1	2	3
y	0.5	−0.5	−1.5	−2.5	−3.5

2 student's graphs of values above

3 $y = x - 2$

4 (a) no   (b) yes   (c) yes

    (d) no   (e) no   (f) no

    (g) yes (horizontal lines)

    (h) yes (vertical lines)

5 (a) $m=1$ (b) $m=-1$

    (c) $m=-1$ (d) $m=\frac{6}{7}$

    (e) $m=2$ (f) $m=0$

    (g) undefined

    (h) $m=\frac{1}{16}$

6 (a) $m=3, c=-4$

    (b) $m=-1, c=-1$

    (c) $m=-\frac{1}{2}, c=5$

    (d) $m=1, c=0$

    (e) $m=\frac{1}{2}, c=\frac{1}{4}$

    (f) $m=\frac{4}{5}, c=-2$

    (g) m is undefined, $c=7$

    (h) $m=-3, c=0$

    (i) $m=-\frac{1}{3}, c=+\frac{14}{3}$

    (j) $m=-1, c=-4$

    (k) $m=1, c=-4$

    (l) $m=-2, c=5$

    (m) $m=-2, c=-20$

7 (a) $y=-x$ (b) $y=\frac{1}{2}x$

    (c) $y=2.5$ (d) $y=-2x-1$

    (e) $y=\frac{1}{2}x-1$ (f) $y=2x+1$

    (g) $x=2$ (h) $y=-\frac{1}{3}x+2$

    (i) $y=-2x$ (j) $y=x+4$

    (k) $y=3x-2$ (l) $y=x-3$

8 (a) $x=2, y=-6$

    (b) $x=6, y=3$

    (c) $x=-4, y=6$

    (d) $x=10, y=10$

    (e) $x=\frac{-5}{2}, y=-5$

9 (a) 1   (b) 1   (c) −1

    (d) 2   (e) 0   (f) $\frac{1}{2}$

10 (a) $(0,0)$ (b) $(-1.5, 0.5)$

    (c) $(-2, 3)$ (d) $(5, 10)$

    (e) $(0.5, -3)$ (f) $(1, 1.5)$

Exercise 10.2 A

1 (a) x^2+5x+6 (b) x^2-x-6

    (c) $x^2+12x+35$ (d) $x^2+2x-35$

    (e) x^2-4x+3 (f) $2x^2+x-1$

    (g) $y^2-9y+14$

    (h) $6x^2-7xy+2y^2$

    (i) $2x^4-x^2-3$

    (j) $x^2+x-132$

    (k) $1-\frac{1}{4}x^2$

    (l) $-3x^2+11x-6$

    (m) $-12x^2+14x-4$

2 (a) $x^2+8x+16$

    (b) x^2-6x+9

    (c) $x^2+10x+25$

    (d) y^2-4y+4

    (e) $x^2+2xy+y^2$

    (f) $4x^2-4xy+y^2$

    (g) $9x^2-12x+4$

    (h) $4x^2-12xy+9y^2$

    (i) $4x^2+20x+25$

    (j) $16x^2-48x+36$

    (k) $9-6x+x^2$

    (l) $16-16x+4x^2$

    (m) $36-36y+9y^2$

3 (a) x^2-25

    (b) $4x^2-25$

    (c) $49y^2-9$

    (d) x^4-y^4

    (e) $9x^2-16$

    (f) x^6-4y^4

    (g) $16x^4y^4-4z^4$

    (h) $4x^8-4y^2$

    (i) $16x^2y^4-25y^2$

    (j) $64x^6y^4-49z^4$

Exercise 10.2 B

1 (a) $(x+2)(x+2)$

    (b) $(x+4)(x+3)$

    (c) $(x+3)(x+3)$

    (d) $(x+1)(x+4)$

    (e) $(x+3)(x+5)$

    (f) $(x-1)(x-8)$

    (g) $(x-5)(x-3)$

    (h) $(x-1)(x-3)$

    (i) $(x-26)(x-1)$

    (j) $(x-8)(x+1)$

    (k) $(x+5)(x-2)$

    (l) $(x+4)(x-8)$

    (m) $(x-3)(x-4)$

    (n) $(x+4)(x-3)$

    (o) $(x+9)(x-6)$

2 (a) $5(x+2)(x+1)$

    (b) $3(x-4)(x-2)$

    (c) $3x(x-3)(x-1)$

    (d) $5(x-2)(x-1)$

    (e) $x(x+10)(x+2)$

    (f) $x^2y(x+2)(x-1)$

    (g) $x(x+7)(x-2)$

    (h) $3(x-3)(x-2)$

    (i) $-2(x+4)(x-6)$

    (j) $2(x+7)(x-8)$

3 (a) $(x+3)(x-3)$

    (b) $(4+x)(4-x)$

    (c) $(x+5)(x-5)$

    (d) $(7+x)(7-x)$

    (e) $(3x+2y)(3x-2y)$

    (f) $(9-2x)(9+2x)$

    (g) $(x+3y)(x-3y)$

    (h) $(11y+12x)(11y-12x)$

    (i) $(4x+7y)(4x-7y)$

    (j) $2(x+3)(x-3)$

    (k) $2(10+x)(10-x)$

    (l) $(x^2+y)(x^2-y)$

    (m) $(5+x^8)(5-x^8)$

    (n) $(xy+10)(xy-10)$

    (o) $\left(\frac{5x}{y^2}+\frac{8w}{z}\right)\left(\frac{5x}{y^2}-\frac{8w}{z}\right)$

    (p) $(5x^5+1)(5x^5-1)$

    (q) $(1+9x^2y^3)(1-9x^2y^3)$

Exercise 10.2 C

1 (a) $x=0$ or $x=3$

    (b) $x=-2$ or $x=2$

    (c) $x=0$ or $x=2$

    (d) $x=0$ or $x=-\frac{2}{3}$

    (e) $x=-1$ or $x=1$

    (f) $x=-\frac{7}{2}$ or $x=\frac{7}{2}$

    (g) $x=-\frac{1}{2}$ or $x=\frac{1}{2}$

    (h) $x=-4$ or $x=-2$

    (i) $x=-4$ or $x=-1$

(j) $x = 5$ or $x = -1$
(k) $x = 5$ or $x = -4$
(l) $x = -10$ or $x = 2$
(m) $x = 5$ or $x = 3$
(n) $x = 20$ or $x = -3$
(o) $x = 7$ or $x = 8$
(p) $x = 10$
(q) $x = 2$

Mixed exercise

1 (a) $y = \frac{1}{2}x$

x	−1	0	2	3
y	−0.5	0	1	1.5

(b) $y = -\frac{1}{2}x + 3$

x	−1	0	2	3
y	3.5	3	2	1.5

(c) $y = 2$

x	−1	0	2	3
y	2	2	2	2

(d) $y - 2x - 4 = 0$

x	−1	0	2	3
y	2	4	8	10

All four plotted on the same graph.

2 (a) $m = -2, c = -1$
(b) $m = 1, c = -6$
(c) $m = 1, c = 8$
(d) $m = 0, c = -\frac{1}{2}$
(e) $m = -\frac{2}{3}, c = 2$
(f) $m = -1, c = 0$

3 (a) $y = x - 3$ **(b)** $y = -\frac{2}{3}x + \frac{1}{2}$
(c) $y = -x - 2$ **(d)** $y = -\frac{4}{5}x - 3$
(e) $y = 2x - 3$ **(f)** $y = -x + 2$
(g) $y = 2$ **(h)** $x = -4$

4 $A\ 0, B\ 1, C\ 2, D\ 1, E\ 4$

5 (a) $y = -2x - 6$ **(b)** $y = 7$
(c) $y = \frac{4}{3}x + 4$ **(d)** $x = -10$
(e) $y = -x$ **(f)** $y = -3$

6 (a)

t	0	2	4	6
D	0	14	28	42

(b)

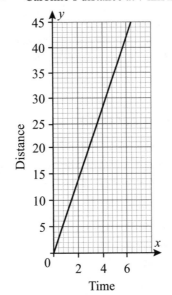

Caroline's distance at 7 km/h

(c) $y = 7x$ **(d)** 7
(e) (i) 3 hours   **(ii)** 1 h 24 min
     (iii) 48 min
(f) (i) 21 km   **(ii)** 17.5 km
     (iii) 5.25 km
(g) 7 hours

7

	(a)	(b)
(i)	1	(0.5, 6.5)
(ii)	2	(0, 5)
(iii)	−1	(1, 3)
(iv)	$-\frac{4}{3}$	(−0.5, 3)
(v)	undefined	(−1.5, 0.25)

8 (a) $x^2 - 16x + 64$
(b) $2x^2 - 2$
(c) $9x^2 - 12xy + 4y^2$
(d) $1 - 12y + 36y^2$
(e) $9x^2 - 4$
(f) $4x^2 + 20x + 25$
(g) $9x^4 y^2 + 6x^2 y + 1$
(h) $x^2 + xy + \frac{1}{4}y^2$
(i) $x^2 - \frac{1}{4}$
(j) $\frac{1}{x^2} - 4$

(k) $10x - 45$
(l) $-2x^3 + 16x^2 - 8x$
(m) $2x^3 + 8x^2 + 16x$

9 (a) $a(a+2)(a-2)$
(b) $(x^2+1)(x+1)(x-1)$
(c) $(x-2)(x+1)$
(d) $(x-1)(x-1)$
(e) $(2x-3y+2z)(2x-3y-2z)$
(f) $(x+12)(x+4)$
(g) $\left(x^2 + \frac{x}{2}\right)\left(x^2 - \frac{x}{2}\right)$
(h) $(x+1)(x-6)$
(i) $4(x+3)(x-4)$
(j) $2(x-3)(x-4)$
(k) $5(1+2x^8)(1-2x^8)$
(l) $3(x+3)(x+2)$

10 (a) $x = -5$ or $x = -1$
(b) $x = -2$ or $x = 2$
(c) $x = 2$ or $x = 1$
(d) $x = -1$
(e) $x = 5$ or $x = -1$
(f) $x = 2$

Chapter 11

Exercise 11.1 A

1 (a) 5 cm   **(b)** 17 cm
   (c) 12 mm   **(d)** 10 cm
   (e) 1.09 cm   **(f)** 0.45 cm
   (g) 8.49 cm   **(h)** 6.11 cm

2 (a) 55.7 mm   **(b)** 14.4 cm
   (c) 5.29 cm   **(d)** 10.9 mm
   (e) 9.85 cm   **(f)** 9.33 cm

3 (a) no   **(b)** yes   **(c)** no
   (d) yes

4 (a) $\sqrt{32} = 5.66$
   (b) $\sqrt{18} = 4.24$
   (c) $\sqrt{32} = 5.66$
   (d) $\sqrt{180} = 13.4$
   (e) 3
   (f) $\sqrt{45} = 6.71$

Exercise 11.1 B

1 20 mm

2 44 cm

3 height = 86.6 mm, area = 4330 mm²

4 13 m and 15 m

5 0.7 m

Exercise 11.2

1 (a) 2.24 cm   (b) 6 mm
   (c) 7.5 mm   (d) 6.4 cm
   (e) $y = 6.67$ cm, $z = 4.8$ cm
   (f) $x = 5.59$ cm, $y = 13.6$ cm
   (g) $x = 9$ cm, $y = 24$ cm
   (h) $x = 50$ cm, $y = 20$ cm

2 $\angle ABC = \angle ADE$ (corr $\angle$ are equal)
   $\angle ACB = \angle AED$ (corr $\angle$ are equal)
   $\angle A = \angle A$ (common)
   $\therefore \triangle ABC$ is similar to $\triangle ADE$

3 25.5 m

Exercise 11.3

1 (a) $x = 18$ cm
   (b) $x = 27$ cm, $y = 16$ cm

2 9:4

3 (a) 254.48 cm²
   (b) 529 mm²

4 (a) $x = 2$ cm   (b) $x = 15$ cm

5 28 000 cm³

6 (a) 5:1   (b) 25:1
   (c) 125:1

Exercise 11.4

1 (a) $\triangle ABC$ is congruent to $\triangle ZXY$ (SAS)
   (b) although the two triangles look
     to be the same size, there are no
     marks to confirm this to be the
     case so we cannot be certain they
     are congruent
   (c) $\triangle XYZ$ is congruent to $\triangle ONM$ (ASA)
   (d) $\triangle DEF$ is congruent to $\triangle RQP$ (ASA)
   (e) $\triangle ACB$ is congruent to $\triangle ACD$ (RHS)
   (f) $\triangle PMN$ is congruent to $\triangle NOP$ (SSS
     or SAS)
   (g) $\triangle PRQ$ is congruent to $\triangle ZYX$ (SAS)
   (h) $\triangle ABC$ is congruent to $\triangle EDC$ (ASA)

2 $PO = PO$ (common)
   $MP = NO$ (given)
   $MO = NP$ (diagonals of isosceles
   trapezium are equal)
   $\triangle MPO$ is congruent to $\triangle NOP$ (SSS)

3 $\angle CDB = \angle DBE = \angle BEA$ (alt $\angle$ equal)
   $\angle BAE = \angle CBD$ (corr $\angle$ equal)
   $AE = BD$ (given)
   $\triangle BAE$ is congruent to $\triangle CBD$ (ASA)
   $AB = BC$
   $\therefore AB = \dfrac{1}{2} AC$

Mixed exercise

1 (a) sketch   (b) 130 m

2 $10^2 = 6^2 + 8^2 \therefore \triangle ABC$ is right-angled
   (converse Pythagoras)

3 (a) $\sqrt{18} = 4.24$
   (b) $\sqrt{20} = 4.47$
   (c) $\sqrt{8} = 2.83$
   (d) 5
   (e) 3.5

4 P = 2250 mm

5 (a) $x = 3.5$ cm
   (b) $x = 63°$, $y = 87°$
   (c) $x = 12$ cm

6 (a) 4:1
   (b) 1:9

7 18 cm²

8 23 750 mm²

9 (a) 3 cm
   (b) height = 12 cm, area of base =
     256 cm²

10 (a) $\triangle ABC$ is congruent to $\triangle HGI$ (RHS)
    (b) $\triangle ABC$ is congruent to $\triangle DEF$
      (ASA)
    (c) $\triangle ACB$ is congruent to $\triangle EDF$ (SAS)
    (d) $\triangle CAB$ is congruent to $\triangle GIH$ (SAS)

11 5.63 m

12 (a)

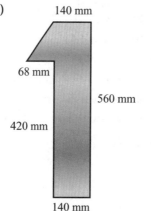

   (b) 156 mm

Chapter 12

Exercise 12.1

1

	(a)	(b)	(c)	(d)	(e)	(f)
mean	6.14	27.44	13.08	5	4.89	5.22
median	6	27	13	5	5	5
mode	6	27 and 38	12	no mode	4	6

2 (a) (iii) and (vi)
   (b) sensible answer from student,
     e.g. different sets can still add up
     to the same total as another set. If
     divided by the same number they
     will have the same mean.

3 255

4 15

5 Need to know how many cows there
   are to work out mean litres of milk
   produced per cow.

6 (a) 2.78   (b) 1

7 (a) $20.40   (b) $6   (c) $10
   (d) 2 (only the category B workers)
   (e) The mean is between $20 and $40
     so the statement is true.

Exercise 12.2

1 (a) mean = 4.3, median = 5,
     mode = 2 and 5.
     The data is bimodal and the lower
     mode (2) is not representative of
     the data.
   (b) mean = 3.15, median = 2,
     mode = 2.
     The mean is not representative
     of the data because it is too high.
     This is because there are some
     values in the data set that are
     much higher than the others.
     (This gives a big range, and when
     the range is big, the mean is
     generally not representative.)
   (c) mean = 17.67, median = 17,
     no mode.
     There is no mode, so this cannot be
     representative of the data. The mean
     and median are similar, so they are
     both representative of the data.

2 (a) mean = 12.8, median = 15, mode = 17, range = 19

(b) mode too high, mean not reliable as range is large

3 (a) Runner B has the faster mean time; he or she also achieved the faster time, so would technically be beating Runner A.

(b) A is more consistent with a range of only 2 seconds (B has a range of 3.8 seconds).

Exercise 12.3

1

Score	Frequency	Score × frequency (fx)
0	6	0
1	6	6
2	10	20
3	11	33
4	5	20
5	1	5
6	1	6
Total	40	90

(a) 2.25   **(b)** 3   **(c)** 2

(d) 6

2

Data set	A	B	C
mean	3.5	46.14	4.12
median	3	40	4.5
mode	3 and 5	40	6.5

Exercise 12.4

1 (a)

Marks (m)	Mid point	Frequency (f)	Frequency × midpoint
$0 \leq m < 10$	5	2	10
$10 \leq m < 20$	15	5	75
$20 \leq m < 30$	25	13	325
$30 \leq m < 40$	35	16	560
$40 \leq m < 50$	45	14	630
$50 \leq m < 60$	55	13	715
Total		63	2315

(b) $36.74 \approx 37$
(c) $30 \leq m < 40$
(d) $30 \leq m < 40$

2

Words per minute (w)	Mid point	Frequency	f × midpoint
$31 \leq w < 36$	33.5	40	1340
$36 \leq w < 41$	38.5	70	2695
$41 \leq w < 46$	43.5	80	3480
$46 \leq w < 51$	48.5	90	4365
$51 \leq w < 55$	53.5	60	3210
$55 \leq w < 60$	58.5	20	1170
Total		360	16 260

(a) 45.17
(b) $46 \leq w < 51$
(c) $41 \leq w < 46$
(d) 29

Exercise 12.5

1 (a) $Q_1 = 47$, $Q_2 = 55.5$, $Q_3 = 63$, IQR = 16

(b) $Q_1 = 8$, $Q_2 = 15$, $Q_3 = 17$, IQR = 9

(c) $Q_1 = 0.7$, $Q_2 = 1.05$, $Q_3 = 1.4$, IQR = 0.7

(d) $Q_1 = 1$, $Q_2 = 2.5$, $Q_3 = 4$, IQR = 3

Mixed exercise

1 (a) mean 6.4, median 6, mode 6, range 6

(b) mean 2.6, median 2, mode 2, range 5

(c) mean 13.8, median 12.8, no mode, range 11.9

2 (a) 19   **(b)** 9 and 10   **(c)** 5.66

3 C – although B's mean is bigger it has a larger range. C's smaller range suggests that its mean is probably more representative.

4 (a) 4.82 cm³   **(b)** 5 cm³
(c) 5 cm³

5 (a) 36.47 years
(b) $40 \leq a < 50$
(c) $30 \leq a < 40$
(d) don't know the actual ages

6 (a) 19
(b) 5
(c) $Q_1 = 18$, $Q_3 = 23$, IQR = 5
(d) fairly consistent, so data not spread out

7 (a) 15 scores fell into the bottom 60% of marks
(b) Less than half students scored above the 60th percentile, so you can assume the marks overall were pretty low.

Chapter 13
Exercise 13.1

1 student's own diagrams

2 (a) 2600 m   **(b)** 230 mm
(c) 820 cm   **(d)** 2450.809 km
(e) 20 mm   **(f)** 0.157 m

3 (a) 9080 g   **(b)** 49 340 g
(c) 500 g   **(d)** 0.068 kg
(e) 0.0152 kg   **(f)** 2.3 tonne

4 (a) 19 km   100 m
(b) 9015 cm   15 cm
(c) 435 mm   2 mm
(d) 492 cm   63 cm
(e) 635 m   35 m
(f) 580 500 cm   500 cm

5 (a) 1200 mm²   **(b)** 900 mm²
(c) 16 420 mm²   **(d)** 370 000 m²
(e) 0.009441 km² **(f)** 423 000 mm²

6 (a) 69 000 mm³
(b) 19 000 mm³
(c) 30 040 mm³
(d) 4 815 000 cm³
(e) 0.103 cm³
(f) 0.0000469 m³

7 220 m

8 110 cm

9 42 cm

10 88 (round down as you cannot have part of a box)

Exercise 13.2

1

Name	Time in	Time out	Lunch	(a) Hours worked	(b) Daily earnings
Dawoot	$\frac{1}{4}$ past 9	Half past five	$\frac{3}{4}$ hour	$7\frac{1}{2}$ hours	$55.88
Nadira	8:17 a.m.	5:30 p.m.	$\frac{1}{2}$ hour	8 h 43 min	$64.94
John	08:23	17:50	45 min	8 h 42 min	$64.82
Robyn	7:22 a.m.	4:30 p.m.	1 hour	8 h 8 min	$60.59
Mari	08:08	18:30	45 min	9 h 37 min	$71.64

2 6 h 25 min

3 20 min

4 (a) 5 h 47 min   (b) 10 h 26 min
   (c) 12 h 12 min   (d) 14 h 30 min

5 (a) 09:00   (b) 1 hour   (c) 09:30
   (d) 30 minutes
   (e) It would arrive late at Peron Place at 10:54 and at Marquez Lane at 11:19.

Exercise 13.3

1 The upper bound is 'inexact' so 42.5 in table means < 42.5

	Upper bound	Lower bound
(a)	42.5	41.5
(b)	13325.5	13324.5
(c)	450	350
(d)	12.245	12.235
(e)	11.495	11.485
(f)	2.55	2.45
(g)	395	385
(h)	1.1325	1.1315

2 (a) $71.5 \leq h < 72.5$
   (b) Yes, it is less than 72.5 (although it would be impossible to measure to that accuracy).

3 (a) 27.52 m²
   (b) upper bound: 28.0575 m²
     lower bound: 26.9875 m²

4 (a) $195.5\,\text{cm} \leq h < 196.5\,\text{cm}$
     $93.5\,\text{kg} \leq m < 94.5\,\text{kg}$

   (b) maximum speed =

$$\frac{\text{greatest distance}}{\text{shortest time}} = \frac{405}{33.5}$$

     $= 12.09\,\text{m/s}$

5 (a) upper bound of area: 15.5563 cm²
     lower bound of area: 14.9963 cm²
   (b) upper bound of hypotenuse: 8.0910 cm
     lower bound of hypotenuse: 7.9514 cm

Exercise 13.4

1 (a) 1 unit = 100 000 rupiah
   (b) (i) 250 000
      (ii) 500 000
      (iii) 2 500 000
   (c) (i) Aus $80
      (ii) Aus $640

2 (a) temperature in degrees F against temperature in degrees C
   (b) (i) 32 °F   (ii) 50 °F
      (iii) 210 °F
   (c) oven could be marked in Fahrenheit, but of course she could also have experienced a power failure or other practical problem
   (d) Fahrenheit scale as 50 °C is hot, not cold

3 (a) 9 kg   (b) 45 kg
   (c) (i) 20 kg   (ii) 35 kg
      (iii) 145 lb

Exercise 13.5

1 (a) (i) US$1 = ¥76.16
      (ii) £1 = NZ$1.99
      (iii) €1 = IR69.10
      (iv) Can$1 = €0.71
      (v) ¥1 = £0.01
      (vi) R1 = US$0.12
   (b) (i) 2490.50   (ii) 41 460
      (iii) 7540.15
   (c) (i) 9139.20   (ii) 52 820
      (iii) 145 632

Mixed exercise

1 (a) 2700 m   (b) 690 mm
   (c) 6000 kg   (d) 0.0235 kg
   (e) 263 000 mg   (f) 29 250 ml
   (g) 0.24 l   (h) 1000 mm²
   (i) 0.006428 km²   (j) 7 900 000 cm³
   (k) 29 000 000 m³   (l) 0.168 cm³

2 23 min 45 s

3 2 h 19 min 55 s

4 $1.615\,\text{m} \leq h < 1.625\,\text{m}$

5 (a) No, that is lower than the lower bound of 45
   (b) Yes, that is within the bounds

6 (a) 3.605 cm to 3.615 cm
     2.565 cm to 2.575 cm
   (b) lower bound of area: 9.246825 cm²
     upper bound of area: 9.308625 cm²
   (c) lower: 9.25 cm², upper: 9.31 cm²

7 (a) conversion graph showing litres against gallons (conversion factor)
   (b) (i) 45 l   (ii) 112.5 l
   (c) (i) 3.33 gallons
      (ii) 26.67 gallons
   (d) (i) 48.3 km/gal and 67.62 km/gal
      (ii) 10.62 km/l and 14.87 km/l

8 €892.06

9 (a) US$1 = IR49.81   (b) 99 620
   (c) US$249.95

10 £4239.13

Chapter 14

Exercise 14.1 A

1 (a)

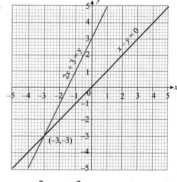

$x = -3,\ y = -3$

(b)

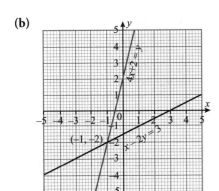

$x = -1, y = -2$

(c)

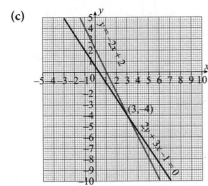

$x = 3, y = -4$

(d)

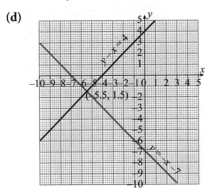

$x = -5.5, y = -1.5$

(e)

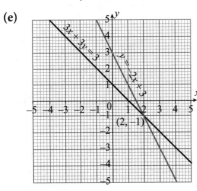

$x = 2, y = -1$

2 (a) (A) $y = -x + 4$

(B) $y = \dfrac{3}{2}x + 6$

(C) $y = -4x - 2$

(D) $y = x$

(E) $y = x - 4$

(F) $y = -2$

(b) (i) $(-2, 6)$ (ii) $(-2, -2)$

(iii) $(4, 0)$

3 (a) $x = 4, y = 2$

(b) $x = -1, y = 2$

(c) $x = 0, y = 4$

(d) $x = 3, y = 1$

4 (a) $x = 6, y = -1$

(b) $x = 1, y = 2$

(c) $x = 18, y = -8$

(d) $x = 1, y = 1\dfrac{1}{3}$

(e) $x = 3, y = -1$

(f) $x = 3, y = 7$

5 (a) $x = 2, y = 1$

(b) $x = 2, y = 2$

(c) $x = 2, y = -1$

(d) $x = 3, y = 2$

(e) $x = 3, y = 2.5$

(f) $x = 4, y = 2$

(g) $x = 5, y = 3$

(h) $x = 0.5, y = -0.5$

(i) $x = -9, y = -2$

6 a chocolate bar costs $1.20 and a box of gums $0.75

7 number of students is 7

8 6 quarters and 6 dimes

Exercise 14.1 B

1 (a) $x = -3, y = 4$

(b) $x = -1, y = \dfrac{1}{3}$

(c) $x = 3, y = -4$

(d) $x = 15, y = 30$

(e) $x = 4, y = 2$

(f) $x = \dfrac{15}{7}, y = \dfrac{12}{7}$

2 (a) $c + d = 15$

(b) 3 desks and 12 chairs

Exercise 14.2

1 (a)

![number line from -5 to 5, closed dot at 4]
$-5 \ -4 \ -3 \ -2 \ -1 \ 0 \ 1 \ 2 \ 3 \ 4 \ 5$

(b)

![number line from -5 to 5, closed dot at -2]
$-5 \ -4 \ -3 \ -2 \ -1 \ 0 \ 1 \ 2 \ 3 \ 4 \ 5$

(c)

![number line, open dot at -3.5]
$-4 \ -3.5 \ -3 \quad -2 \quad -1 \quad 0 \quad 1$

(d)

![number line with closed dots at 1.2 and 2.8]
$1 \ 1.2 \ 1.4 \ 1.6 \ 1.8 \ 2 \ 2.2 \ 2.4 \ 2.6 \ 2.8 \ 3$

(e)

![number line with closed dot at -4, arrow to left]
$-7 \ -6 \ -5 \ -4 \ -3 \ -2 \ -1 \ 2 \ 0 \ 1$

(f)

![number line with open dot at -3, arrow to right]
$-5 \ -4 \ -3 \ -2 \ -1 \ 0 \ 1 \ 2 \ 3 \ 4 \ 5$

(g)

![number line with closed dot at -2, arrow to left]
$-4 \ -3.5 \ -3 \quad -2 \quad -1 \quad 0 \quad 1$

(h)

![number line with open dot at 0.75, closed dot at 1.25]
$0.25 \quad 0.75 \quad 1.25 \quad 1.75$
$0 \quad 0.5 \quad 1 \quad 1.5 \quad 2$

(i)

![number line with closed dot at 4, open dot at 6]
$-2 \ -1 \ 0 \ 1 \ 2 \ 3 \ 4 \ 5 \ 6 \ 7$

2 (a) 3, 4

(b) $-2, -1, 0, 1, 2, 3$

(c) 2

(d) $-1, 0, 1, 2, 3$

(e) 0, 1, 2, 3, 4

(f) 4, 5, 6, 7, 8, 9

3 (a) $x \le -2$ (b) $x > 11$

(c) $x \ge 4$ (d) $x \le 52$

(e) $x \ge 9$ (f) $x > 73$

(g) $x > 9\dfrac{1}{4}$ (h) $e \ge -3$

(i) $r < 11\dfrac{1}{2}$ (j) $x \ge 45$

(k) $g < 9\dfrac{1}{4}$ (l) $y \le \dfrac{10}{11}$

(m) $n > 31$ (n) $n > -2$

(o) $x \le -6\dfrac{1}{28}$

Exercise 14.3

1 (a)

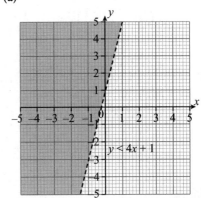

$y < 4x + 1$

(b)

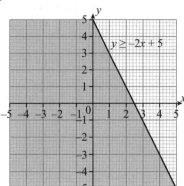

$y \geq -2x + 5$

(c)

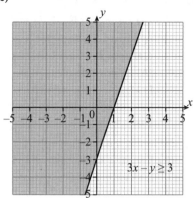

$3x - y \geq 3$

3 **(a)** $y \geq 2x - 1$
  (b) $y < -4x + 3$
  (c) $y > -\dfrac{1}{2}x$
  (d) $y \geq -x - 3$

4

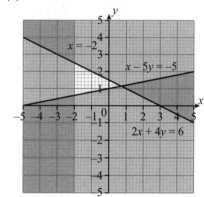

$2x + 3y = 6$ $x - y = 0$ $y = -1$

(c)

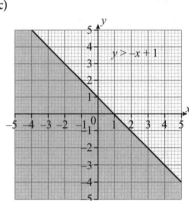

$y > -x + 1$

(d)

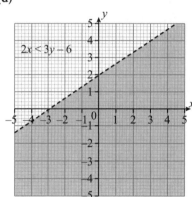

$2x < 3y - 6$

5 **(a)**

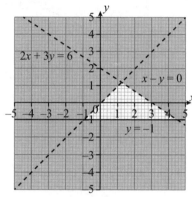

$x = -2$ $x - 5y = -5$ $2x + 4y = 6$

2 **(a)**

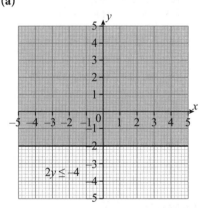

$2y \leq -4$

(e)

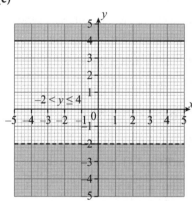

$-2 < y \leq 4$

(b) $(-2, 2), (-2, 1), (-1, 2), (-1, -1),$
$(0, 1)$

Exercise 14.4

1

(b)

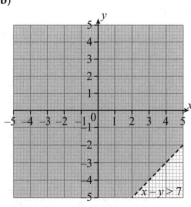

$x - y \geq 7$

(f)

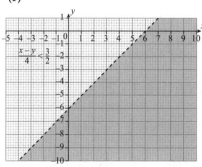

$\dfrac{x - y}{4} < \dfrac{3}{2}$

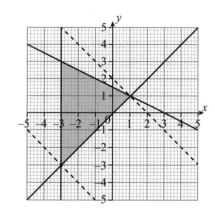

2 (a)

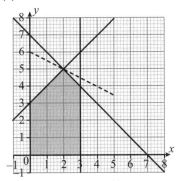

(b) greatest posible value is at the point (2, 5) so $2y + x = 12$

3 let x = number of chocolate fudge cakes and y = number of vanilla fudge cakes

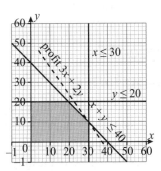

to maximise profit $x = 30$ and $y = 10$
maximum profit = $110

4 let x = number of litres of orange and y = number of litres of lemon

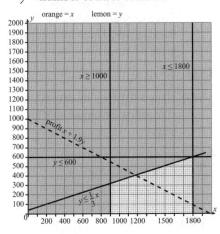

maximum income ($2940) when $x = 1800$ and $y = 600$

Exercise 14.5

1 (a) $(x+3)^2 - 5$
   (b) $(x-2)^2 + 3$
   (c) $(x+7)^2 - 5$
   (d) $(x-6)^2 - 6$
   (e) $(x+5)^2 - 8$
   (f) $(x+11)^2 + 20$
   (g) $(x+12)^2 - 23$
   (h) $(x-8)^2 - 7$
   (i) $(x+9)^2 + 12$
   (j) $(x-1)^2 + 9$
   (k) $(x-4)^2 - 21$
   (l) $(x+10)^2 - 17$

2 (a) $x = 6, x = -1$
   (b) $x = 3, x = -2$
   (c) $x = 3, x = 1$
   (d) $x = 7, x = -1$
   (e) $x = 15.81, x = 0.19$
   (f) $x = -6.85, x = -0.15$
   (g) $x = 0.11, x = -9.11$
   (h) $x = -3.70, x = -7.30$
   (i) $x = 11.05, x = -9.05$

3 (a) $x = 2, x = -0.5$
   (b) $x = 3, x = 1$
   (c) $x = 2.53, x = -0.53$
   (d) $x = 3, x = -0.5$
   (e) $x = 7.47, x = -1.47$
   (f) $x = -2.27, x = 1.77$

Exercise 14.6

1 (a) $x = 10$ or 4
   (b) $x = 6$ or -20
   (c) $x = 1$ or -6
   (d) $x = 3$ or 5
   (e) $x = 4$ or -1
   (f) $x = 2$
   (g) $x = 2$ or -6
   (h) $x = -5$
   (i) $x = 2$ or -4
   (j) $x = 6$ or -2
   (k) $x = 4$ or 5
   (l) $x = 5$ or -8

2 (a) $x = -0.76$ or -5.24
   (b) $x = 1.56$ or -2.56
   (c) $x = -4.76$ or -9.24
   (d) $x = 7.12$ or -1.12
   (e) $x = -2.17$ or -7.83
   (f) $x = -0.15$ or -6.85

(g) $x = -7.20$ or -16.80
(h) $x = -3.70$ or -7.30
(i) $x = 4.19$ or -22.19
(j) $x = 4.32$ or -2.32
(k) $x = 8.58$ or -0.58
(l) $x = 11.05$ or -9.05

3 (a) $x = 5.46$ or -1.46
   (b) $x = 1.67$ or -3.5
   (c) $x = 1.31$ or 0.19
   (d) $x = 5$ or -2.5
   (e) $x = 2.25$ or 1
   (f) $x = 1.77$ or -1.27
   (g) $x = 0.80$ or -0.14
   (h) $x = 10.65$ or 5.35
   (i) $x = 9.91$ or -0.91
   (j) $x = 0.5$ or -3
   (k) $x = -0.67$ or -1.5
   (l) $x = 1$ or -0.75

4 numbers are 57 and 58 or -58 and -57

5 dimensions are $12\,\text{cm} \times 18\,\text{cm}$

Exercise 14.7

1 (a) $(2x - 3)(x + 1)$
   (b) $(3x +1)^2$
   (c) $(2x - 3)^2$
   (d) $(2x + 1)(3x - 5)$
   (e) $(4x - 3)(x + 1)$
   (f) $(7x - 1)(2x - 7)$
   (g) $(x + 5)(3x - 4)$
   (h) $(2x - 1)(3x + 7)$
   (i) $(3x + 5)(x - 5)$
   (j) $(3x - 11)(x + 6)$
   (k) $(5x + 3)(3x - 5)$
   (l) $(8x + 1)(x + 3)$

2 (a) $(2x + 3)^2$
   (b) $\frac{1}{2}(2x+1)(2x-1)$ or
   $\left(x+\frac{1}{2}\right)(2x+1)$
   (c) $2(5x + 2)^2$
   (d) $(2x + y)(3x - 5y)$
   (e) $(4x^2 - 3)(x^2 + 1)$
   (f) $2(2x - 1)(3x + 1)$
   (g) $2(1 - 2x)(1 + x)$
   (h) $(x + 3)(x + 2)$
   (i) $(3x + 8)(x - 4)$
   (j) $2(3x - 11)(x + 6)$
   (k) $(4x - 3)(x + 1)$
   (l) $(8x + y)(x + 3y)$

Exercise 14.8

1 (a) $\dfrac{x}{7}$ (b) 3

   (c) $\dfrac{1}{7}$ (d) $\dfrac{2x}{5}$

   (e) $\dfrac{8z}{3}$ (f) $\dfrac{2}{y}$

   (g) $\dfrac{2x}{3y}$ (h) $\dfrac{1}{5ab}$

   (i) $\dfrac{2b}{3a}$

2 (a) $\dfrac{x+3}{x}$ (b) $\dfrac{a-b}{a+b}$

   (c) $\dfrac{2x+y}{x}$ (d) $\dfrac{3x+1}{x-5}$

   (e) $\dfrac{a+2}{a}$ (f) $\dfrac{a+b}{a+2b}$

   (g) $\dfrac{x+5}{x+2}$ (h) x^2-3

   (i) $\dfrac{7}{3}$

3 (a) $\dfrac{x^2}{6}$ (b) $\dfrac{y^2}{6}$

   (c) $\dfrac{35}{a^2}$ (d) $\dfrac{5xy}{2}$

   (e) $\dfrac{a}{c}$ (f) $(b+1)(b-1)$

   (g) $\dfrac{1}{42}$ (h) $\dfrac{4-x}{3}$

   (i) $\dfrac{-2-3x}{2x+1}$

4 (a) $\dfrac{3x+2y}{xy}$ (b) $\dfrac{13p+2}{8p}$

   (c) $\dfrac{29}{10p}$ (d) $\dfrac{7}{p+1}$

   (e) $\dfrac{5x+7}{(x+2)(x+1)}$ (f) $\dfrac{18-5m}{6}$

   (g) $\dfrac{9x-17}{(x-3)(x+2)(x-1)}$

   (h) $\dfrac{17-x}{x(x-3)(x+4)}$

   (i) $\dfrac{5-3x}{(2x-3)(x+1)(x-1)}$

Mixed exercise

1 $x=2, y=-5$

2 $x=-2, y=5$

3 \$5000 at 5% and \$10 000 at 8%

4 (a) $x>-5$ (b) $x\le-1$

5

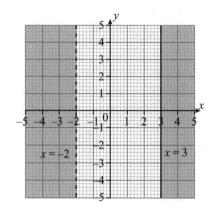

6

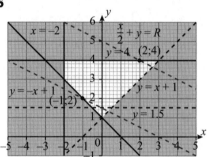

the integer solutions are:

least, $x=-1, y=2$, giving $\dfrac{x}{2}+y=1.5$

greatest, $x=2, y=4$, giving $\dfrac{x}{2}+y=5$

7 (a) $x(x-2y)$
   (b) $(a^2+b)(a^2-b)$
   (c) $(x-5)(x+11)$
   (d) $(2y-1)(y+7)$
   (e) $-2(x+1)(2x-3)$
   (f) $(x-6)(x+3)$

8 (a) $a=1.30$ or -2.30
   (b) $x=1.33$ or -1
   (c) $x=3$ or -5
   (d) $x=0.67$ or 1
   (e) $x=1$ or -0.625
   (f) $x=1$

9 (a) $x=-2$ or 0.4

   (b) $x=\dfrac{q\pm\sqrt{q^2-4pr}}{2p}$

10 (a) $\dfrac{x-y}{x+y}$

   (b) $2-x$

   (c) $\dfrac{5+2p}{10p^2}$

   (d) $\dfrac{3xy}{2}$

   (e) $\dfrac{xy^3z}{4}$

   (f) $\dfrac{45a^2+16a-50}{30a}$

   (g) $\dfrac{(x+2)(x-1)}{x(x+4)}$

   (h) $\dfrac{1}{2x-1}$

   (i) $\dfrac{-6}{(2x+1)(x+5)(x-1)}$

Chapter 15

Exercise 15.1

1 (a) length $=10\,\text{cm}$, width $=7\,\text{cm}$
   (b) length $=14.4\,\text{cm}$, width $=7\,\text{cm}$

2 (a) length $=9.14\,\text{cm}$, width $=5.5\,\text{cm}$
   (b) Yes. The length of the mini pitch $=$ width of standard pitch and $2\times$ width of mini pitch $<$ length of standard pitch. It is possible to have two mini pitches on a standard pitch so, with three standard pitches, up to six matches could take place at the same time.

3 (a) $\dfrac{1}{200}$ or $\dfrac{1}{150}$
   (b) (i) and (ii) diagram drawn using student's scale including $\times$ for net posts

4 (a) student's scale drawing – diagonal distance $=11.3\,\text{m}$
   (b) using Pythagoras' theorem

Exercise 15.2

1 (a) $090°$
   (b) $225°$
   (c) $315°$

2 (a) $250°$ (b) $310°$ (c) $135°$

3 student's drawing
  (a) 223°   **(b)** 065°
  (c) 11 km   **(d)** 13 km

Exercise 15.3

1

	(a)	(b)	(c)	(d)
hypotenuse	c	z	f	q
opp(A)	a	y	g	p
adj(A)	b	x	e	r

2 **(a)** opp(30°) = x cm
    adj(60°) = x cm
    opp(60°) = adj(30°) = y cm
  (b) adj(40°) = q cm
    opp(50°) = q cm
    opp(40°) = adj(50°) = p cm

3 **(a)** 0.65   **(b)** 1.43   **(c)** 5.14
  (d) 0.41   **(e)** 0

4 **(a)** $\tan A = \frac{3}{4}$ **(b)** $\tan x = \frac{2}{3}, \tan y = \frac{3}{2}$
  (c) $\tan 55° = \frac{1}{d}, \tan B = d$
  (d) $\tan y = \frac{5}{12}, \angle X = (90 - y)°, \tan X = \frac{12}{5}$
  (e) $AC = 2$ cm, $\tan B = \frac{4}{3}, \tan C = \frac{3}{4}$

5 **(a)** $x = 1.40$ cm
  (b) $y = 19.29$ m
  (c) $c = 3.32$ cm
  (d) $a = 13$ m
  (e) $x = 35.70$ cm

6 **(a)** 26.6°   **(b)** 40.9°   **(c)** 51.3°
  (d) 85.2°   **(e)** 14.0°   **(f)** 40.9°
  (g) 79.7°   **(h)** 44.1°

7 **(a)** 16°   **(b)** 46°   **(c)** 49°
  (d) 23°   **(e)** 38°

8 **(a)** hyp = y, adj(θ) = z, $\cos\theta = \frac{z}{y}$
  (b) hyp = c, adj(θ) = b, $\cos\theta = \frac{b}{c}$
  (c) hyp = c, adj(θ) = a, $\cos\theta = \frac{a}{c}$
  (d) hyp = p, adj(θ) = r, $\cos\theta = \frac{r}{p}$
  (e) hyp = x, adj(θ) = z, $\cos\theta = \frac{z}{x}$

9 **(a)** $\sin A = \frac{7}{13}, \cos A = \frac{12}{13}, \tan A = \frac{7}{12}$
  (b) $\sin B = \frac{5}{11}, \cos B = \frac{19.6}{22}, \tan B = \frac{10}{19.6}$
  (c) $\sin C = \frac{3}{5}, \cos C = \frac{4}{5}, \tan C = \frac{3}{4}$

(d) $\sin D = \frac{63}{65}, \cos D = \frac{16}{65}, \tan D = \frac{63}{16}$

(e) $\sin E = \frac{84}{85}, \cos E = \frac{13}{85}, \tan E = \frac{84}{13}$

10 **(a)** 45°   **(b)** 64°   **(c)** 57°
  (d) 60°   **(e)** 30°   **(f)** 27°

11 4.86 m

12 **(a)** $x = 30°$ and $y = 4.69$ cm
  (b) $x = 3$ m and $y = 53.1°$
  (c) $x = 48.2°$
  (d) $x = 22.9°$ and $y = 8.90$ cm

Exercise 15.4

1 1.68 m
2 **(a)** 30°   **(b)** 33°

Exercise 15.5

1 **(a)** $-\cos 68°$ **(b)** $\sin 24°$
  (c) $\cos 105°$ **(d)** $\sin 55°$
  (e) $\cos 135°$ **(f)** $\sin 35°$
  (g) $-\cos 60°$ **(h)** $\sin 82°$
  (i) $-\cos 125°$ **(j)** $-\cos 50°$

2 **(a)** $\theta = 15°$ or 165°
  (b) $\theta = 124°$
  (c) $\theta = 52°$ or 128°
  (d) $\theta = 70°$
  (e) $\theta = 20°$ or 160°
  (f) $\theta = 48°$
  (g) $\theta = 39°$
  (h) $\theta = 110°$
  (i) $\theta = 7°$ or 173°
  (j) $\theta = 84°$ or 96°

Exercise 15.6

1 **(a)** $x = 40.4°$ **(b)** $x = 18.5$
  (c) $x = 61.2°$ **(d)** $x = 18.2$
  (e) $x = 7.1$ **(f)** $x = 28.1°$
  (g) $x = 22.5°$ **(h)** $x = 8.3$
  (i) $x = 14.0°$

2 **(a)** $x = 6.3$ cm **(b)** $x = 6.8$ cm
  (c) $x = 4.4$ cm **(d)** $x = 13.2$ cm
  (e) $x = 8.7$ cm **(f)** $x = 10.8$ cm

3 **(a)** $\theta = 82.4°$ **(b)** $\theta = 23.1°$
  (c) $\theta = 33.3°$ **(d)** $\theta = 28.9°$
  (e) $\theta = 38.4°$ **(f)** $\theta = 82.5°$

4 $\cos B = \dfrac{a^2 + c^2 - b^2}{2ac}$

5 **(a)** $\theta = 66.4°$ **(b)** $\theta = 43.2°$
  (c) $\theta = 60.7°$ **(d)** $\theta = 31.1°$

6 **(a)** $a = 2.9$ m   **(b)** $z = 3.7$ cm
  (c) $m = 9.2$ m   **(d)** $r = 5.0$ cm

Exercise 15.7

1 **(a)** 11.2 cm²   **(b)** 25.4 cm²
  (c) 17.0 cm²   **(d)** 70.4 cm²
  (e) 3.8 cm²   **(f)** 24.6 cm²

2 44.9 cm²

3 **(a)** $x = 115°$ and area = 31.7 cm²
  (b) $x = 108°$ and area = 43.0 cm²
  (c) $x = 122.2°$ and area = 16.3 cm²

Exercise 15.8

1 **(a)** 90°   **(b)** 5 cm
  (c) 36.9°   **(d)** 4 cm
  (e) 9.85 cm   **(f)** 66.0°
  (g) 10.3 cm   **(h)** 16.9°

2 **(a)** 21.2 m   **(b)** 10.6 m
  (c) 21.2 m   **(d)** 18.4 m

3 **(a)** 9.80 cm   **(b)** 24.1°

Mixed exercise

1 **(a)** $x = 37.6°$
  (b) $x = 44.0°$
  (c) $x = 71.4°$

2 35.3°

3 $AB = 300$ m

4 $AC \approx 41.6$ cm

5 ≈ 16 m

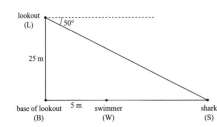

6 $RS = 591$ m

Chapter 16

Exercise 16.1

1 **(a)** E   **(b)** C   **(c)** A
  (d) D   **(e)** B

2 **(a)** student's own line (line should go close to (160, 4.2) and (175, 5.55)); answers (b) and (c) depend on student's best fit line
(b) ≈ 4.7 m
(c) between 175 cm and 185 cm
(d) fairly strongly positive
(e) taller athletes can jump further

3 **(a)** distance (m)
(b)
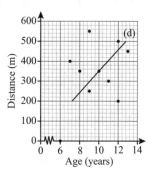

(c) weak positive
(e) 12 years old
(f) Not very reliable because correlation is very weak
(g) 600 m

Mixed exercise

1 **(a)** the number of accidents for different speeds
(b) average speed
(c) answers to (c) depend on student's best fit line
  (i) ≈ 35 accidents
  (ii) < 40 km/h
(d) strong positive
(e) there are more accidents when vehicles are travelling at a higher average speed

2 **(a)** there a strong negative correlation at first, but this becomes weaker as the cars get older
(b) 0–2 years
(c) it stabilises around the $6000 level
(d) 2–3 years
(e) $5000–$8000

Chapter 17

Exercise 17.1

1 $19.26

2 $25 560

3 **(a)** $930.75 **(b)** $1083.75
  (c) $765 **(d)** $1179.38
4 $1203.40
5 $542.75
6 **(a)** $625 **(b)** $25 **(c)** $506.50

Exercise 17.2

1 **(a)** $7.50 **(b)** $160 **(c)** $210
  (d) $448 **(e)** $343.75

2 5 years

3 2.8%

4 $2800 more

5 $2281 more

6 **(a)** $7.50 **(b)** $187.73
  (c) $225.75 **(d)** $574.55
  (e) $346.08

7 $562.75

8 $27 085.85

Exercise 17.3

1 **(a)** $100 **(b)** $200 **(c)** $340
  (d) $900

2 $300

3 $500

4 $64.41

5 **(a)** $179.10
  (b) $40.04
  (c) $963.90

Mixed exercise

1 **(a)** 12 h **(b)** 40 h **(c)** $25\frac{1}{2}$ h

2 **(a)** $1190 **(b)** $1386 **(c)** $1232

3 **(a)** $62 808 **(b)** $4149.02

4 **(a)**

Years	Simple interest	Compound interest
1	300	300
2	600	609
3	900	927.27
4	1200	1125.09
5	1500	1592.74
6	1800	1940.52
7	2100	2298.74
8	2400	2667.70

(b) $92.74
(c) student's own graph; a comment such as, the amount of compound interest increases faster than the simple interest

5 $862.50

6 $3360

7 **(a)** $1335, $2225
  (b) $1950, $3250
  (c) $18 000, $30 000

8 **(a)** $4818 **(b)** 120%

9 $425
10 $211.20
11 $43.36 (each)
12 $204

Chapter 18

Exercise 18.1

1

x		–3	–2	–1	0	1	2	3
(a)	$y = -x^2 + 2$	–7	–2	1	2	1	–2	–7
(b)	$y = x^2 - 3$	6	1	–2	–3	–2	1	6
(c)	$y = -x^2 - 2$	–11	–6	–3	–2	–3	–6	–11
(d)	$y = -x^2 - 3$	–12	–7	–4	–3	–4	–7	–12
(e)	$y = x^2 + \frac{1}{2}$	9.5	4.5	1.5	0.5	1.5	4.5	9.5

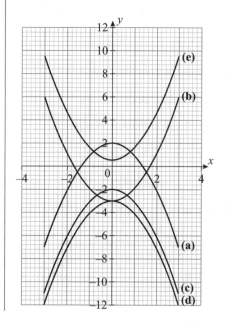

2 (a) $y = 3 + x^2$ **(b)** $y = x^2 + 2$
(c) $y = x^2$ **(d)** $y = -x^2 + 3$
(e) $y = -x^2 - 4$

3 (a)

x	-2	-1	0	1	2	3	4	5
$y = x^2 - 3x + 2$	12	6	2	0	0	2	6	12

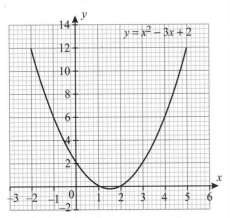

(b)

x	-3	-2	-1	0	1	2	3
$y = x^2 - 2x - 1$	14	7	2	-1	-2	-1	2

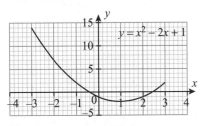

(c)

x	-2	-1	0	1	2	3	4	5	6
$y = -x^2 + 4x + 1$	-11	-4	1	4	5	4	1	-4	-11

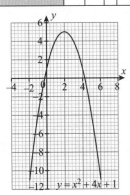

4 (a) 8 m
(b) 2 seconds

(c) 6 m
(d) just short of 4 seconds
(e) 3 seconds

Exercise 18.2

1 (a)

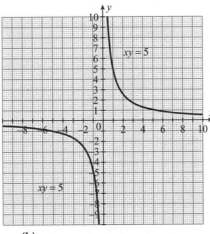

(b)

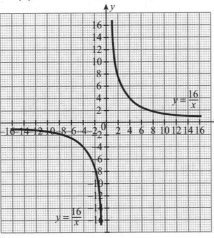

(c)

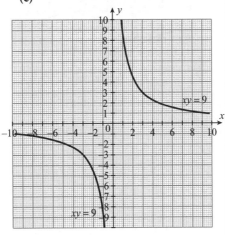

(d)

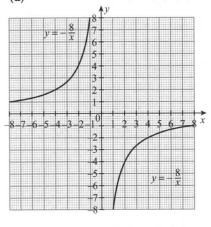

(e)

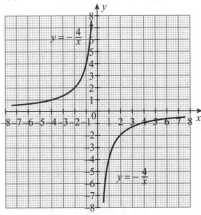

2 (a)

Length	1	2	3	4	6	8	12	24
Width	24	12	8	6	4	3	2	1

(b)

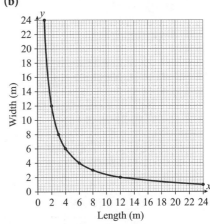

(c) the curve represents all the possible measurements for the rectangle with an area of 24 m²
(d) ≈ 3.4 m

Exercise 18.3

1 (a) −2 or 3   **(b)** −1 or 2
  (c) −3 or 4

2 (a)

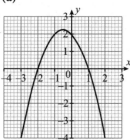

  (b) (i)   −2 or 1
    (ii) ≈ −1.6 or 0.6
    (iii) ≈ −2.6 or 1.6

3 (a)

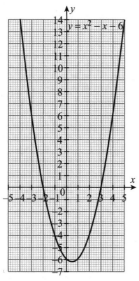

  (b) (i) 0 or 1
    (ii) −2 or 3
    (iii) −3 or 4

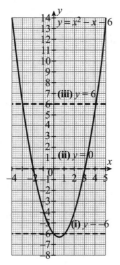

Exercise 18.4

1 (a)

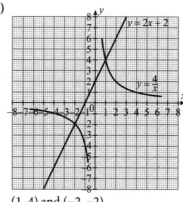

  (1, 4) and (−2, −2)

  (b)

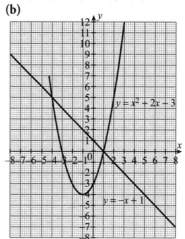

  (−4, 5) and (1, 0)

  (c)

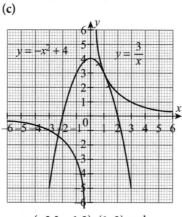

  ≈ (−2.3, −1.3), (1, 3) and
  (1.3, 2.3)

2 (a)

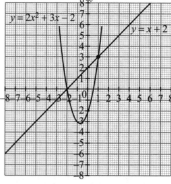

  (−2, 0) and (1, 3)

  (b)

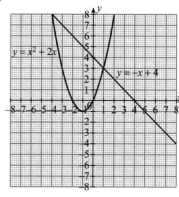

  (−4, 8) and (1, 3)

  (c)

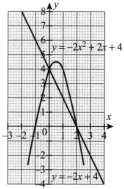

  (0, 4) and (2, 0)

  (d)

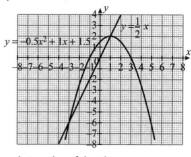

  (−3, −6) and (1, 2)

Exercise 18.5

1

x	-5	-4	-3	-2	-1	0	1	2	3	4	5
(a) $y = x^3 - 4x^2$	-225	-128	-63	-24	-5	0	-3	-8	-9	0	25
(b) $y = x^3 + 5$	-120	-59	-22	-3	4	5	6	13	32	69	130
(c) $y = -2x^3 + 5x^2 + 5$	380	213	104	41	12	5	8	9	-4	-43	-120
(d) $y = -x^3 + 4x^2 - 5$	220	123	58	19	0	-5	-2	3	4	-5	-30
(e) $y = x^3 + 2x - 10$	-145	-82	-43	-22	-13	-10	-7	2	23	62	125
(f) $y = 2x^3 + 4x^2 - 7$	-157	-71	-25	-7	-5	-7	-1	25	83	185	343
(g) $y = -x^3 - 3x^2 + 6$	56	22	6	2	4	6	2	-14	-48	-106	-194
(h) $y = -3x^3 + 5x$	350	172	66	14	-2	0	2	-14	-66	-172	-350

(a)

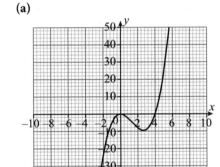

$y = x^3 - 4x^3$

(b)

$y = x^3 + 5$

(c)

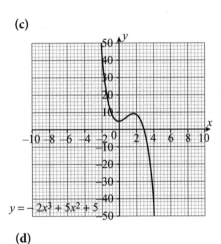

$y = -2x^3 + 5x^2 + 5$

(d)

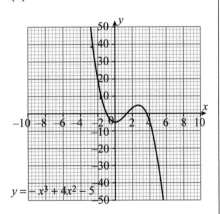

$y = -x^3 + 4x^2 - 5$

(e)

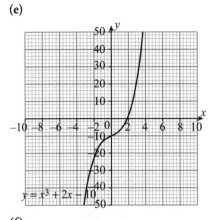

$y = x^3 + 2x - 10$

(f)

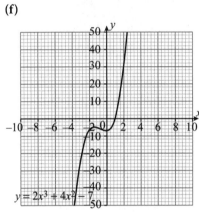

$y = 2x^3 + 4x^2 - 7$

(g)

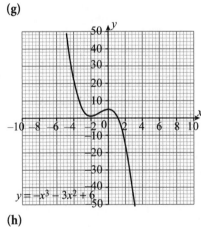

$y = -x^3 - 3x^2 + 6$

(h)

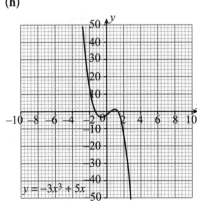

$y = -3x^3 + 5x$

2 (a)

x	−2.5	−2	−1.5	−1	−0.5	0	0.5	1	1.5	2	2.5	3	4	5	6
y	−36.875	−18	−4.625	4	8.625	10	8.875	6	2.125	−2	−5.625	−8	−6	10	46

(b)

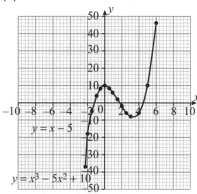

(b)

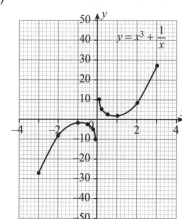

(c) (i) $x = -1.3$, 1.8 or 4.5
   (ii) $x = 0$ or 5
   (iii) $x = -1.6$, 2.1 or 4.5

3

	x	−3	−2	−1	−0.5	−0.2	−0.1	0	0.1	0.2	0.5	1	2	3
(a)	$y = x - \dfrac{1}{x}$	−2.67	−1.5	0	1.5	4.8	9.9		−9.9	−4.8	−1.5	0	1.5	2.67
(b)	$y = x^3 + \dfrac{1}{x}$	−27.33	−8.5	−2	−2.125	−5.008	−10.001		10.001	5.008	2.125	2	8.5	27.33
(c)	$y = x^2 + 2 - \dfrac{4}{x}$	12.33	8	7	10.25	22.04	42.01		−37.99	−17.96	−5.75	−1	4	9.67
(d)	$y = 2x + \dfrac{3}{x}$	−7	−5.5	−5	−7	−15.4	−30.2		30.2	15.4	7	5	5.5	7
(e)	$y = x^3 - \dfrac{2}{x}$	−26.33	−7	1	3.875	9.992	19.99		−19.99	−9.992	−3.875	−1	7	26.33
(f)	$y = x^2 - x + \dfrac{1}{x}$	11.67	5.5	1	−1.25	−4.76	−9.89		9.91	4.84	1.75	1	2.5	6.33

(d)

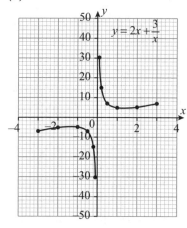

(e)

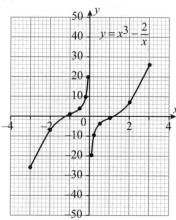

(a)

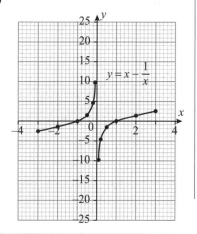

(c)

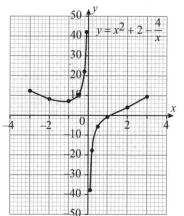

(f)

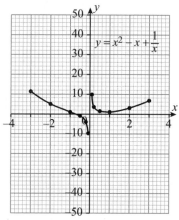

4 (a)

x	−4	−3	−2	−1	0	1	2	3	4
$y = 2^x$	0.0625	0.125	0.25	0.5	1	2	4	8	16
$y = 2^{-x}$	16	8	4	2	1	0.5	0.25	0.125	0.0625

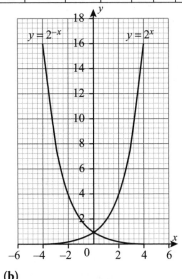

(b)

x	0	0.2	0.4	0.6	0.8	1
$y = 10^x$	1	1.58	2.51	3.98	6.31	10
$y = 2x - 1$	−1	−0.6	−0.2	0.2	0.6	1

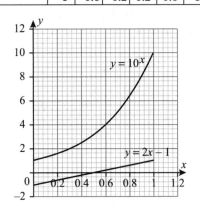

5 (a) & (b) (i)

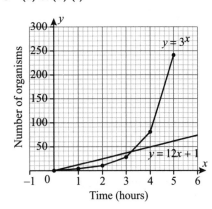

(b) (ii) 12 per hour
(c) (i) ≈ 3.4 hours   (ii) ≈ 42

Exercise 18.6

1

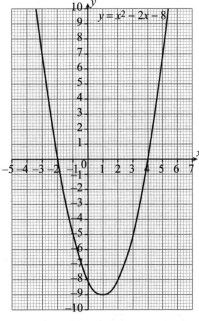

(a) −2
(b) 6 and −6

2 (a)

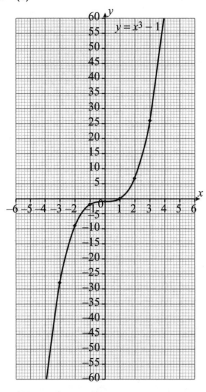

(b) gradient = 12

3 answers should be close to: with light ≈ 1.4 cm per day, without light ≈ 1 cm per day

Mixed exercise

1 (a) A: $y = 3x - 2$

   B: $y = -x^2 + 3$

   C: $y = -\dfrac{x}{4} - 5\dfrac{1}{4}$

(b) (i) $(-1, -5)$
   (ii) answer should be the point of intersection of graphs A and C.
(c) maximum value $y = 3$

2 (a)

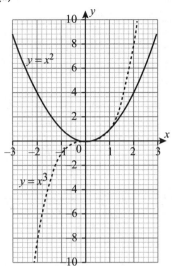

(b) (0, 0) and (1, 1)
(c) (i) $x = 2$ or $x = -2$
　　(ii) $x = -2$
(d) gradient for $y = x^2$ when $x = 2$ is 4
　　and gradient for $y = x^3$ when
　　$x = 2$ is 12

3 (a) $y = -\dfrac{4}{x}$　　**(b)** $y = x$
(c)

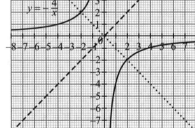

Chapter 19

Exercise 19.1

1 (a)

A 　　　B

C 　　　D

E　　　F

G

H has no line symmetry

(b) A = 0, B = 3, C = 4, D = 4, E = 5,
　　F = 2, G = 2, H = 2

2 (a) 2, student's diagram
(b) 2

3 student's own diagrams but as an
　example:

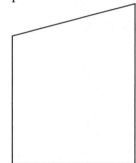

Exercise 19.2

1 (a) 3　　　**(b)** 4

(c) infinite number corresponding to
　　the number of diameters of the
　　circle face
(d) as per part (c)　　　**(e)** 2
(f) 3 (5 if face is a square)
(g) 1
(h) infinite number corresponding to
　　the number of diameters of the
　　sphere

2 (a) 4　　**(b)** 3　　**(c)** 1
(d) infinite　**(e)** 4　　**(f)** 8

Exercise 19.3

1 (a) $x = 25°$　**(b)** $x = 160°$, $y = 20°$

2 6.5 cm

3 (a) 49.47 cm　　**(b)** 177.72 cm

Exercise 19.4

1 (a) 15° (isosceles Δ)
(b) 150° (angles in a Δ)
(c) 35° ($\angle$MON = 80°, and ΔMNO in
　　isosceles, so $\angle$NMO = $\angle$NOM =
　　50°, so $\angle$MPN = 35°)
(d) 105° ($\angle$PON = 210° so $\angle$PMN =
　　105° – half the angle at the centre)

2 (a) 55° (angles in same segment)
(b) 110° (angle at centre twice angle
　　at circumference)
(c) 25° ($\angle$ABD = $\angle$ACD, opposite
　　angles of intersecting lines AC
　　and BD, so third angle same)

3 $\angle$DAB = 65°, $\angle$ADC = 115°,
　$\angle$DCB = 115°, $\angle$CBA = 65°

4 35°

5 59.5°

6 144°

7 (a) 22°　　**(b)** 116°　　**(c)** 42°

8 (a) 56°　　**(b)** 68°　　**(c)** 52°

Exercise 19.5

DIAGRAMS ARE NOT TO SCALE BUT
STUDENTS' SHOULD BE WHERE
REQUESTED

1
(a)　　　　　　　　**(b)**

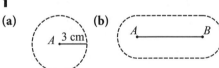

(c)

2

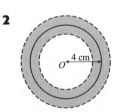

3

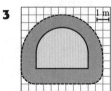

4

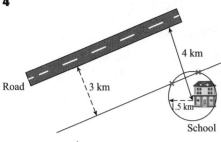

5

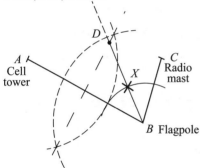

6 NOT TO SCALE – note that on student drawing point X should be 2 cm (10 m) from B.

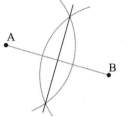

Mixed exercise

1

(a) (i) **(ii)** none

(b) (i) **(ii)** none

(c) (i)  **(ii)** four

(d) (i) **(ii)** eight

(e) (i) 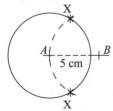 **(ii)** none

2 (a) a hexagonal prism
   (b) the axis of rotational symmetry
   (c) 6
   (d) 7

3 (a) $w = 72°$ (base angle isosceles $\triangle OCB$), $x = 90°$ (angle in semi-circle), $y = 62°$ (angles in a $\triangle$) $z = 18°$ (base angle isosceles $\triangle ODC$)
   (b) $x = 100°$ (reflex $\angle ADB = 200°$, angle at circumference = half angle at centre)
   (c) $x = 29°$ ($\angle ADB$ is angle in a semi-circle so $\angle BDC = 90°$, then angles in a $\triangle$)
   (d) $x = 120°$ (angle at centre), $y = 30°$ (base angle isosceles $\triangle$)

4 (a) $x = 7.5$ cm, $y = 19.5$ cm
   (b) $x = 277.3$ mm, $y = 250$ mm

5 NOT TO SCALE

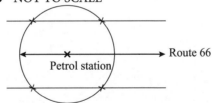

6 NOT TO SCALE

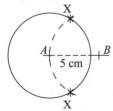

Chapter 20

Exercise 20.1

1 (a)

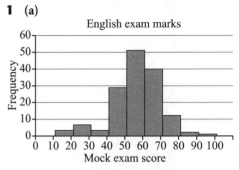

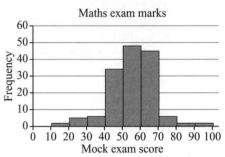

(b) 51–60   **(c)** 51–60
(d) students to compare based on histograms, but possible comments are: The modal value for both subjects is the same but the number in the English mode is higher than the Maths. Maths has more students scoring between 40 and 70 marks. Maths has more students scoring more than 90 marks and fewer scoring less than 20.

2 (a) bars are touching, scale on horizontal axis is continuous, vertical axis shows frequency
   (b) 55   **(c)** 315   **(d)** 29–31
   (e) scale does not start from 0

3

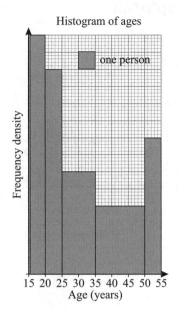

Histogram of ages

4 (a) 300   (b) 480   (c) 100

Exercise 20.2

1 (a)

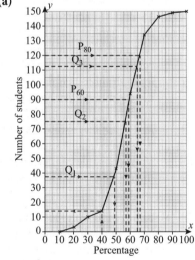

(b) Median = 57%, Q_1 = 49% and
Q_3 = 65%
(c) IQR = 16
(d) 91%
(e) 60% of students scored at least
59%; 80% of the students scored
at least 67%

2 (a) 166 cm
(b) Q_1 = 158, Q_3 = 176
(c) 18
(d) 12.5%

Mixed exercise

1 (a)

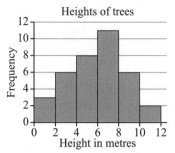

Heights of trees

(b) 19   (c) 6–8 metres

2 (a)

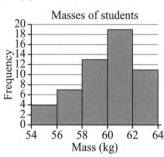

Masses of students

(b) 60–62 kg
(c) 7.4%
(d) 10 kg

3

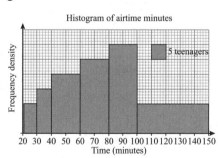

Histogram of airtime minutes

4 (a) 6.5 cm
(b)

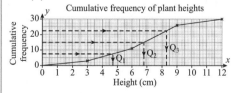

Cumulative frequency of plant heights

median height = 6.8 cm
(c) IQR = 8.3 – 4.7 = 3.6

Chapter 21

Exercise 21.1

1 (a) 3:4   (b) 6:1
(c) 7:8   (d) 1:5   (e) 1:4

2 (a) $x = 9$ (b) $x = 4$
(c) $x = 16$ (d) $x = 3$
(e) $x = 4$ (f) $x = 1.14$
(g) $x = 1.875$ (h) $x = 2.67$
(i) $x = 7$ (j) $x = 13.33$

3 60 cm and 100 cm

4 (a) 20 ml oil and 30 ml vinegar
(b) 240 ml oil and 360 ml vinegar
(c) 300 ml oil and 450 ml vinegar

5 60°, 30° and 90°

6 810 mg

Exercise 21.2 A

1 (a) 1:2.25   (b) 1:3.25   (c) 1:1.8

2 (a) 1.5:1   (b) 5:1
(c) 5:1

Exercise 21.2 B

1 240 km

2 30 m

3 (a) 5 cm
(b) 3.5 cm

4 (a) it means one unit on the map is
equivalent to 700 000 of the same
units in reality
(b)

Map distance (mm)	10	71	50	80	1714	2143
Actual distance (km)	7	50	35	56	1200	1500

5 (a) 4:1   (b) 14.8 cm
(c) 120 mm or 12 cm

Exercise 21.3

1 25.6 l

2 11.5 km/l

3 (a) 78.4 km/h
(b) 520 km/h
(c) 240 km/h

4 (a) 5 h   (b) 9 h 28 min
   (c) 40 h   (d) 4.29 min

5 (a) 150 km   (b) 300 km
   (c) 3.75 km   (d) 18 km

Exercise 21.4

1 (a) (i) 100 km
      (ii) 200 km
      (iii) 300 km
   (b) 100 km/h
   (c) vehicle stopped
   (d) 250 km
   (e) 125 km/h

2 (a) 2 hours
   (b) 190 min = 3 h 10 min
   (c) 120 km/h
   (d) (i) 120 km
      (ii) 80 km
   (e) 48 km/h
   (f) 40 min
   (g) 50 min
   (h) 53.3 − 48 = 5.3 km/h
   (i) Pam 12 noon, Dabilo 11:30 a.m.

3 (a) (i) 40 km/h
      (ii) 120 km/h
   (b) 3.5 min
   (c) 1200 km/h^2
   (d) 6 km

4 (a) 0–30 s, $\frac{5}{6}$ m/s^2
   (b) after 70 s, 0.5 m/s^2
   (c) 90 km/h
   (d) 2 km

Exercise 21.5

1 (a) Yes, $\frac{A}{B} = \frac{1}{150}$
   (b) No, $\frac{8}{15}$ is not $= \frac{1}{2}$
   (c) Yes, $\frac{A}{B} = \frac{10}{1}$

2 (a) $175   (b) $250

3 $12.50

4 60 m

5 (a) 75 km   (b) 375 km
   (c) 3 h 20 min

6 (a) 15 litres (b) 540 km

7 (a) inversely proportional

   (b) (i) $2\frac{1}{2}$ days
      (ii) $\frac{1}{2}$ day

8 (a) 12 days (b) 5 days

9 5 h 30 min

10 1200 km/h

Exercise 21.6

1 (a) $k = 7$
   (b) $a = 84$

2 ratio of m to T is constant, $\frac{m}{T} = 0.4587$, so m varies directly with T

3 (a) $F = 40$
   (b) $m = 4.5$

4 $a = 2$, $b = 8$, $c = 1\frac{1}{3}$

5 (a) $y = 2$ (b) $x = 0.5$

6 (a) $y = 2x^2$ (b) $y = 1250$
   (c) $x = 9$

7 (a) $y\sqrt{x} = 80$
   (b) $y = 8$
   (c) $x = 15.49$

8 (a) $b = 40$ (b) $a = 17\frac{7}{9}$

9 (a) $y = 2.5$ (b) $x = 2$

10 (a) $xy = 18$ for all cases, so relationship is inversely proportional
   (b) $xy = 18$ or $y = \frac{18}{x}$
   (c) $y = 36$

Exercise 21.7

1 $300

2 $72 000

3 (a) $51 000 (b) $34 000

4 14 350

Mixed exercise

1 (a) 90 mm, 150 mm and 120 mm
   (b) Yes, $(150)^2 = (90)^2 + (120)^2$

2 1:50

3 (a) (i) 85 km
      (ii) 382.5 km
      (iii) 21.25 km

   (b) (i) 0.35 h
      (ii) 4.7 h
      (iii) 1.18 h

4 (a) 150 km
   (b) after 2 hours; stopped for 1 hour
   (c) 100 km/h
   (d) 100 km/h
   (e) 500 km

5 (a) 20 seconds
   (b) 2 m/s^2
   (c) 200 m
   (d) 100 m

6 4.5 min

7 187.5 g

8 (a) $P = \frac{k}{V}$ or $PV = k$
   (b) $P = 80$

9 (a) 7:4   (b) 54.86 mm

Chapter 22

Exercise 22.1 A

1 (a) $x - 4$
   (b) $P = 4x - 8$
   (c) $A = x^2 - 4x$

2 (a) $S = 5x + 2$
   (b) $M = \frac{5x + 2}{3}$

3 (a) $x + 1$, $x + 2$
   (b) $S = 3x + 3$

4 (a) $x + 2$ (b) $x - 3$
   (c) $S = 3x - 1$

Exercise 22.1 B

1 14

2 9 cm

3 80 silver cars, 8 red cars

4 father = 35, mother = 33 and Nadira = 10

5 breadth = 13 cm, length = 39 cm

6 X cost 90c, Y cost $1.80 and Z cost 30c

7 9 years

8 97 tickets

Exercise 22.2

1 (a) $V = U + T - W$

(b) $V = \dfrac{U - T^2}{3} - W$ or

$V = \dfrac{1}{3}\left(U - T^2 - 3W\right)$

(c) $B = \dfrac{C}{A}$

(d) $B = AC$

(e) $Q = \pm\sqrt{2P}$

(f) $Q = \pm\sqrt{\dfrac{P}{2}}$

(g) $Q = \pm\sqrt{\dfrac{P}{R}}$

(h) $P = \dfrac{Q^2}{2}$

(i) $P = \dfrac{Q^2}{R}$

(j) $P = Q^2 + R$

(k) $Q = \dfrac{R^2}{P}$

2 (a) $I = \dfrac{V}{R}$

(b) 20 amps

3 (a) $r = \sqrt{\dfrac{A}{\pi}}$ (note, radius cannot be negative)

(b) $r = 5.64\,\text{mm}$

4 (a) $F = \dfrac{9}{5}C + 32$

(b) $80.6\,^\circ\text{F}$

(c) $323\,\text{K}$

Exercise 22.3

1 (a) 11   (b) -1

(c) 5   (d) $2m + 5$

2 (a) $f(x) = 3x^2 + 5$

(b) (i) 17

(ii) 53

(iii) 113

(c) $f(2) + f(4) = 17 + 53 = 70 \neq f(6)$ which is $= 113$

(d) (i) $3a^2 + 5$

(ii) $3b^2 + 5$

(iii) $3(a + b)^2 + 5$

(e) $a = \pm 3$

3 (a) $h(x) = \sqrt{5 - x}$

(b) (i) $h(1) = \pm 2$

(ii) $h(-4) = \pm 3$

4 (a) $4(x - 5)$

(b) $4x - 5$

5 18

6 (a) $f^{-1}(x) = x - 4$

(b) $f^{-1}(x) = x + 9$

(c) $f^{-1}(x) = \dfrac{x}{5}$

(d) $f^{-1}(x) = -2x$

7 (a) $\dfrac{x}{2} - 3$

(b) $\dfrac{x - 3}{2}$

(c) $2(x + 3)$

(d) $2x + 3$

(e) $2x + 3$

(f) $2(x + 3)$

Mixed exercise

1 10

2 41, 42, 43

3 4 years

4 Nathi has \$67 and Cedric has \$83

5 Sindi puts in \$40, Jonas \$20 and Mo \$70

6 44 children

7 (a) $b = \dfrac{9a - 26}{8}$

(b) $b = \dfrac{a^2 - 4}{17}$

8 $f^{-1}(x) = \dfrac{5x + 3}{2}$

9 (a) $f^{-1}(x) = \dfrac{x - 4}{3}$

(b) 3

(c) $a = 6$

(d) $9x + 16$

(e) 37

Chapter 23

Exercise 23.1 A

1

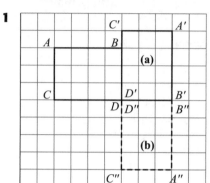

2

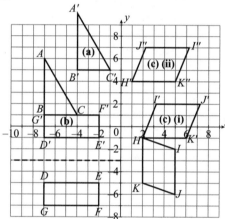

3

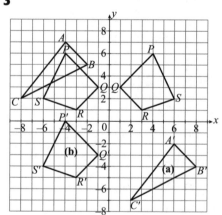

4 A: $y = 5$

B: $x = 0$

C: $y = -1.5$

D: $x = -6$

5

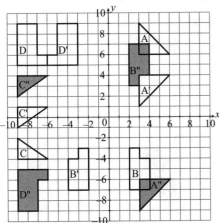

6 possible answers are:

for *ABC*: rotate 90° clockwise about *B* then reflect in the line $x = -6$

for *MNOP*: rotate 90° clockwise about (2, 1) then reflect in the line $x = 5.5$

Exercise 23.1 B

1 A: centre (0, 2), scale factor 2
B: centre (1, 0), scale factor 2
C: centre (−4, −7), scale factor 2
D: centre (9, −5), scale factor $\frac{1}{4}$

2

(a)

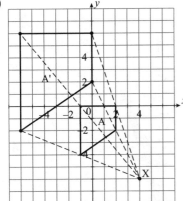

(b)

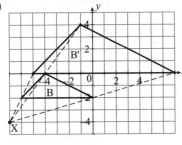

(c)

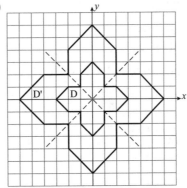

(d)

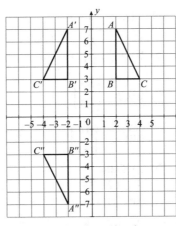

Exercise 23.1 C

1 **(a)**

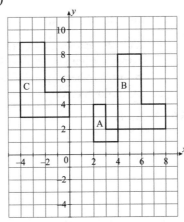

(b) rotation 180° about (0, 0)

2 **(a)**

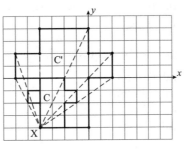

(b) enlargement scale factor 2, using (8, −1) as centre

3 **(a)**

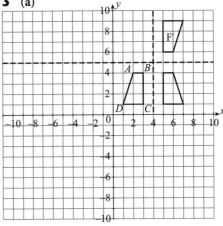

(b) rotation 180° about (4, 5)

Exercise 23.2 A

1 **(a)** $\overrightarrow{AB} = \begin{pmatrix} 5 \\ 0 \end{pmatrix}$ **(b)** $\overrightarrow{BC} = \begin{pmatrix} 4 \\ 0 \end{pmatrix}$

(c) $\overrightarrow{AE} = \begin{pmatrix} 0 \\ -6 \end{pmatrix}$ **(d)** $\overrightarrow{BD} = \begin{pmatrix} -1 \\ -6 \end{pmatrix}$

(e) $\overrightarrow{DB} = \begin{pmatrix} 1 \\ 6 \end{pmatrix}$ **(f)** $\overrightarrow{EC} = \begin{pmatrix} 9 \\ 6 \end{pmatrix}$

(g) $\overrightarrow{CD} = \begin{pmatrix} -5 \\ -6 \end{pmatrix}$ **(h)** $\overrightarrow{BE} = \begin{pmatrix} -5 \\ -6 \end{pmatrix}$

(i) they are equal

(j) $\begin{pmatrix} 9 \\ 0 \end{pmatrix}$ **(k)** $\begin{pmatrix} -5 \\ -6 \end{pmatrix}$

(l) Yes

2

(a)

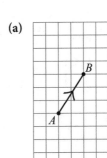

(b)

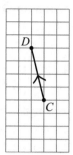

(c)

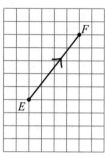

(d)

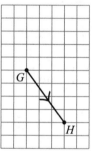

3 A $\begin{pmatrix} 8 \\ 1 \end{pmatrix}$ B $\begin{pmatrix} 2 \\ 3 \end{pmatrix}$ C $\begin{pmatrix} 4 \\ -3 \end{pmatrix}$

D $\begin{pmatrix} -3 \\ -3 \end{pmatrix}$ E $\begin{pmatrix} 9 \\ 3 \end{pmatrix}$

Exercise 23.2 B

1 (a) $\begin{pmatrix} -8 \\ 16 \end{pmatrix}$ (b) $\begin{pmatrix} 2 \\ 6 \end{pmatrix}$ (c) $\begin{pmatrix} 0 \\ 12 \end{pmatrix}$

(d) $\begin{pmatrix} -1 \\ 7 \end{pmatrix}$ (e) $\begin{pmatrix} -2 \\ 1 \end{pmatrix}$ (f) $\begin{pmatrix} -1 \\ 4 \end{pmatrix}$

(g) $\begin{pmatrix} -4 \\ 18 \end{pmatrix}$ (h) $\begin{pmatrix} -8 \\ 22 \end{pmatrix}$ (i) $\begin{pmatrix} 0 \\ -20 \end{pmatrix}$

(j) $\begin{pmatrix} 10 \\ -16 \end{pmatrix}$

2 (a) $-a$ (b) $2b$ (c) $-a + c$
(d) $2c$ (e) $2b$ (f) $2c$

(g) b (h) $-c$ (i) $-7a + 7c$
(j) $\frac{b}{2} + 3c$

3 (a) – (e) student's own diagrams

4 (a) 6.40 cm
(b) 7.28 cm
(c) 15 cm
(d) 17.69 cm

5 (a) 5.10
(b) 5
(c) 8.06
(d) 9.22

6 (a) A(–6, 2), B (–2, –4), C (5, 1)

(b) $\overrightarrow{AB} = \begin{pmatrix} 4 \\ -6 \end{pmatrix}$

$\overrightarrow{BC} = \begin{pmatrix} 7 \\ 5 \end{pmatrix}$

$\overrightarrow{CA} = \begin{pmatrix} -11 \\ 1 \end{pmatrix}$

7 (a) $\overrightarrow{XZ} = x + y$
(b) $\overrightarrow{ZX} = -x - y$
(c) $\overrightarrow{MZ} = \frac{1}{2}x + y$

8 (a) (i) $x = \begin{pmatrix} 2 \\ 7 \end{pmatrix}$

(ii) $y = \begin{pmatrix} -3 \\ -3 \end{pmatrix}$

(iii) $z = \begin{pmatrix} 10 \\ -4 \end{pmatrix}$

(b) (i) 7.28
(ii) 4.24
(iii) 21.5

9 (a) (i) $\overrightarrow{XY} = b - a$
(ii) $\overrightarrow{AD} = \frac{1}{2}(a + b)$
(iii) $\overrightarrow{BC} = 2(b - a)$

(b) $\overrightarrow{XY} = b - a$ and, $\overrightarrow{BC} = 2(b - a)$
so they are both multiples of
$(b - a)$, and hence parallel, and
$\overrightarrow{BC}$ is double $\overrightarrow{XY}$

10 28.2(3sf)

Exercise 23.3

1 (a)

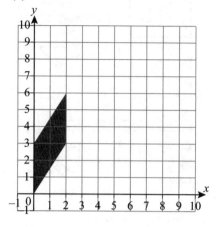

(b)

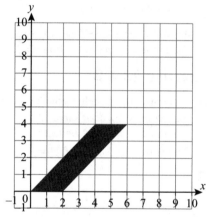

(c)

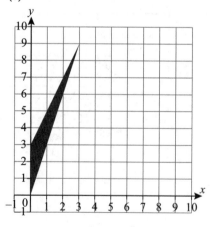

(d)

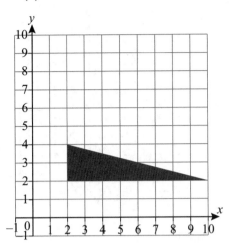

2 **(a)** shear, x-axis invariant, shear factor 1.5

(b) 2-way stretch: stretch of scale factor 4, invariant line $x = 1$ and stretch of scale factor 2, invariant line $y = 2$

(c) shear, $x = 0$ (y-axis) invariant, scale factor 0.75

(d) shear, line $y = 4$ invariant, shear factor 1

Exercise 23.4

1 **(a)** $\begin{pmatrix} 0 & 6 & 5 \\ 7 & 2 & -3 \end{pmatrix}$

(b) $\begin{pmatrix} -2 & -2 & 1 \\ 1 & 4 & -3 \end{pmatrix}$

(c) $\begin{pmatrix} 2 & 2 & -1 \\ -1 & -4 & 3 \end{pmatrix}$

2 **(a)** -12 **(b)** $\dfrac{-1}{12}\begin{pmatrix} 8 & -5 \\ -4 & 1 \end{pmatrix}$

3 **(a)** $AB = \begin{pmatrix} 3 & 9 \\ 9 & -1 \end{pmatrix}$ and $BA = \begin{pmatrix} 6 & -6 \\ -10 & -4 \end{pmatrix}$; so $AB \neq BA$

(b) **(i)** -6
(ii) -84

4 **(a)** $\begin{pmatrix} 7 & 0 & -3 \\ 11 & 0 & 4 \end{pmatrix}$

(b) $\begin{pmatrix} 3 & -9 & 0 \\ 12 & 6 & -3 \end{pmatrix}$

(c) $\begin{pmatrix} -12 & -6 & 6 \\ -14 & 4 & -10 \end{pmatrix}$

5 **(a)** $x = 3$ **(b)** $\dfrac{1}{5}\begin{pmatrix} 4 & -1 \\ -3 & 2 \end{pmatrix}$

Exercise 23.5

1 **(a)** **(i)** reflection in the y-axis
(ii) shear with x-axis invariant and shear factor 2

(b) **(i)** $\begin{pmatrix} -1 & 0 \\ 0 & 1 \end{pmatrix}$

(ii) $\begin{pmatrix} 1 & 2 \\ 0 & 1 \end{pmatrix}$

2 **(a)** R' (2, 8)

(b) a stretch parallel to the y-axis (x-axis invariant), scale factor 4

3 **(a)** enlargement, scale factor 3, centre of enlargement the origin

(b) $\begin{pmatrix} -3 & 0 \\ 0 & 3 \end{pmatrix}$

4 $\begin{pmatrix} 3 & 0 \\ 0 & -3 \end{pmatrix}$

Mixed exercise

1 **(a)** **(i)** reflect in the line $x = -1$

(ii) rotate 90° clockwise about the origin

(iii) reflect in the line $y = -1$

(b) **(i)** rotate 90° anticlockwise about (0, 0) then translate $\begin{pmatrix} -2 \\ -1 \end{pmatrix}$

(ii) reflect in the line $y = -1$ then translate $\begin{pmatrix} -8 \\ 0 \end{pmatrix}$

(iii) rotate 180° about origin then translate $\begin{pmatrix} 6 \\ 0 \end{pmatrix}$

(iv) reflect in the line $x = 0$ (y-axis) then translate $\begin{pmatrix} 0 \\ -2 \end{pmatrix}$

---

2 **(a)** & **(b)**

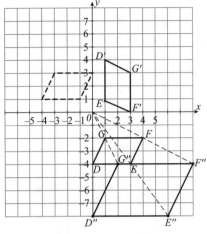

3

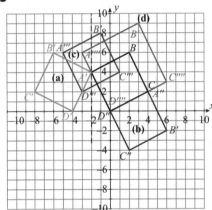

(a) B' $(-6, -6)$ **(b)** B' $(6, -2)$
(c) B' $(-1, 8)$ **(d)** B' $(3, 9)$

4 **(a)** **(i)** $\begin{pmatrix} 6 \\ 12 \end{pmatrix}$ **(ii)** $\begin{pmatrix} 0 \\ -8 \end{pmatrix}$

(iii) $\begin{pmatrix} 1 \\ 10 \end{pmatrix}$ **(iv)** $\begin{pmatrix} 12 \\ 0 \end{pmatrix}$

(b) **(i)**

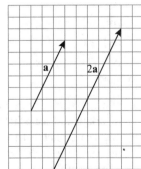

(ii)

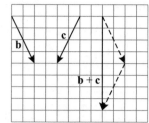

(iii)

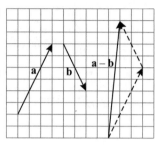

(iv)

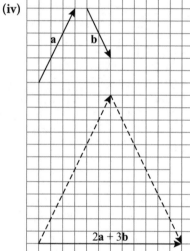

5 (a) (i) $\overrightarrow{ED} = y$
   (ii) $\overrightarrow{DE} = -y$
   (iii) $\overrightarrow{FB} = x + y$
   (iv) $\overrightarrow{EF} = x - y$
   (v) $\overrightarrow{FD} = 2y - x$

(b) 4. 47

6 (a) one-way stretch with y-axis invariant and scale factor of 2
   (b) one-way stretch with x-axis invariant and scale factor of 2
   (c) a shear with x-axis invariant and shear factor = 3
   (d) a shear with y-axis invariant, shear factor = 2

7

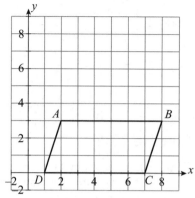

8

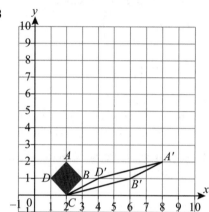

9 (a) $\begin{pmatrix} 2 & 5 \\ 4 & 3 \end{pmatrix}$

(b) $\begin{pmatrix} 0 & -1 \\ 0 & -1 \end{pmatrix}$

(c) $\begin{pmatrix} 5 & 7 \\ 4 & 8 \end{pmatrix}$

(d) $\begin{pmatrix} 7 & 5 \\ 6 & 6 \end{pmatrix}$

(e) $|\mathbf{P}| = -3$

(f) $\mathbf{P}^{-1} = \begin{pmatrix} -\dfrac{1}{3} & \dfrac{2}{3} \\ \dfrac{2}{3} & -\dfrac{1}{3} \end{pmatrix}$

10 $a = 7$, $b = 2$ and $c = -9$

11 (a) & (c)

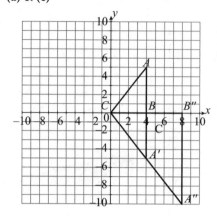

(b) $\begin{pmatrix} 1 & 0 \\ 0 & -1 \end{pmatrix}$

(d) $\begin{pmatrix} 2 & 0 \\ 0 & 2 \end{pmatrix}$

(e) $\begin{pmatrix} 2 & 0 \\ 0 & -2 \end{pmatrix}$

Chapter 24
Exercise 24.1

1

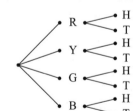

2

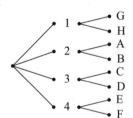

3 (a) & (b)

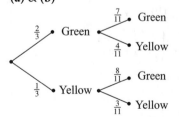

Exercise 24.2

1 (a)

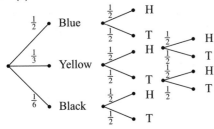

(b) $\frac{1}{4}$ (c) $\frac{1}{12}$ (d) $\frac{5}{12}$

2 (a)

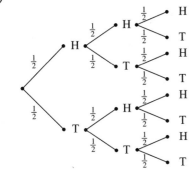

(b) $\frac{1}{8}$ (c) $\frac{1}{2}$

(d) $\frac{1}{2}$

(e) 0, not possible on three coin tosses

Mixed exercise

1 (a) & (b)

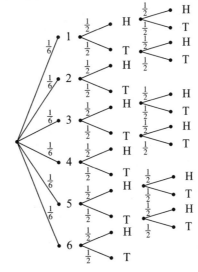

(c) $\frac{1}{8}$ (d) $\frac{1}{12}$

2 (a) & (b)

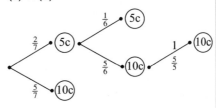

(c) $\frac{5}{7}$ (d) $\frac{1}{21}$

(e) 1 (there are no 5c coins left)